Everyman, I will go with thee,
and be thy guide

William Shakespeare

THE TEMPEST

Edited by
JOHN F. ANDREWS

Foreword by
SIR JOHN GIELGUD

EVERYMAN
J. M. DENT · LONDON
CHARLES E. TUTTLE
VERMONT

Text © 1991 by Doubleday Book & Music Clubs, Inc.

Textual revisions, revisions to notes, introduction, note on
text, chronology, and all end matter © J. M. Dent 1994 and
Charles E. Tuttle Co. 1994

First published in Everyman by J. M. Dent 1994
Published by permission of GuildAmerica Books, an imprint
of Doubleday Book and Music Clubs, Inc.

Photoset by Deltatype Ltd, Ellesmere Port, Cheshire
Printed in Great Britain by
The Guernsey Press Co. Ltd, Guernsey, C.I.
for
J. M. Dent
Orion Publishing Group
Orion House
5 Upper St Martin's Lane, London WC2H 9EA
and
Charles E. Tuttle Co.
28 South Main Street, Rutland, Vermont
05701 – USA

British Library Cataloguing-in-Publication Data is available
upon request

ISBN 0 460 87455 1

CONTENTS

NOTE ON AUTHOR AND EDITOR

WILLIAM SHAKESPEARE is held to have been born on St George's Day, 23 April 1564. The eldest son of a prosperous glove-maker in Stratford-upon-Avon, he was probably educated at the town's grammar school.

Tradition holds that between 1585 and 1592, Shakespeare first became a schoolteacher and then set off for London. By 1594 he was a leading member of the Lord Chamberlain's Men, helping to direct their business affairs, as well as being a playwright and actor. In 1598 he became a part-owner of the company, which was the most distinguished of its age. However, he maintained his contacts with Stratford, and his family seem to have remained there.

From about 1610 he seems to have grown increasingly involved in the town's affairs, suggesting a withdrawal from London. He died on 23 April 1616, in his 53rd year, and was buried at Holy Trinity two days later.

JOHN F. ANDREWS has recently completed a 19-volume edition, *The Guild Shakespeare*, for the Doubleday Book and Music Clubs. He is also the editor of a 3-volume reference set, *William Shakespeare: His World, His Work, His Influence*, and the former editor (1974–85) of the journal *Shakespeare Quarterly*. From 1974 to 1984, he was director of Academic Programs at the Folger Shakespeare Library in Washington and Chairman of the Folger Institute.

CHRONOLOGY OF SHAKESPEARE'S LIFE

Year[1]	Age	Life
1564		Shakespeare baptized 26 April at Stratford-upon-Avon
1582	18	Marries Anne Hathaway
1583	19	Daughter, Susanna, born
1585	21	Twin son and daughter, Hamnet and Judith, born
1590–1	26	*The Two Gentlemen of Verona* & *The Taming of the Shrew*
1591	27	*2 & 3 Henry VI*
1592	28	*Titus Andronicus* & *1 Henry VI*
1592–3		*Richard III*
1593	29	*Venus and Adonis* published
1594	30	*The Comedy of Errors. The Rape of Lucrece* published
1594–5		*Love's Labour's Lost*
1595	31	*A Midsummer Night's Dream, Romeo and Juliet,* & *Richard II.* An established member of Lord Chamberlain's Men
1596	32	*King John.* Hamnet dies
1596–7		*The Merchant of Venice* & *1 Henry IV*

[1] It is rarely possible to be certain about the dates at which plays of this period were written. For Shakespeare's plays, this chronology follows the dates preferred by Stanley Wells and Gary Taylor, the editors of *The Oxford Shakespeare*. Publication dates are given for poetry and books.

CHRONOLOGY OF HIS TIMES

Year	Literary Context	Historical Events
1565–7	Golding, Ovid's *Metamorphoses*, tr.	Elizabeth I reigning
1574	*A Mirror for Magistrates* (3rd ed.)	
1576	London's first playhouse built	
1578	John Lyly, *Euphues*	
1579	North, Plutarch's *Lives*, tr.	
	Spenser, *Shepherd's Calender*	
1587	Marlowe, *I Tamburlaine*	Mary Queen of Scots executed
1588	Holinshed's *Chronicles* (2nd ed.)	Defeat of Spanish Armada
1589	Kyd, *Spanish Tragedy*	Civil war in France
	Marlowe, *Jew of Malta*	
1590	Spenser, *Faerie Queene*, Bks I–III	
1591	Sidney, *Astrophel and Stella*	Proclamation against Jesuits
1592	Marlowe, *Dr Faustus* & *Edward II*	Scottish witchcraft trials
		Plague closes theatres from June
1593	Marlowe killed	
1594	Nashe, *Unfortunate Traveller*	Theatres reopen in summer
1594–6		Extreme food shortages
1595	Sidney, *An Apologie for Poetry*	Riots in London
1596		Calais captured by Spanish
		Cadiz expedition

[2] A schoolmaster would earn around £20 a year at this time.

Year	Literary Context	Historical Events
1597	Bacon, *Essays*	
1598	Marlowe and Chapman, *Hero and Leander* Jonson, *Every Man in his Humour*	Rebellion in Ireland
1599	Children's companies begin playing Thomas Dekker's *Shoemaker's Holiday*	Essex fails in Ireland
1601	'War of the Theatres' Jonson, *Poetaster*	Essex rebels and is executed
1602		Tyrone defeated in Ireland
1603	Florio, Montaigne's *Essays*, tr.	Elizabeth I dies, James I accedes Raleigh found guilty of treason
1604	Marston, *The Malcontent*	Peace with Spain
1605	Bacon, *Advancement of Learning*	Gunpowder plot
1606	Jonson, *Volpone*	
1607	Tourneur, *The Revenger's Tragedy*, published	Virginia colonized Enclosure riots
1609		Oath of allegiance Truce in Netherlands
1610	Jonson, *Alchemist*	
1611	Authorised Version of the Bible Donne, *Anatomy of the World*	
1612	Webster, *White Devil*	Prince Henry dies
1613	Webster, *Duchess of Malfi*	Princess Elizabeth marries
1614	Jonson, *Bartholomew Fair*	
1616	Folio edition of Jonson's plays	

Biographical note, chronology and plot summary compiled by John Lee, University of Bristol, 1993.

FOREWORD BY SIR JOHN GIELGUD

As a very young actor, I was engaged in the early 1920s to play the part of Ferdinand for a few performances at the Savoy Theatre in London by Robert Courtneidge, whose daughter Rosaline was to play Miranda. Courtneidge presented a short Shakespeare season every year starring Henry Baynton, who was then a popular provincial actor with a romantic appeal. Following the examples of Sir Frank Benson and Sir Herbert Beerbohm Tree, Baynton decided to give prominence to Caliban, finding, as did most managers and actors at that time, that Prospero was merely a tedious old bore. I have never found him so. (Benson hung upside down, with a fish in his mouth, while Tree staged a final tableau in which he was left desolate on the island watching the receding ship as it sailed back to Italy.)

A few years later, Tree's daughter Viola went into management and presented a very unhappy production of the play, which I had gone to see with high hopes but in which I was sadly disappointed. The Prospero was Henry Ainley, previously outstanding as Malvolio and Leontes under Granville Barker, but apparently bewildered in attempting Prospero, despite a sonorous delivery in his beautiful voice, and perhaps distracted by an Ariel (a charming but unsatisfactory musical comedy actress named Winifred Barnes) who flew about and hovered above him on a wire. The Caliban, a fine actor, Louis Calvert, was made up to look like an animal, and walked about on all-fours. Only the young lovers (Joyce Carey and Francis Lister) shed a few moments of beauty and romantic style, while the scenery, evidently resuscitated from Tree's version of the play many years before, did little to rescue a disastrous failure.

When I first attempted the part of Prospero at the Old Vic, in 1930, I was only 26, but extremely fortunate in my director,

Harcourt Williams, and enormously helped by the imaginative skills of Leslie French and Ralph Richardson, who were Ariel and Caliban respectively. I became increasingly devoted to the play, and was to act Prospero in three subsequent productions on the stage under three fine directors, George Devine, Peter Brook and Peter Hall, over a number of years. Finally, two years ago, I played the part again for the director Peter Greenaway, in his controversial film entitled *Prospero's Books*, a most fascinating and rewarding experience. Each time, I had to re-examine my previous performance, but tried to profit by the different ideas of the directors, actors, and designers with whom I came to be associated. Since I have never directed the play myself, I have always been too busy concentrating on my own part to examine in detail the scenes in which Prospero does not appear (both the conspiracy scenes of the usurping lords, and the low-life comedians who conspire with Caliban to destroy Prospero). The long dialogue between Prospero and Miranda at the beginning of the play is something of a problem for the actors and audience alike. The speeches are long and involved, though so essential to the understanding of the plot. Curiously enough, I felt that this was one of the most successful scenes in Greenaway's film, greatly helped by the closeups, angles of the camera, and its visual beauty.

I once spent a somewhat exhausting half hour discussing the play with Jonathan Miller when we chanced to meet at Nice Airport while we were both waiting to board a plane. I had recently seen his production of the play at the Mermaid Theatre in London, in which he seemed to have concentrated on the colonial implications of the 'still-vex'd Bermooths', and he was derisive of all the 'magic nonsense' as he called it, so naturally we argued to little purpose. I was greatly taken by a suggestion of Professor Glynne Wickham, with whom I talked at Bristol when we were giving the play there. He thought that Shakespeare intended the end of the play to flatter the new king, James I; that, in the masque, Iris was to represent Queen Elizabeth (referring to the famous 'Rainbow' portraits of her), Juno for James's Queen, and that Ariel is finally freed to ascend into Heaven, as a kind of John the

Baptist, to herald the deification of Prospero, celebrating his triumphant welding of England and Scotland into a single kingdom.

The play is, of course, intensely difficult to stage successfully with so many possible pitfalls to be avoided. The shipwreck should surely be very simply suggested and the speeches must be audible despite the competition of the background storm. I am sure that Ariel should be acted by a boy or a very young man, though at various times, at the Vic and Stratford, both Elsa Lanchester (Charles Laughton's wife) and Margaret Leighton were very successful in the part. The lovers must combine youth and beauty with style and breeding, and the comics kept in reasonable check, not forgetting their sinister intent. The late Arthur Lowe was a superb Stephano in the Peter Brook production. Jack Hawkins, Denis Quilley and Alec Clunes all played Caliban in productions with me, all fine performances, though I felt Richardson surpassed them all. Needless to say how important it is to mingle the fantasy, songs and magnificent language – both poetry and prose – with the powerful suggestions of evil, repentance and forgiveness which bind the whole play together. And then, in the epilogue, the beautiful fable is crowned with a poignant simplicity and charm.

Sir John Gielgud

SIR JOHN GIELGUD's first stage appearance was playing the role of the Herald in *Henry V*. He has since appeared in such diverse Shakespearean roles as Hamlet, Shylock, Antony, King Lear, Prospero, Julius Caesar, and Richard II, and directed productions of *Hamlet, Romeo and Juliet, The Merchant of Venice,* and *Twelfth Night,* among many others.

EDITOR'S INTRODUCTION TO
The Tempest

The Tempest is a drama about the uses of display, and it draws to a fitting close with an ageing showman's reflections on the 'Magic' that has long enabled him to flourish as a behind-the-scenes manipulator. Like a ducal impresario, this purveyor of special effects has ransacked the 'Globe' for spectacles to ornament his crowd-pleasing extravaganzas. Like a shrewd carnival proprietor, he has conjured up 'Music', 'Viands', and 'golden Palaces'. Like a skilled sorcerer, an alchemist of the mind and imagination, he has exploited the secrets of an 'Art' that works with 'great creating Nature' (*The Winter's Tale*, IV.iv.88) to impress and move others and to summon forth a 'new World' too 'brave' and wondrous to be regarded as merely 'Natural'.

But now this instigator of haunting 'Noises' and edifying 'Visions' is compelled to take stock. With the prescience of a seasoned astrologer, he divines that his 'Charms' are about to be 'o'er-thrown'. He discerns that his flaccid 'Sails' will soon depend upon the 'Breath' he can solicit from forces beyond his ken. And he confides that, like a 'Deceiver' whose devices have been discovered, he will wind up in 'Despair' unless he be 'reliev'd by Prayer'.

For all his magisterial aura, the wizard who orchestrates *The Tempest*'s culminating 'Pageant' is a self-confessed fraud: the vulnerable if ostensibly omnipotent human being beneath the persona of a domestic and political patriarch, the insecure if stern principal of a 'Vanity' that repeatedly directs our attention to the nervous ventriloquist on the far side of the rear stage curtain.

The name this wonder-worker carries is Prospero, and he presides over a 'bare Island' with analogies to the 'Wooden O' (*Henry V*, Prologue, line 13), the three-tiered amphitheatre that accommodated public performances by His Majesty's Servants in Southwark, a suburb of early seventeenth-century London. Like a manager of the King's Men, as these Servants were known to their fellows, he oversees his attendant ministers as a troupe of 'Actors'. By his deployment of their skills he weaves subtle illusions out of 'thin Air'. He conducts puppet-like playthings through mazes as intricate 'as ere Men trod'. He wields fierce 'Vexations' and restorative 'Dreams'. He erects 'solemn Temples' and fills the Heavens with 'Cloud-capp'd Tow'rs'. And in the process he prompts his audience to ponder the relationship between the protagonist's own doings and those of the poet who begot him.

When Shakespeare penned Prospero's lines, he was nearing the end of a distinguished career as England's foremost knitter of riddling 'Distractions'. He was shortly to bid adieu to the 'Cell' in which he had plotted so many diversions, and he no doubt looked forward to the tranquillity he expected to repossess when he retired to the 'Dukedom' of his birth. He may have suspected that he would enjoy his reclaimed state only briefly before he too commended his soul into the hands of a higher authority. He may thus have intuited that he would be 'Wise hereafter' to devote 'Every third Thought' to his 'Grave'. All we know is that, whatever his thoughts and motives, he took the occasion to produce a drama that gives eloquent expression to Everyman's yearning for 'Sea-change', for a 'second Life' to gainsay 'the dark Backward and Abysm of Time' and confer his spirit to eternity.

The Tempest is by no means unique in its preoccupation with the search for an antidote to the anxieties provoked by mutability and mortality. The same concern pervades *Love's Labour's Lost*, *King Lear*, and Shakespeare's Sonnets. Variations on it animate *Richard II*, *As You Like It*, *Twelfth Night*, *Hamlet*, *Antony and Cleopatra*, and several other plays. But it resonates with greatest intensity in *Pericles*, *Cymbeline*, *The Winter's Tale*, and *Henry VIII*, the four late works that commentators now link with the drama a venerable tradition interprets, rightly or wrongly, as the playwright's benediction to the 'Fancies' that have given his 'little Life' focus.

The tragicomedies with which Shakespeare completed his

tenure as a man of the theatre are normally classified today as 'Romances'. Though they all have what can be defined as happy endings, they differ from his earlier comedies and tragicomedies in the earnestness with which they engage the grim realities of 'State and Woe' (*Henry VIII*, Prologue, line 3). In *Pericles*, *Cymbeline*, and *Henry VIII*, for example, we either witness or hear reports of the demise of *dramatis personae*, and in *The Tempest* we feel that death is a real danger until the moment when Prospero's own 'Release' is effected.

The term 'Romance' might appear to suggest sentimental escapism. But Shakespeare's experiments in the genre force us to confront a universe in which even the most ordinary pilgrimages are fraught with real peril. As a group these dramatic works reverberate with intimations of the ominous, and they frequently imply that the only way to evade life's snares is through some benign suspension of Nature's usual functions.

Taken together, these late tragicomedies offer a panoramic view of the human condition. Often they do so by emphasizing that the occurrences they depict are widely dispersed in time, location, and circumstance, as in *Pericles*, *Cymbeline*, and *The Winter's Tale*. On other occasions they do so by basing their events upon action that took place in the murky past, as in *The Tempest*, or by orienting their action to events that will transpire in some remote future, as in *Henry VIII*.

Most of them contain incidents that seem wildly implausible, if not shocking, as when a horrified Antigonus exits pursued by a bear in *The Winter's Tale*; and they rely heavily on storms, shipwrecks, and other 'acts of God' to propel the narrative forward. In patterns that recall *The Comedy of Errors*, a proto-Romance from Shakespeare's earlier years, families are scattered on land or at sea, doomed to wander and then astonishingly reunited at the close. Terrible calamities are but narrowly averted, and then only because of reversals that stem from sudden changes of heart or from unprecedented visitations by 'the Powres above' (*Cymbeline*, V.v.467). Cordelia-like daughters, maidens with symbolic names or pseudonyms (Marina in *Pericles*, Fidele in *Cymbeline*, Perdita in *The Winter's Tale*,

Miranda in *The Tempest*), intervene as instruments of special grace, restoring hope and perception to fathers who have lost their bearings and would otherwise perish in their guilt and grief.

Rather than conceal their improbability or disguise their artifice, Shakespeare's Romances tend to revel in it, on the one hand reminding theatregoers that what they are witnessing is only make-believe, on the other hand laying the foundation for some climactic marvel that will turn out to have been the *raison d'être* of the drama. In these works what initially appear to be opaque 'Fumes', impenetrable to 'Clearer Reason' (*The Tempest*, V.i.67–68), suddenly transfigure themselves into designer clouds with silver linings. 'Things Dying' there may be, but in the cosmos of these new-style mystery plays they almost always become metamorphosed into, or serve as precursors of, 'Things new-borne' (*The Winter's Tale*, III.iii.117).

Like the Tragedies, the Romances are suffused with suffering; but in a way that sets them apart from most of the Tragedies, they depict pain as purgative and even beautifying. In the Romances 'the Seas threaten' and they sometimes drown; but in the last analysis they show themselves to be 'Merciful'. For if there is a first principle of Romance ecology, it would seem to be this: that anything that can be made 'Rich and Strange' will be recycled and refined until it emerges as an emblem of the Providence that burnished it and made it lustrous (*The Tempest*, V.i.177, I.ii.399).

The earliest recorded performance of *The Tempest* was at Whitehall on 1 November 1611, but the script was probably staged at the Blackfriars, if not the Globe, prior to that date. It was not the last of Shakespeare's dramatic works, of course, but the valedictory note it sounds has always made it seem as if it should have been. It has steadily attracted the interest of those in search of the 'real' Shakespeare. It has delighted generations of viewers with its besotted clowns and celestial pyrotechnics. It has fostered more than its share of artistic offspring. And it will long maintain a special hold on the memories of those who share its devotion to the fragile glories of an 'Art' that can fulfil its destiny only by dissolving into the 'Air' that brought it into being.

But if this philosophical drama is a study of what the Prince of Denmark calls 'the Purpose of Playing' (*Hamlet*, III.ii.24), it is also a meditation on the 'baseless Fabric' of the 'Isle' an 'unworthy Scaffold' (*Henry V,* Prologue, line 10) attempts to confine within its charmed circle. And whether we think of Caliban's tormented domicile as a dot in the Mediterranean or as a counterpart to the 'still-vext Bermoothes' in the eye of an Atlantic hurricane, it is difficult to resist the inference that what the playwright is really representing in *The Tempest* is a microcosm of the marbled gem our own bold voyages have revealed to Earth's inhabitants as a precious 'demi-Paradise' against the silent backdrop of an ever-deepening void.

In June of 1609, under the auspices of the Virginia Company, whose members were acquaintances of the intrepid spirits in Shakespeare's own global enterprise, a group of entrepreneurs sailed from Plymouth to transport a newly appointed Governor to England's first permanent settlement in the Americas. As it happened, the ships encountered a terrible storm, and on 24 July the vessel carrying Sir Thomas Gates foundered off the coast of the Bermudas. To the amazement of everyone who had been on the flagship, there were no casualties. To their further surprise, 'the Devil's Islands' on which they had landed proved remarkably 'temperate'. Not only did all the mariners survive; by May of 1610 they had pieced together two pinnaces and completed their journey to Jamestown, Virginia.

Before the year was out several accounts of the Bermuda adventure, including William Strachey's *True Repertory of the Wrack*, were circulating in London. They all praised Providence for a rescue that seemed little short of miraculous, and they generated a spiritual climate that Shakespeare freely invoked when he conceived *The Tempest*. When it suited his design he alluded to details his audience would recognize from the recent English forays into 'unpath'd Waters' (*The Winter's Tale*, IV.iv.581). But he also took material from other travel narratives, among them tales of Magellan's and Drake's encounters with the Patagonians of South America, who worshipped a god named Setebos; and he immersed himself in reactions to those narratives as he read works such as John Florio's 1603 translation of Michel de Montaigne's essays on cannibals and other topics. For the storm that opens the play he recalled the New Testament story (Acts 27) about the Apostle Paul's role in saving the occupants of a Roman sailing vessel. For the meanderings of the Neapolitans after their arrival on Prospero's island, he drew parallels with the Exodus of the children of Israel from captivity in Egypt and their wanderings in the wilderness that frustrate their quest for the Promised Land. Meanwhile, as usual, he borrowed at will from Ovid's *Metamorphoses*, which he probably read both in Latin and in Arthur Golding's 1567 English version. And, as in *Antony and Cleopatra,* he incorporated both structural paradigms and incidental themes from the *Aeneid*.

In many respects the enveloping frame of *The Tempest* reiterates Virgil's epic. The playwright suggests analogies between the odyssey that Alonso and his companions undertake from Tunis to Naples and the mission that conveyed Aeneas from Dido's Carthage to the Latium that would become his new Troy. By doing so Shakespeare reminds us that these latter-day Trojans can gain their destination only by negotiating a 'Vast' (*The Winter's Tale*, I.i.35) that is totally unfamiliar to them.

According to its only aboriginal (a character the First Folio cast list for *The Tempest* describes as a 'salvage and deformed slave'), the 'Isle' on which the grounded Italians find themselves in Shakespeare's play is 'full of Noises'. But on one point the observant Caliban is incorrect: not all the 'Sounds' to be heard here are 'sweet Airs that give Delight and hurt not'. The acrimonious Duke who has ruled for twelve years and who commissions these disturbances appears at times to be a spiteful Lear – more sinned against than sinning, to be sure, but at first unable to register the degree to which his own neglect has contributed to the 'Evil Nature' he awakened in a perfidious recipient of his favour. As a result of the intemperance Prospero displays in his initial conversation with Ariel, an obedient sprite who has never done anything to offend his master, the old man comes across as an iron-fisted despot. He then behaves so imperiously with the gentle Ferdinand, and even with his own daughter, the 'admir'd Miranda', that we can't help speculating about the agitation that appears to underlie his presumably beneficent ministrations. And notwithstanding Prospero's comments about a surly 'Monster' who is supposedly incapable of the least 'Print of Goodness', the exchanges *we* witness suggest that Caliban's ruler may finally be disclosing more than he perceives when he says 'this Thing of Darkness I / Acknowledge mine'.

There can be no question that the lord of *The Tempest* was expected to cut an imposing figure on the Shakespearean stage. Like Duke Senior in the Forest of Arden in *As You Like It*, he is an exile who has profited from pastoral adversity; and like Duke Vincentio in *Measure for Measure*, he endeavours to model himself on the Good Shepherd. But though his effects on the lives of others turn out in general to be salutary, he fails in at least one of his aims: he never extracts so much as an admission of wrongdoing, let alone any expression of remorse, from his faithless brother. And if it is eventually Prospero who achieves the drama's 'most majestic Vision', he attains it only by way of a psychological and spiritual progress that depends upon his forswearing 'Vengeance' for the 'rarer Action' of a compassionate 'Virtue'.

What Prospero hopes to bestow on the play's other characters, friend and foe alike, is a spirit of 'Grace' and an informed understanding of each person's own 'Meaning'. Before he can attend to the needs of lesser mortals, however, the isle's physician must first address his own ills. He must take part with the 'nobler Reason' that is his only salve for a 'Fury' that continually threatens to sabotage his well-intentioned 'Project'. He must submit himself to the truth in Ariel's hint that to be fully human is, in the end, to be humane. Eventually Prospero breaks his 'Staff' and drowns his 'Book'; but even then the once and future Duke of Milan leaves us asking if he has really learned all he'll need to know if he aspires to leave a renewable 'Island' behind him and bequeath a bounteous 'Dukedom' to posterity.

Shortly after he finished *The Tempest*, if not before, Shakespeare appears to have retired from London to New Place, the house he had purchased more than a decade before in his native Stratford. Two years later, when he was back in the capital for an early performance of *Henry VIII*, the final play to bear his name as sole author, he was probably on hand to see 'the great Globe' burn to the ground, leaving 'not a Rack behind'. A year later a second theatre stood on the site its predecessor had occupied, but by 1616 the man who would become renowned as the world's foremost playwright was permanently at rest, in the church where he had been christened a little more than half a century earlier.

Some time prior to 1623, a monument to Shakespeare was placed above his tomb in Holy Trinity Church, and that tribute is still on view today. But of course the poet's greatest memorial is the legacy he left in works that will keep his 'Art' potent forever. In the words and actions that invigorate his poems and plays, in the revivals that enrich our theatres and silver screens, in the offshoots to be enjoyed in the efforts of later writers, and in the influence Shakespeare continues to exercise in one cultural sphere after another, the genius behind *The Tempest* remains a 'brave God' who 'bears celestial Liquor'.

John F. Andrews, 1994

THE TEXT OF THE EVERYMAN SHAKESPEARE

Background

THE EARLY PRINTINGS OF SHAKESPEARE'S WORKS

Many of us enjoy our first encounter with Shakespeare when we're introduced to *Julius Caesar* or *Macbeth* at school. It may therefore surprise us that neither of these tragedies could ever have been read, let alone studied, by most of the playwright's contemporaries. They began as scripts for performance and, along with seventeen other titles that never saw print during Shakespeare's lifetime, they made their inaugural appearance as 'literary' works seven years after his death, in the 1623 collection we know today as the First Folio.

The Folio contained thirty-six titles in all. Of these, half had been issued previously in the small paperbacks we now refer to as quartos.* Like several of the plays first published in the Folio, the most trustworthy of the quarto printings appear to have been set either from Shakespeare's own manuscripts or from faithful copies of them. It's not impossible that the poet himself prepared some of these works for the press, and it's intriguing to imagine him reviewing proof-pages as the words he'd written for actors to speak and embody were being transposed into the type that readers would filter through their eyes, minds, and imaginations. But, alas, there's no indisputable evidence that Shakespeare had any direct involvement with the publication of these early editions of his plays.

What about the scripts that achieved print for the first time in the Folio? Had the dramatist taken any steps to give the permanency of book form to those texts? We don't know. All we

---

* Quartos derived their name from the four-leaf units of which these small books were comprised: large sheets of paper that had been folded twice after printing to yield four leaves, or eight pages. Folios, volumes with twice the page-size of quartos, were put together from two-leaf units: sheets that had been folded once after printing to yield four pages.

can say is that when he fell fatally ill in 1616, Shakespeare was denied any opportunities he might otherwise have taken to ensure that his 'insubstantial Pageants' survived the mortal who was now slipping into the 'dark Backward and Abysm of Time'.

Fortunately, two of the playwright's colleagues felt an obligation, as they put it, 'to procure his Orphans Guardians'. Sometime after his death John Heminge (or Heminges) and Henry Condell made arrangements to preserve Shakespeare's theatrical compositions in a manner that would keep them vibrant for all time. They dedicated their endeavour to two noblemen who had helped see England's foremost acting company through some of its most trying vicissitudes. They solicited several poetic tributes for the volume, among them a now-famous eulogy by fellow writer Ben Jonson. They commissioned an engraved portrait of Shakespeare to adorn the frontispiece. And they did their utmost to display the author's dramatic works in a style that would both dignify them and make them accessible to 'the great Variety of Readers'.

As they readied Shakespeare's plays for the compositors who would set them into stately Folio columns, Heminge and Condell (or editors designated to carry out their wishes) revised and augmented many of the entrances, exits, and other stage directions in the manuscripts. They divided most of the works into acts and scenes.* For a number of plays they appended 'Names of the Actors', or casts of characters. Meanwhile they made every effort to guarantee that the Folio printers had reliable copy-texts for each of the titles: authoritative manuscripts for the plays that had not been published previously, and good quarto printings (annotated in some instances to insert staging details, mark script changes, and add supplementary material) for the ones that had been issued prior to the Folio. For several titles they supplied texts that were substantively different from, if not always demonstrably superior to, the quarto versions that preceded them.

Like even the most accurate of printings that preceded it, the

---

* The early quartos, reflecting the unbroken sequence that probably typified Elizabethan and Jacobean performances of the plays, had been printed without the structural demarcations usual in Renaissance editions of classical drama.

Folio collection was flawed by minor blemishes. But it more than fulfilled the purpose of its generous-minded compilers: 'to keep the memory of so worthy a Friend and Fellow alive as was our Shakespeare'. In the process it provided a publishing model that remains instructive today.

MODERN EDITIONS OF THE PLAYS AND POEMS

When we compare the First Folio and its predecessors with the usual modern edition of Shakespeare's works, we're more apt to be impressed by the differences than by the similarities. Today's texts of Renaissance drama are normally produced in conformity with twentieth-century standards of punctuation and usage; as a consequence they look more neat, clean, and, to our eyes, 'right' than do the original printings. Thanks to an editorial tradition that extends back to the early eighteenth century and beyond, most of the rough spots in the early printings of Shakespeare have long been smoothed away. Textual scholars have ferreted out redundancies and eradicated inconsistencies. They've mended what they've perceived to be errors and oversights in the playscripts, and they've systematically attended to what they've construed as misreadings by the copyists and compositors who transmitted these playscripts to posterity. They've added '[Within]' brackets and other theatrical notations. They've revised stage directions they've judged incomplete or inadequate in the initial printings. They've regularized disparities in the speech headings. They've gone back to the playwright's sources and reinstated the proper forms for many of the character and place names which a presumably hasty or inattentive author got 'wrong' as he conferred identities on his dramatis personae and stage locales. They've replaced obsolete words like *bankrout* with their modern heirs (in this case *bankrupt*). And in a multitude of other ways they've accommodated Shakespeare to the tastes, interests, and expectations of latter-day readers.

The results, on the whole, have been splendid. But interpreting the artistic designs of a complex writer is always problematical, and the task is especially challenging when that writer happens to have been a poet who felt unconstrained by many of the 'rules' that more conventional dramatists respected. The undertaking becomes further complicated when new rules, and new criteria of linguistic and social correctness, are imposed by subsequent generations of artists and critics.

To some degree in his own era, but even more in the neoclassical period (1660–1800) that came in its wake, Shakespeare's most ardent admirers thought it necessary to apologize for what Ben Jonson hinted at in his allusion to the 'small Latin, and less Greek' of an untutored prodigy. To be sure, the 'sweet Swan of Avon' sustained his popularity; in fact his reputation rose so steadily that by the end of the eighteenth century he'd eclipsed Jonson and his other peers and become the object of near-universal Bardolatry. But in the theatre most of his plays were being adapted in ways that were deemed advisable to tame their supposed wildness and bring them into conformity with the decorum of a society that took pride in its refinement. As one might expect, some of the attitudes that induced theatre proprietors to metamorphose an unpolished poet from the provinces into something closer to an urbane man of letters also influenced Shakespeare's editors. Persuaded that the dramatist's works were marred by crudities that needed expunging, they applied their ministrations to the canon with painstaking diligence.

Twentieth-century editors have moved away from many of the presuppositions that guided a succession of earlier improvers. But a glance at the textual apparatus accompanying virtually any modern publication of the plays and poems will show that emendations and editorial procedures deriving from such fore-bears as the sets published by Nicholas Rowe (1709), Alexander Pope (1723–5, 1728), Lewis Theobald (1733, 1740, 1757), Thomas Hanmer (1743–5, 1770–1), Samuel Johnson (1765), Edward Capell (1768), George Steevens (1773), and Edmond Malone (1790) retain a strong hold on today's renderings of the playwright's works. The consequence is a 'Shakespeare' who offers the tidiness we've come to expect in our libraries of treasured authors, but not necessarily the playwright a reader of the Second Quarto of *Romeo and Juliet* in 1599 would still be able to recognize as a contemporary.

OLD LIGHT ON THE TOPIC

Over the last two decades we've learned from art curators that paintings by Old Masters such as Michelangelo and Rembrandt look a lot brighter when centuries of grime are removed from their surfaces – when hues that had become dulled with soot and other extraneous matter are allowed to radiate again with something approximating their pristine luminosity. We've learned from conductors like Christopher Hogwood that there are aesthetic rewards to be gained from a return to the scorings and instruments with which Renaissance and Baroque musical compositions were first presented. We've learned from twentieth-century experiments in the performance of Shakespeare's plays that an open, multi-level stage, analogous to that on which the scripts were originally enacted, does more justice to their dramaturgical techniques than does a proscenium auditorium devised for works that came later in the development of Western theatre. We've learned from archaeological excavations in London's Bankside area that the foundations of playhouses such as the Rose and the Globe look rather different from what many historians had expected. And we're now learning from a close scrutiny of Shakespeare's texts that they too look different, and function differently, when we accept them for what they are and resist the impulse to 'normalize' features that strike us initially as quirky, unkempt, or unsophisticated.

The Aims that Guide the Everyman *Text*

Like other modern editions of the dramatist's plays and poems, The Everyman Shakespeare owes an incalculable debt to the scholarship that has led to so many excellent renderings of the author's works. But in an attempt to draw fresh inspiration from the spirit that animated those remarkable achievements at the outset, the Everyman edition departs in a number of respects from the usual post-Folio approach to the presentation of Shakespeare's texts.

RESTORING SOME OF THE NUANCES OF RENAISSANCE PUNCTUATION

In its punctuation, Everyman attempts to give equal emphasis to sound and sense. In places where Renaissance practice calls for heavier punctuation than we'd normally employ – to mark the caesural pause in the middle of a line of verse, for instance – Everyman sometimes retains commas that other modern editions omit. Meanwhile, in places where current practice usually calls for the inclusion of commas – after vocatives and interjections such as 'O' and 'alas', say, or before 'Madam' or 'Sir' in phrases such as 'Ay Madam' or 'Yes Sir' – Everyman follows the original printings and omits them.

Occasionally the absence of a comma has a significant bearing on what an expression means, or can mean. At one point in *Othello*, for example, Iago tells the Moor 'Marry patience' (IV.i.90). Inserting a comma after 'Marry', as most of today's editions do, limits Iago's utterance to one that says 'Come now, have patience.' Leaving the clause as it stands in the Folio, the way the Everyman text does, permits Iago's words to have the additional, agonizingly ironic sense 'Be wed to Patience.'

The early texts generally deploy exclamation points quite sparingly, and the Everyman text follows suit. Everyman also follows the early editions, more often than not, when they use question marks in places that seem unusual by current standards: at the ends of what we'd normally treat as exclamations, for example, or at the ends of interrogative clauses in sentences that we'd ordinarily denote as questions in their entirety.

The early texts make no orthographic distinction between simple plurals and either singular or plural possessives, and there are times when the context doesn't indicate whether a word spelled *Sisters*, say, should be renedered *Sisters*, *Sisters'*, or *Sister's* in today's usage. In such situations the Everyman edition prints the word in the form modern usage prescribes for plurals.

REVIVING SOME OF THE FLEXIBILITY OF RENAISSANCE SPELLING

Spelling had not become standardized by Shakespeare's time, and that meant that many words could take a variety of forms. Like James Joyce and some of the other innovative prose and verse stylists of our own century, Shakespeare revelled in the freedom a largely unanchored language provided, and with that in mind Everyman retains original spelling forms (or adaptations of those forms that preserve their key distinctions from modern spellings) whenever there is any reason to suspect that they might have a bearing on how a word was intended to be pronounced or on what it meant, or could have meant, in the playwright's day. When there is any likelihood that multiple forms of the same word could be significant, moreover, the Everyman text mirrors the diversity to be found in the original printings.

In many cases this practice affects the personalities of Shakespeare's characters. One of the heroine's most familiar questions in *Romeo and Juliet* is 'What's in a Name?' For two and a half centuries readers – and as a consequence actors, directors, theatre audiences, and commentators – have been led to believe that Juliet was addressing this query to a Romeo named 'Montague'. In fact 'Montague' *was* the name Shakespeare found in his principal source for the play. For reasons that will become apparent to anyone who examines the tragedy in detail, however, the playwright changed his protagonist's surname to 'Mountague', a word that plays on both 'mount' and 'ague' (fever). Setting aside an editorial practice that began with Lewis Theobald in the middle of the eighteenth century, Everyman resurrects the name the dramatist himself gave Juliet's lover.

Readers of *The Merchant of Venice* in the Everyman set will be amused to learn that the character modern editions usually identify as 'Lancelot' is in reality 'Launcelet', a name that calls attention to the clown's lusty 'little lance'. Like Costard in *Love's Labour's Lost*, another stage bumpkin who was probably played by the actor Will Kemp, Launcelet is an upright 'Member of the

Commonwealth'; we eventually learn that he's left a pliant wench 'with Child'.

Readers of *Hamlet* will find that 'Fortinbras' (as the name of the Prince's Norwegian opposite is rendered in the First Folio and in most modern editions) appears in the earlier, authoritative 1604 Second Quarto of the play as 'Fortinbrasse'. In the opening scene of that text a surname that meant 'strong in arms' in French is introduced to the accompaniment of puns on *brazen*, in the phrase 'brazon Cannon', and on *metal*, in the phrase 'unimprooued mettle'. In the same play readers of the Everyman text will encounter 'Ostricke', the ostrich-like courtier who invites the Prince of Denmark to participate in the fateful fencing match that draws *Hamlet* to a close. Only in its final entrance direction for the obsequious fop does the Second Quarto call this character 'Osrick', the name he bears in all the Folio text's references to him and in most modern editions of Shakespeare's most popular tragedy.

Readers of the Everyman *Macbeth* will discover that the fabled 'Weird Sisters' appear only as the 'weyward' or 'weyard' Sisters. Shakespeare and his contemporaries knew that in his *Chronicles of England, Scotland, and Ireland* Raphael Holinshed had used the term 'weird sisters' to describe the witches who accost Macbeth and Banquo on the heath; but no doubt because he wished to play on *wayward*, the playwright changed their name to *weyward*. Like Samuel Johnson, who thought punning vulgar and lamented Shakespeare's proclivity to seduction by this 'fatal Cleopatra', Lewis Theobald saw no reason to retain the playwright's weyward spelling of the witches' name. He thus restored the 'correct' form from Holinshed, and editors ever since have generally done likewise.

In many instances Renaissance English had a single spelling for what we now define as two separate words. For example, *humane* combines the senses of 'human' and 'humane' in modern English. In the First Folio printing of *Macbeth* the protagonist's wife expresses a concern that her husband is 'too full o'th' Milke of humane kindnesse'. As she phrases it, *humane kindnesse* can mean several things, among them 'humankind-ness', 'human kindness', and 'humane kindness'. It is thus a reminder that to be true to his or her own 'kind' a human being must be 'kind' in the sense we now attach to 'humane'. To disregard this logic, as the protagonist and his wife will soon prove, is to disregard a principle as basic to the cosmos as the laws of gravity.

In a way that parallels *humane*, *bad* could mean either 'bad' or 'bade', *borne* either 'born' or 'borne', *ere* either 'ere' (before) or 'e'er' (ever), *least* either 'least' or 'lest', *lye* either 'lie' or 'lye', *nere* either 'ne'er' or 'near' (though the usual spellings for the latter were *neare* or *neere*), *powre* either 'pour' or 'power', *then* either 'than' or 'then', and *tide* either 'tide' or 'tied'.

There were a number of word-forms that functioned in Renaissance English as interchangeable doublets. *Travail* could mean 'travel', for example, and *travel* could mean 'travail'. By the same token, *deer* could mean *dear* and vice versa, *dew* could mean *due*, *hart* could mean *heart*, and (as we've already noted) *mettle* could mean *metal*.

A particularly interesting instance of the equivocal or double meanings some word-forms had in Shakespeare's time is *loose*, which can often become either 'loose' or 'lose' when we render it in modern English. In *The Comedy of Errors* when Antipholus of Syracuse compares himself to 'a Drop / Of Water that in the Ocean seeks another Drop' and then says he will 'loose' himself in quest of his long-lost twin, he means both (a) that he will release himself into a vast unknown, and (b) that he will lose his own identity, if necessary, to be reunited with the brother for whom he searches. On the other hand, in *Hamlet* when Polonius says he'll 'loose' his daughter to the Prince, he little suspects that by so doing he will also lose his daughter.

In some cases the playwright employs word-forms that can be translated into words we wouldn't think of as related today: *sowre*, for instance, which can mean 'sour', 'sower', or 'sore', depending on the context. In other cases he uses forms that do have modern counterparts, but not counterparts with the same potential for multiple connotation. For example, *onely* usually means 'only' in the modern sense; but occasionally Shakespeare gives it a figurative, adverbial twist that would require a nonce word such as 'one-ly' to replicate in current English.

In a few cases Shakespeare employs word-forms that have only seeming equivalents in modern usage. For example, *abhominable*, which meant 'inhuman' (derived, however incorrectly, from *ab*, 'away from', and *homine*, 'man') to the poet and his contemporaries, is not the same word as our *abominable* (ill-omened, abhorrent). In his advice to the visiting players Hamlet complains about incompetent actors who imitate 'Humanity so abhominably' as to make the characters they depict seem unrecognizable as men. Modern readers who don't realize the distinction between Shakespeare's word and our own, and who see *abominable* on the page before them, don't register the full import of the Prince's satire.

Modern English treats as single words a number of word-forms that were normally spelled as two words in Shakespeare's time. What we render as *myself*, for example, and use primarily as a reflexive or intensifying pronoun, is almost invariably spelled *my self* in Shakespeare's works; so also with *her self*, *thy self*, *your self*, and *it self* (where *it* functions as *its* does today). Often there is no discernible difference between Shakespeare's usage and our own. At other times there is, however, as we are reminded when we come across a phrase such as 'our innocent self' in *Macbeth* and think how strained it would sound in modern parlance, or as we observe when we note how naturally the self is objectified in the balanced clauses of the Balcony Scene in *Romeo and Juliet*:

> Romeo, doffe thy name,
> And for thy name, which is no part of thee,
> Take all my selfe.

Yet another difference between Renaissance orthography and our own can be exemplified with words such as *today*, *tonight*, and *tomorrow*, which (unlike *yesterday*) were treated as two words in Shakespeare's time. In *Macbeth* when the Folio prints 'Duncan comes here to Night', the unattached *to* can function either as a preposition (with *Night* as its object, or in this case its destination) or as the first part of an infinitive (with *Night* operating figuratively as a verb). Consider the ambiguity a Renaissance reader would have detected in the original publication of one of the most celebrated soliloquies in all of Shakespeare:

> To morrow, and to morrow, and to morrow,
> Creeps in this petty pace from day to day,
> To the last Syllable of Recorded time:
> And all our yesterdayes, have lighted Fooles
> The way to dusty death.

Here, by implication, the route 'to morrow' is identical with 'the way to dusty death', a relationship we miss if we don't know that for Macbeth, and for the audiences who first heard these lines spoken, *to morrow* was not a single word but a potentially equivocal two-word phrase.

RECAPTURING THE ABILITY TO HEAR WITH OUR EYES

When we fail to recall that Shakespeare's scripts were designed initially to provide words for people to hear in the theatre, we sometimes overlook a fact that is fundamental to the artistic structure of a work like *Macbeth*: that the messages a sequence of sounds convey through the ear are, if anything, even more significant than the messages a sequence of letters, punctuation marks, and white spaces on a printed page transmit through the eye. A telling illustration of this point, and of the potential for ambiguous or multiple implication in any Shakespearean script, may be found in the dethronement scene of *Richard II*. When Henry Bullingbrook asks the King if he is ready to resign his crown, Richard replies 'I, no no I; for I must nothing be.' Here the punctuation in the 1608 Fourth Quarto (the earliest text to print this richly complex passage) permits each *I* to signify either 'ay' or 'I' (*I* being the usual spelling for 'ay' in Shakespeare's time). Understanding *I* to mean 'I' permits additional play on *no*, which can be heard (at least in its first occurrence) as 'know'. Meanwhile the second and third soundings of *I*, if not the first, can also be heard as 'eye'. In the context in which this line occurs, that sense echoes a thematically pertinent passage from Matthew 18:9: 'if thine eye offend thee, pluck it out'.

But these are not all the implications *I* can have here. It can also represent the Roman numeral for '1', which will soon be reduced, as Richard notes, to 'nothing' (0), along with the speaker's title, his worldly possessions, his manhood, and eventually his life. In Shakespeare's time, to become 'nothing' was, *inter alia*, to be emasculated, to be made a 'weaker vessel' (1 Peter 3:7) with 'no thing'. As the Fool in *King Lear* reminds another monarch who has abdicated his throne, a man in want of an 'I' is impotent, 'an O without a Figure' (I.iv.207). In addition to its other dimensions, then, Richard's reply is a statement that can be formulated mathematically, and in symbols that anticipate the binary system behind today's computer technology: '1, 0, 0, 1, for 1 must 0 be.'

Modern editions usually render Richard's line 'Ay, no; no, ay; for I must nothing be.' Presenting the line in that fashion makes good sense of what Richard is saying. But as we've seen, it doesn't make total sense of it, and it doesn't call attention to Richard's paradoxes in the same way that hearing or seeing three undifferentiated *I*'s is likely to have done for Shakespeare's contemporaries. Their culture was more attuned than ours is to the oral and aural dimensions of language, and if we want to appreciate the special qualities of their dramatic art we need to train ourselves to 'hear' the word-forms we see on the page. We must learn to recognize that for many of what we tend to think of as fixed linkages between sound and meaning (the vowel 'I', say, and the word 'eye'), there were alternative linkages (such as the vowel 'I' and the words 'I' and 'Ay') that could be just as pertinent to what the playwright was communicating through the ears of his theatre patrons at a given moment. As the word *audience* itself may help us to remember, people in Shakespeare's time normally spoke of 'hearing' rather than 'seeing' a play.

In its text of *Richard II*, the Everyman edition reproduces the title character's line as it appears in the early printings of the tragedy. Ideally the orthographic oddity of the repeated *I*'s will encourage today's readers to ponder Richard's utterance, and the play it epitomizes, as a characteristically Shakespearean enigma.

OTHER ASPECTS OF THE EVERYMAN TEXT

Now for a few words about other features of the Everyman text.

One of the first things readers will notice about this edition is its bountiful use of capitalized words. In this practice as in others, the Everyman exemplar is the First Folio, and especially the works in the Folio sections billed as 'Histories' and 'Tragedies'.* Everyman makes no attempt to adhere to the Folio printings with literal exactitude. In some instances the Folio capitalizes words that the Everyman text of the same passage lowercases; in other instances Everyman capitalizes words not uppercased in the Folio. The objective is merely to suggest something of the flavour, and what appears to have been the rationale, of Renaissance capitalization, in the hope that today's audiences will be made continually aware that the works they're contemplating derive from an earlier epoch.

Readers will also notice that instead of cluttering the text with stage directions such as '[Aside]' or '[To Rosse]', the Everyman text employs unobtrusive dashes to indicate shifts in mode of address. In an effort to keep the page relatively clear of words not supplied by the original printings, Everyman also exercises restraint in its addition of editor-generated stage directions. Where the dialogue makes it obvious that a significant action occurs, the Everyman text inserts a square-bracketed phrase such as '[Fleance escapes]'. Where what the dialogue implies is subject to differing interpretations, however, the Everyman text provides a facing-page note to discuss the most plausible inferences.

Like other modern editions, the Everyman text combines into

---

* The quarto printings employ far fewer capital letters than does the Folio. Capitalization seems to have been regarded as a means of recognizing the status ascribed to certain words (*Noble*, for example, is almost always capitalized), titles (not only King, Queen, Duke, and Duchess, but Sir and Madam), genres (tragedies were regarded as more 'serious' than comedies in more than one sense), and forms of publication (quartos, being associated with ephemera such as 'plays', were not thought to be as 'grave' as the folios that bestowed immortality on 'works', writings that, in the words of Ben Jonson's eulogy to Shakespeare, were 'not of an age, but for all time').

'shared' verse lines (lines divided among two or more speakers) many of the part-lines to be found in the early publications of the plays. One exception to the usual modern procedure is that Everyman indents some lines that are not components of shared verses. At times, for example, the opening line of a scene stops short of the metrical norm, a pentameter (five-foot) or hexameter (six-foot) line comprised predominantly of iambic units (unstressed syllables followed by stressed ones). In such cases Everyman uses indentation as a reminder that scenes can begin as well as end in mid-line (an extension of the ancient convention that an epic commences *in media res*, 'in the midst of the action'). Everyman also uses indentation to reflect what appear to be pauses in the dialogue, either to allow other activity to transpire (as happens in *Macbeth*, II.iii.87, when a brief line 'What's the Business?' follows a Folio stage direction that reads *'Bell rings. Enter Lady'*) or to permit a character to hesitate for a moment of reflection (as happens a few seconds later in the same scene when Macduff responds to a demand to 'Speak, speak' with the reply 'O gentle Lady, / 'Tis not for you to hear what I can speak').

Everyman preserves many of the anomalies in the early texts. Among other things, this practice pertains to the way characters are depicted. In *A Midsummer Night's Dream*, for example, the ruler of Athens is usually identified in speech headings and stage directions as 'Theseus', but sometimes he is referred to by his title as 'Duke'. In the same play Oberon's merry sprite goes by two different names: 'Puck' and 'Robin Goodfellow'.

Readers of the Everyman edition will sometimes discover that characters they've known, or known about, for years don't appear in the original printings. When they open the pages of the Everyman *Macbeth*, for example, they'll learn that Shakespeare's audiences were unaware of any woman with the title 'Lady Macbeth'. In the only authoritative text we have of the Scottish tragedy, the protagonist's spouse goes by such names as 'Macbeth's Lady', 'Macbeth's Wife', or simply 'Lady', but at no time is she listed or mentioned as 'Lady Macbeth'. The same is true of the character usually designated 'Lady Capulet' in modern editions of

Romeo and Juliet. 'Capulet's Wife' makes appearances as 'Mother', 'Old Lady', 'Lady', or simply 'Wife'; but she's never termed 'Lady Capulet', and her husband never treats her with the dignity such a title would connote.

Rather than 'correct' the grammar in Shakespeare's works to eliminate what modern usage would categorize as solecisms (as when Mercutio says 'my Wits faints' in *Romeo and Juliet*), the Everyman text leaves it intact. Among other things, this principle applies to instances in which archaic forms preserve idioms that differ slightly from related modern expressions (as in the clause 'you are too blame', where 'too' frequently functions as an adverb and 'blame' is used, not as a verb, but as an adjective roughly equivalent to 'blameworthy').

Finally, and most importantly, the Everyman edition leaves unchanged any reading in the original text that is not manifestly erroneous. Unlike other modern renderings of Shakespeare's works, Everyman substitutes emendations only when obvious problems can be dealt with by obvious solutions.

The Everyman *Text of* The Tempest

Modern editions of *The Tempest* derive from the printing of the play that opened the 1623 First Folio. Happily, the Folio text presents few difficulties, and from all indications the script behind it was scrivener Ralph Crane's 'fair copy' of the playwright's own rendering of the drama.

Crane was evidently responsible for polished versions of several Shakespearean works, among them *The Two Gentlemen of Verona*, *The Merry Wives of Windsor*, *The Winter's Tale*, and at least parts of *2 Henry IV*, *Measure for Measure*, *Timon of Athens*, and *Cymbeline*. The texts in which Crane appears to have had a hand are all competently divided into acts and scenes, and in most cases they are followed by rosters of dramatis personae. At the same time they are marked by a proclivity to 'massed entry' stage directions (scene-commencing stage directions in which all the characters who will figure in that scene are listed at the outset rather than as they appear), and occasionally by mid-scene stage directions that are slightly out of sync with the dialogue.

As a scribe, Crane seems to have been prone to heavier than usual punctuation. He frequently employs full stops, colons, and semicolons in places where modern usage would call either for commas or for no punctuation at all. He tends to bracket parenthetical words, appositives, and exclamations. And he resorts to far more hyphens than we would opt for today (as illustrated by phrases such as 'bemockt-at-Stabs', 'borne-Devill', 'dark-backward', 'peg-thee', 'Turphie-Mountaines', and 'wide-chopt-rascall'). In a way that anticipates current practice, he inserts apostrophes to mark the elision of words or syllables (as in ''Pray' for 'I pray', or ''bove' for 'above'). He also uses apostrophes to identify metrical contractions (as in the spelling 'I'am', which occurs in a context where the conventions of iambic pentameter would call for a gliding one-syllable sound roughly equivalent to 'I'm').

Like other twentieth-century editions of *The Tempest*, the Everyman text disregards a number of features in the Folio printing that reflect Crane's eccentricities as a scribe. Whenever a peculiar Folio form might be construed as authentically Shakespearean, however, the Everyman text reproduces it. In accordance with this principle, Everyman retains a number of anomalies that other editions emend, among them *busy lest* (III.i.15), *creadulous* (II.ii.155), *fowl* (I.ii.258), *Plumbe* (III.iii.65), *Rariety* (II.i.42), *rediculous* (II.ii.174), *Roalties* (I.ii.110), and *sty-me* (I.ii.341). In keeping with its customary procedure, Everyman also preserves such spellings as *abhominable* ('abominable'), *aboord* ('aboard'), *bad* ('bade'), *blew* ('blue'), *borne* ('born'), *chast* ('chaste'), *Divel* ('devil'), *ere* ('ere' or 'e'er'), *foorth* ('forth'), *Gate* ('gait'), *Harts* ('hearts'), *hether* ('hither'), *Humane* ('human'), *I* ('ay'), *least* ('lest'), *loose* ('lose'), *onely* ('only'), *ought* ('aught'), *prethee* or *'prethee* ('prithee' or 'prythee'), *President* ('precedent'), *powre* ('pour' or 'power'), *queint* ('quaint'), *Raign* ('rain', 'reign', or 'rein'), *shews* ('shows'), *Sprights* ('sprites'), *sower/sowre* ('sore', 'sour', or 'sower'), *steeded* ('steaded'), *to night* ('tonight'), *Vassail* ('vassal'), *vild* ('vile'), *waigh'd* ('weigh'd'), and *where* ('whe'er').

In a few cases the Everyman text emends the First Folio text. In the lines singled out below, the first entry, in boldface type, is the reading to be found in Everyman and in most of today's editions; the second entry is the reading to be found in the First Folio (F1).

I.i.	64	**wi'th'** with' (compare I.ii.112, where F1 reads 'with')
I.ii.	60	**foul** fowle (so also in I.ii.62, IV.i.183)
	99	**exact** (like exact. Like
	262	**Month** moneth
	286	**Service.** service,
	305	**Heart** hart
II.i.	112	**to** too (so also in IV.i.206)
IV.i.	124	***Juno ... employment.*** Placed after line 127 in F1.
V.i.	72	**Didst** Did (The catchword at the bottom of the preceding page in F1 strongly suggests that *Didst* was what the Folio compositor would have read in the manuscript from which he drew.)
Epilogue	2	**own,** own.

In a number of instances Everyman adheres to, or construes, the text of F1 in ways that set it apart from other twentieth-century publications of *The Tempest*. In the roster that follows, the first entry, in boldface type, is the reading to be found in the Everyman rendering of the play; the second entry is the reading adopted by some, if not most, modern editions. Unless otherwise specified, the first entry also represents the Folio reading.

I.i.	7	**Harts** hearts
	9	***Ferdinando*** *Ferdinand*
	13	**Boson** bosun
	22	**Counsellor** councillor
	24	**Present** presence
	35	**borne** born (so also in I.ii.283, II.i.231, IV.i.188)
	54	**MARINER** MARINERS (*Mari.* in F1)
	57	**I am** I'm (*I'am* in F1)

I.ii.
3 **powre** pour (compare III.iii.73, 90, IV.i.38)
7 **Creature** creatures
45 **, then** than
58 **onely** only (so also in I.ii.98, II.i.217, III.ii.102, IV.i.210)
62 **Foul-play** foul play
87 **not?** not!
110 **Roalties** royalties
152 **you?** you!
159 **Divine,** divine.
165 **steeded** steaded
173 **Princess** princess'
194 **bad** bade
197 **Waste** waist
201 **Lightning** lightnings
205 **Seem** Seemed
234 **Flote** float
248 **made thee** made
249 **did** didst
258 **fowl** foul
261 **so:** so?
265 **Humane** human (so also in I.ii.284, 345, III.iii.33, V.i.20)
269 **blew** blue (so also in IV.i.80)
282 **he** she
298 **Spryting** spriting
320 **ere** e'er (so also in III.i.89, III.iii.101, V.i.241, 288)
324 **to night** tonight (compare III.ii.32, III.iii.14, 17)
341 **sty-me** sty me
356 **vild** vile
372 **Vassail** vassal
378 **bear the Burthen** the burthen bear
383 ARIEL **Hark** Hark
384 **cry Cockadiddle-dow** *Cry* [within] Cock-a-diddle-dow
387 **Island, sitting** island. Sitting
388 **Wrack.** wrack,
406 **Eye** eyes
407 **What** What,
449 **least** lest (so also in IV.i.169)

II.i.
15 **Dollor** dollar
37 **looks?** looks!
  Green? green!
42 **Rariety** rarety (compare II.i.44)
79 **I** Ay (so also in II.i.85, 258, III.i.88, V.i.293)

	89	**Marriage.** marriage?
	114	**Waigh'd** Weigh'd
	117	**Business** business'
	122	**Plaister** plaster
	134	**Borne** bourn
	163	**Metal** mettle
	171	**Heavy.** heavy?
	173	**asleep?** asleep!
	181	**them?** them!
	213	**throws** throes
	222	**you?** you!
	250	**Advancement?** advancement!
	257	**Conscience.** conscience?
	273	**President** precedent
II.ii.	9	**moe** mow
	77	**'prethee** prithee (so also in II.ii.123)
	122	**scap'd?** 'scap'd!
	155	**creadulous** credulous
	168	**abhominable** abominable
	174	**rediculous** ridiculous
	179	**Marmazet** marmoset
	180	**Philbirts** filberts
III.i.	2	**set** sets
	14	**busy lest** busilest
	47	**Peetless** peerless
	61	**would not** would, not
	62	**wodden** wooden
	93	**with all** withal
III.ii.	3	**Servant** servant- (so also in III.ii.5, 9)
	18	**Lieutenant** lieutenant,
	32	**to day** today
	37	**Natural?** natural!
	68	**this?** this!
	83	**Murren** murrain
	119	**troule** troll
	124	**cout** scout
III.iii.	29	**Islands** islanders
	65	**Plumbe** plume
IV.i.	9	**her of** her off *or* hereof
	13	**Guest** gift
	17	**Right** rite

19 **barrain** barren
20 **Sower** sour (compare V.i.37)
38 **Powre** power (compare I.ii.3)
52 **Raign** rein *or* reign
53 **Abstenious** abstemious
61 **Fetches** vetches
63 **thetch'd** thatch'd
66 **chast** chaste
68 **Pole** poll
69 **stirrile** sterile
83 **gras'd** grass'd
102 **Gate** gait
134 **Sicklemen** sicklemen,
136 **Holly Day** holiday
147 **Sir,** sir.
164 **I thank thee,** I thank thee. (In many editions this clause is designated as one that Prospero addresses to Ferdinand and Miranda.)
182 **filthy** filthy-
193 **on them** them on
207 **hudwink** hoodwink
209 **loose** lose (so also in IV.i.249, V.i.176)
232 **Let's** Let't
252 **lay to** lay-to

V.i.
4 **Sixt** sixth
Hower hour
11 **boudge** budge
14 **Brim full** brimful
15 **Him that you** Him you
23 **sharply,** sharply
37 **sowre** sour (compare IV.i.20)
39 **Mushrumps** mushrooms
46 **strong** strong-
59 **Brain's** brains, (braines F1)
60 **Boil** boil'd
75 **entertain** entertain'd
81 **Shore** shores
94 **Bow** bough
111 **Where** Whe'er
124 **nor** not
181 **here?** here!
182 **is?** is!
190 **Advise** advice

197 **Forgiveness?** forgiveness!
232 **gingling** jingling
247 **(Which ... shortly single)** Which ... shortly, single
261 **is?** is!
271 **rob'd** robb'd

THE TEMPEST

NAMES OF THE ACTORS

ALONSO, King of Naples
FERDINAND, his Son
SEBASTIAN, Alonso's Brother
PROSPERO, the right Duke of Millaine (Milan)
ANTONIO, his Brother, the usurping Duke of Millaine
MIRANDA, Daughter to Prospero
GONZALO, an honest old Councillor

ADRIAN
FRANCISCO } Lords

TRINCULO, a Jester
STEPHANO, a drunken Butler
MASTER of a Ship
BOATSWAIN
MARINERS

ARIEL, an airy Spirit

IRIS
CERES
JUNO ⎱ Spirits
NYMPHS
REAPERS

CALIBAN, a salvage (savage) and deformed Slave

This list of the dramatis personae is adapted from the one provided in the First Folio.

I.i   The opening scene takes place aboard a storm-tossed ship at sea.
Though there are echoes of New World islands in the play
(see I.ii.229, where Ariel refers to 'the still-vext Bermoothes'),
most of the geographical references suggest that these
mariners are in the Mediterranean Sea (see I.ii.233–5),
somewhere between North Africa and Italy.

1   **Boatswain** the petty officer in charge of a ship's deck and
riggings. The word is often spelled *bosun* or *boson* (as in line
13) and is usually so pronounced.

2   **Master** shipmaster; captain.
What Cheer? How are you faring?

3   **Good** either (a) good cheer (I'm doing well, thank you), or (b)
good man.
Mariners sailors, shipmen.

3–4   **fall to't yarely** see that you do it promptly.

4   **a ground** aground; into the ground. The ship is near the shore
of an island.

6   **cheerly** spiritedly; energetically.

7   **tend to** attend; pay heed to [and obey]. Variations of this word
occur in I.ii.38, 47, 78, 87, all emphasizing the need to be
alert and avoid any tendency to slothfulness. In this line *yare*
means 'be nimble'. *Harts* may simply be a variant of *Hearts*,
but it could also be a term of endearment, likening the
Boatswain's colleagues to hearty stags.

8   **Whistle** commands.

8–9   **Blow . . . enough** Bestir yourselves until you have burst your
lungs from exertion. Some editors interpret this order as an
apostrophe addressed to the wind; that reading may be
correct, but it is difficult to see why the Boatswain would
want to 'assist the Storm' (line 15) until the ship is ready to be
taken back out to the open waters.

S.D.   **Ferdinando** Ferdinand. Here Shakespeare renders his name in
its Italian form. The Folio form for *Antonio* is *Anthonio*,
another authorial spelling for a name that may have been
pronounced 'Ant-ho-nio' in Shakespeare's theatre.

10   **have Care** (a) be careful, and (b) don't forget that you have
very important passengers in your care (line 20).

11   **Play the Men** Do everything humanly possible to preserve us.

ACT I

Scene 1

A tempestuous noise of Thunder and Lightning heard.
Enter a Ship-master, and a Boatswain.

MASTER   Boatswain.
BOATSWAIN   Here, Master. What Cheer?
MASTER   Good; speak to th' Mariners; fall to't,
yarely, or we run our selves a ground; bestir,
bestir.   *Exit.*   5

Enter Mariners.

BOATSWAIN   Heigh, my Hearts, cheerly, cheerly, my
Harts; yare, yare; take in the Topsail; tend to
th' Master's Whistle; blow till thou burst thy
Wind, if room enough.

Enter Alonso, Sebastian, Antonio, Ferdinando,
Gonzalo, and Others.

ALONSO   Good Boatswain, have Care: where's the   10
Master? Play the Men.
BOATSWAIN   I pray now keep below.
ANTONIO   Where is the Master, Boson?

6

14 **mar** interfere with.

15 **Keep** stay in.

16 **good** an abbreviation of 'good Boatswain' (line 10). Compare
line 3.

18 **Roarers** 'Elements' (line 23); agitated wind and water.

22 **Counsellor** advisor; member of your realm's ruling council.

23–24 **work ... Present** bring about an instant peace in your presence
chamber (the room in which you hold court).

24 **hand** handle; lay hands on.

26 **make ... ready** prepare your soul (with prayers and
confessions). Compare *Hamlet*, I.v.75–79, III.iii.80–95,
V.ii.46–47.

27–28 **if ... hap** if it should happen that 'Mischance' (disaster) befall
you.

32 **his ... Gallows** he illustrates the proverb that a man born to
be hanged need not fear drowning. Compare *The Two
Gentlemen of Verona*, I.i.151–53. Here *Complexion* means
both 'disposition' and 'look'.

33–35 **make ... advantage** let's anchor or moor our hopes on the
cable ('Rope') that determines his destiny, because our own
'Rope' is of scant use.

36 **Case** both (a) situation, and (b) cause. *Case* and *cause* both
derive from the same Latin root, *causa*. Gonzalo is playing
upon the legal sense of *Case*, an implication that befits the
Boatswain's warning that the 'Mischance of the Hour' may
soon deliver the ship's occupants to their appearance before
the highest court at the Last Judgement.

38 **Bring ... Main-course** Use the mainsail (try-sail) to keep the
ship exposed to the wind [and thus away from the island
upon which it threatens to run aground].

39 **A ... Howling** May these screaming passengers die of the
plague.

40 **our Office** the noise we make while doing our jobs ('Office') in
our attempts to keep the ship from being destroyed.

BOATSWAIN   Do you not hear him? You mar our
   Labour,
   Keep your Cabins: you do assist the Storm.   15
GONZALO   Nay, good, be patient.
BOATSWAIN   When the Sea is: hence: what cares
   these Roarers for the name of King? To Cabin;
   silence; trouble us not.
GONZALO   Good, yet remember whom thou hast aboord.   20
BOATSWAIN   None that I more love than my self.
   You are a Counsellor: if you can command these
   Elements to Silence, and work the Peace of the
   Present, we will not hand a Rope more. Use your
   Authority: if you cannot, give Thanks you have   25
   liv'd so long, and make your self ready in your
   Cabin for the Mischance of the Hour, if it so
   hap. – Cheerly, good Hearts. – Out of our way,
   I say.   *Exit.*
GONZALO   I have great Comfort from this Fellow: 30
   methinks he hath no Drowning Mark upon him,
   his Complexion is perfect Gallows. – Stand
   fast, good Fate, to his Hanging; make the Rope
   of his Destiny our Cable, for our own doth
   little advantage. If he be not borne to be   35
   hang'd, our Case is Miserable.

                        Exit [with his Companions].

        Enter Boatswain.

BOATSWAIN   Down with the Top-mast: yare, lower,
   lower. Bring her to Try with Main-course.
                        A Cry within.
   A Plague upon this Howling: they are louder

      Enter Sebastian, Antonio, and Gonzalo.

   than the Weather, or our Office. – Yet again? What   40
   do you here? Shall we give o'er and drown, have
   you a Mind to sink?

8

43 **Pox o'** pox on. Sebastian refers to one form of 'Plague' (line
      39): *Pox* could refer to smallpox, leprosy, syphilis, or other
      loathsome diseases. Here *bawling* means 'vehemently
      screaming', cursing, roaring (see line 18).

44 **incharitable** uncaring (lacking in Christian compassion).
      Compare line 10, and see the note to I.ii.162.

46 **whoreson** whore's son, bastard.

49 **warrant him for** warranty (insure) him against.

50–51 **as ... Wench** either (a) as free-flowing as a menstruating
      woman, or (b) as full of holes as a woman whose lust cannot
      be satisfied (compare *King Lear*, III.vi.28).

52 **Lay ... hold** bring her hold a-hull (hove-to), so that her sails
      will catch the wind.

52–53 **set ... again** position her two sails (her mainsail and her
      foresail) so that she will head back out to sea.

53 **lay her off** get her off this shoreline.

57 **Our ... theirs** out situation is the same as theirs. *Case* echoes
      line 36. *Patience* (here meaning 'tolerance', 'forbearance')
      recalls line 16.

58 **merely** totally. Compare *Hamlet*, I.ii.136–37.

59 **chopt** jawed.

59–60 **would ... Tides** may you suffer an agonizing death by
      drowning. Antonio wants to improve on the practice of letting
      the corpses of hanged pirates lie on the shore until they have
      been washed over three times by incoming tides. Meanwhile
      Gonzalo remains optimistic that everyone on the ship will 'die
      a dry Death' (line 69).

62 **gape ... him** open its mouth to a yawning gulf to gulp him
      down.

63 **split** break apart [on the rocks].

65 **Let's ... him** In what will prove to be a characteristic gesture,
      Sebastian declines to be his brother's keeper (Genesis 4:9).
      Antonio requires little persuasion before he abandons ship
      too.

66 **Furlongs** lengths of 220 yards (distances of one-eighth of a
      mile).

SEBASTIAN   A Pox o' your Throat, you bawling,
  blasphemous, incharitable Dog.
BOATSWAIN   Work you then.   45
ANTONIO   Hang, Cur, hang, you whoreson insolent
  Noisemaker: we are less afraid to be drown'd
  than thou art.
GONZALO   I'll warrant him for Drowning, though the
  Ship were no stronger than a Nutshell, and as   50
  leaky as an unstanch'd Wench.
BOATSWAIN   Lay her a hold, a hold, set her two
  Courses off to Sea again; lay her off.

Enter Mariners wet.

MARINER   All lost, to Prayers, to Prayers, all lost.
BOATSWAIN   What, must our Mouths be cold?   55
GONZALO   The King and Prince, at Prayers; let's
  assist them,
For our Case is as theirs.
SEBASTIAN   I am out of Patience.
ANTONIO   We are merely cheated of our Lives by
    Drunkards.
  This wide-chopt Rascal – would thou mightst lie
    drowning
  The washing of ten Tides.
GONZALO   He'll be hang'd yet,   60
  Though every Drop of Water swear against it,
  And gape at wid'st to glut him.
A confused Noise within.   Mercy on us:
  We split, we split. – Farewell, my Wife and
    Children;
  Farewell, Brother; we split, we split, we split.
ANTONIO   Let's all sink wi'th' King.
SEBASTIAN   Let's take leave of him.
                           Exit [with Antonio].   65
GONZALO   Now would I give a thousand Furlongs of

67–68 **long . . . Furze** types of heather and gorse that can subsist in infertile, dry soils. The Folio prints *firrs*, and it is conceivable, though highly unlikely, that Gonzalo is referring to parched fir trees.

69 **fain** gladly; prefer to. Gonzalo's prayer recalls *The Winter's Tale*, III.iii.6–7.

I.ii This scene takes place in the cell (possibly a cave, as in *As You Like It*, V.iv.204) of Prospero, somewhere on the island near which the mariners have run aground.

1 **Art** magical powers.

2 **allay** lessen; calm. *Roar* recalls I.i.17–18.

3 **powre** pour. But here as elsewhere (see *Macbeth*, I.v.28, I.iii.98, IV.i.18, 63, 79), the Shakespearean spelling plays on *power*; compare III.iii.90, IV.i.38.
    Pitch black tar (proverbially associated with defilement, as in *Love's Labour's Lost*, IV.iii.3, and *Much Ado About Nothing*, III.iii.62).

4 **Welkin's** sky's. Lines 3–5 recall *The Winter's Tale*, III.iii. *Cheek* probably refers to the firmament just above the horizon, where the ground kisses the sky.

6 **brave** proud, handsome. This will prove a key word.

7 **Creature** Miranda probably means 'creatures', but the ship contains one 'noble Creature' who will be of particular interest to her. Compare Romans 8:19 in the 1611 King James Bible, where *creature* refers to the entire 'creation'.

8 **knock** pound. Compare *Macbeth*, I.iii.132–35, II.ii.54–55.

11 **or ere** before.

12 **swallow'd** Miranda's verb echoes I.i.60–62.

13 **fraughting Souls** souls who comprised the cargo (freight). Here *fraughting* also suggests (a) fraught (burdened, 'heavy laden', as in Matthew 11:28), and (b) frightened.
    Be collected compose yourself (calm your anxieties).

16 **in . . . thee** to benefit you. *Care* recalls I.i.10.

18 **naught** nothing.

Sea for an Acre of barren Ground: long Heath,
brown Furze, any thing. The Wills Above be
done, but I would fain die a dry Death.　　　　　*Exit.*

Scene 2

Enter Prospero and Miranda.

MIRANDA　If by your Art, my dearest Father, you
　　have
Put the wild Waters in this Roar, allay them:
The Sky it seems would powre down stinking
　　Pitch
But that the Sea, mounting to th' Welkin's
　　Cheek,
Dashes the Fire out. Oh! I have suffered　　　　　5
With those that I saw suffer: a brave Vessel,
Who had, no doubt, some noble Creature in her,
Dash'd all to pieces. O the Cry did knock
Against my very Heart. Poor Souls, they
　　perish'd.
Had I been any God of power, I would　　　　　10
Have sunk the Sea within the Earth or ere
It should the good Ship so have swallow'd,
　　and
The fraughting Souls within her.
PROSPERO　　　　　　　　　Be collected,
No more Amazement. Tell your piteous Heart
There's no Harm done.
MIRANDA　　　　　　　O Woe the Day.
PROSPERO　　　　　　　　　　No Harm:　　　15
I have done nothing but in Care of thee,
Of thee, my Dear One, thee my Daughter, who
Are Ignorant of what thou art, naught knowing

19 **Of . . . am** where I came from.

19–21 **more . . . Father** anything other than the Prospero who presides over a meagre cell and is no more than a father to you. *Full poor* means 'completely worthless'.

22 **meddle** (a) mingle, and (b) interfere. Compare *Measure for Measure*, V.i.127.

24 **pluck** remove, pull off, strip.

25 **Lie . . . Art** Prospero addresses either his 'Magic Garment' (line 24) or his potent 'Staff' (V.i.54), both of which he probably places on the ground.

26 **Wrack** wreck. But the compassionate Miranda has also suffered the agonies of the *rack*, an instrument of torture.

29 **ordered** both (a) commanded, and (b) arranged.

30 **Perdition** loss (see *The Winter's Tale*, III.iii.31–33). *Perdition* can also mean 'damnation' (eternal loss). *Hair* echoes Matthew 10:29–31, where Jesus assures his disciples that their heavenly Father watches over them with such providence that 'the very hairs of [their] head are all numbered'. Compare lines 212–13, 217.

31 **Betid** betided (with an implicit reminder of the 'tide' to which the ship fell victim), happened. The syntax of lines 29–33 is difficult to anchor; what Prospero appears to mean is that there is no soul lost in the ship whose fate has so troubled Miranda. At this point we cannot tell whether the 'broken Delivery' (*The Winter's Tale*, V.ii.11) is part of Prospero's design or one of the devices Shakespeare uses to suggest that Prospero's emotional state is now making his speech somewhat incoherent. *Betid* echoes I.i.59–60.

33 **know farther** know more. Prospero's phrasing is a reminder that Miranda will soon 'know Father' in a new way; compare lines 15–23.

35 **a bootless Inquisition** an interrogation that gains nothing.

41 **Out . . . old** out of the womb a full three years. Here *Out* can mean 'fully'.

43–44 **Of . . . Remembrance** Tell me any recollection of that prior period that has remained in your memory. *Kept* echoes I.i.15.

Of whence I am, nor that I am more better
Than Prospero, Master of a full poor Cell   20
And thy no greater Father.
MIRANDA   More to know
Did never meddle with my Thoughts.
PROSPERO   'Tis Time
I should inform thee farther. Lend thy Hand
And pluck my Magic Garment from me. – So,
Lie there, my Art. – Wipe thou thine Eyes, have
    Comfort: 25
The direful Spectacle of the Wrack which touch'd
The very Virtue of Compassion in thee
I have with such Provision in mine Art
So safely ordered that there is no Soul,
No not so much Perdition as an Hair   30
Betid to any Creature, in the Vessel
Which thou heardst cry, which thou saw'st sink.
    Sit down,
For thou must now know farther.
MIRANDA   You have often
Begun to tell me what I am, but stopp'd
And left me to a bootless Inquisition,   35
Concluding 'Stay: not yet.'
PROSPERO   The Hour's now come,
The very Minute bids thee ope thine Ear,
Obey, and be attentive. Canst thou remember
A Time before we came unto this Cell?
I do not think thou canst, for then thou wast
    not   40
Out three Years old.
MIRANDA   Certainly, Sir, I can.
PROSPERO   By what? By any other House, or Person?
Of any thing the Image tell me that
Hath kept with thy Remembrance.
MIRANDA   'Tis far off,

45   **Dream, then** dream than. But here, as occasionally elsewhere, *then* can also carry its usual modern sense. Compare *Macbeth*, III.ii.7, III.iv.13, IV.iii.110.

45–46 **an . . . warrants** an image my memory can guarantee to be accurate. Compare I.i.49.

49   **this . . . Mind** this long-buried 'Remembrance' remains alive.

50   **dark Backward . . . Time** pitch-black, unfathomable recesses of Time. *Abysm* means 'abyss' (a primordial, seemingly bottomless pit). For other references to vast, murky, abysmal depths, compare lines 10–13, 44–46, and I.i.59–62, 66–67.

51   **ought ere** anything before.

52   **How . . . mayst** you may also be able to recall how you arrived here.

53   **Year since** years ago.

54   **Millaine** Milan (here, as elsewhere, accented on the first syllable).

55   **of power** with considerable authority. Compare line 10.

56   **a . . . Virtue** an exemplar of chastity. *Piece* recalls *Cymbeline*, V.iv.140, V.v.437, 447, and *The Winter's Tale*, V.iii.38.

59   **no worse issued** the offspring of no worse parentage. Here, as in line 98, *onely* means 'only'.

60   **Foul Play** wickedness, departure from the rules of fair play. Compare *Hamlet*, I.ii.250, *Macbeth*, I.i.9.

62   **heav'd thence** cast out of there. Compare II.i.233, and see *King Lear*, I.i.92–93.

63   **blessedly holp** providentially helped.

64   **Teen** sorrow, grief. Compare *Romeo and Juliet*, I.iii.13.

65   **Which . . . Remembrance** which I cannot remember.
       farther proceed. Compare lines 23, 33.

67   **mark** 'attend' (line 78), pay heed.

68   **perfidious** faithless, treacherous. Compare *Coriolanus*, V.vi.90–91.
       next thy self after you. Compare *The Winter's Tale*, I.ii.171–75.

And rather like a Dream, then an Assurance   45
That my Remembrance warrants. Had I not
Four or five Women once, that tended me?
PROSPERO   Thou hadst; and more, Miranda. But how
   is it
That this lives in thy Mind? What seest thou
   else
In the dark Backward and Abysm of Time?   50
If thou rememb'rest ought ere thou cam'st here,
How thou cam'st here thou mayst.
MIRANDA   But that I do not.
PROSPERO   Twelve Year since, Miranda, twelve Year
   since,
Thy Father was the Duke of Millaine and
A Prince of power.
MIRANDA   Sir, are not you my Father?   55
PROSPERO   Thy Mother was a piece of Virtue, and
She said thou wast my Daughter; and thy Father
Was Duke of Millaine, and his onely Heir
And Princess no worse issued.
MIRANDA   O the Heavens,
What Foul Play had we, that we came from thence?   60
Or Blessed was't we did?
PROSPERO   Both, both, my Girl.
By Foul-play, as thou sayst, were we heav'd
   thence,
But blessedly holp hither.
MIRANDA   O my Heart bleeds
To think o'th' Teen that I have turn'd you to,
Which is from my Remembrance. Please you,
   farther.   65
PROSPERO   My Brother and thy Uncle, call'd
   Antonio
(I pray thee mark me, that a Brother should
Be so perfidious), he, whom next thy self
Of all the World I lov'd, and to him put

70   **Manage . . . State**   management of my city-state.

71   **Signories**   Italian states under ducal rule (from *signior*).

72   **prime**   'first' (line 71) and highest.

73   **liberal Arts**   the *artes liberales* (a Latin phrase defining the
       abstract, reflective studies befitting a freeman), as
       distinguished from the manual *artes serviles* (servile arts) of
       those in bondage to others and therefore limited to the
       non-intellectual labour that characterizes 'rude Mechanicals'
       (see *A Midsummer Night's Dream*, III.ii.8–15, V.i.72–75).
       Prospero refers to various forms of 'book learning'
       (languages, literature, history, science, and philosophy) that
       promote the 'bettering of' a person's 'Mind' (line 90).

75   **cast upon**   Prospero means 'put' (delegated) to, lines 69–70. But
       his phrase echoes *heav'd thence* (line 62) and anticipates *trash*
       (line 81), with the unintended suggestion that 'Government'
       (rule) was something to be 'shuffled off' (*Hamlet*, III.i.64), like
       unwanted clothing, food, or refuse.

77   **rapt**   (a) carried away, (b) wrapped. Compare *Macbeth*, I.iii.55,
       140.

79   **Being . . . Suits**   having learned how to grant requests and
       'advance' (reward) those who flattered him for favours.

81   **trash for over-topping**   (a) check for too much eagerness (as a
       hunting-dog that runs too fast), and (b) lop off excess growth
       (as with a gardener making a trash heap).

83–84 **having . . . Office**   having been given the run of my office
       (position) and the power to turn my officers into his own.
       Office echoes I.i.39–40.

87   **Verdure**   vigour. Compare the vine imagery in *The Comedy of
       Errors*, II.ii.178–85.

90   **Closeness**   (a) privacy, and (b) seclusion from worldly affairs.
       Compare *Cymbeline*, III.v.46.

91–92 **but . . . Rate**   either (a) merely by being sequestered from the
       vulgar tastes of the public, exceeded in value anything that
       less discriminating people thought estimable, or (b) if it had
       not been hidden away from public view, would have been
       rated higher than anything the populace esteemed valuable.

92–93 **in . . . Nature**   in a brother with the potential to prove 'false',
       aroused a latent 'Evil Nature'.

The Manage of my State (as at that Time   70
Through all the Signories it was the first,
And Prospero the prime Duke, being so reputed
In Dignity, and for the liberal Arts
Without a Parallel, those being all my Study),
The Government I cast upon my Brother,   75
And to my State grew Stranger, being
   transported
And rapt in secret Studies. Thy false Uncle —
Dost thou attend me?
MIRANDA   Sir, most heedfully.
PROSPERO — Being once perfected how to graunt
   Suits,
How to deny them, who t' advance, and who   80
To trash for over-topping, new created
The Creatures that were mine, I say, or chang'd
   'em,
Or else new form'd 'em (having both the Key
Of Officer and Office), set all Hearts i'th'
   State
To what Tune pleas'd his Ear, that now he was   85
The Ivy which had hid my princely Trunk
And suck'd my Verdure out on't. Thou attend'st
   not?
MIRANDA   O good Sir, I do.
PROSPERO   I pray thee mark me.
I thus neglecting Worldly Ends (all dedicated
To Closeness and the bettering of my Mind   90
With that which, but by being so Retir'd,
O'er-priz'd all popular Rate), in my false
   Brother
Awak'd an Evil Nature, and my Trust,

94–96 **did . . . was**   did conceive in him a deceit as large as was my trusting 'Confidence' in his honesty and goodness.

97   **sans Bound**   without 'Limit' (line 96), or restraint.
Lorded   rendered lord-like; given the power of a duke.

98   **Revenue**   income (from rents and taxes); here pronounced 're-vén-ue'. *Onely* means 'only', solely; compare line 58.

99   **my . . . exact**   the authority vested in my title might otherwise permit him to extract from the realm.

103–4 **out . . . Prerogative**   as an outgrowth of my having deputized him to execute all the public duties of rulership. Appropriately, lines 103–6 are all 'sans Bound' metrically, with six metrical feet rather than the five feet normal to Shakespeare's dramatic verse. Like Antonio's 'Ambition', Prospero finds his lines 'growing' from pentameters into hexameters.

107   **Screen**   (a) distinction, (b) partition, (c) impediment, (d) disguising. Lines 107–8 give a theatrical twist to Miranda's reference to 'Foul Play' in line 60.

110–11 **of . . . incapable**   he now considers me unable to play a royal role in affairs that pertain to 'Worldly Ends'. *Roalties* is the Folio spelling; it may be compositorial (though, even in a crowded line, he would have had room for a *y* as in line 104), but it is equally likely to be an authorial pun on *role*.

111–12 **confederates . . . Sway**)   plots, arranges (so thirsty was he for complete control of the Milanese dukedom). *Sway* (power) can also refer to the swaying that denotes a loss of stability; compare *King Lear*, I.i.136–40.

114   **Subject . . . Crown**   bow Milan's coronet to Naples' crown.

117   **Condition**   both (a) disposition, character, and (b) stipulation (set of conditions) for the subordination of his city-state to the King of Naples' hegemony. The second sense is primary in line 120. *Mark* echoes lines 67, 88.
th' Event   the consequence; what ensued.

119   **To . . . Grandmother**   to wonder if my grandmother was unfaithful to the noble bed of my grandfather. *Sin* recalls line 101.

Like a good Parent, did beget of him
A Falsehood in its Contrary as great   95
As my Trust was, which had indeed no Limit,
A Confidence sans Bound. He being thus Lorded,
Not onely with what my Revenue yielded
But what my Power might else exact (like one
Who, having into Truth, by telling of it,   100
Made such a Sinner of his Memory
To credit his own Lie), he did believe
He was indeed the Duke, out o'th' Substitution
And Executing th' outward Face of Royalty
With all Prerogative. Hence, his Ambition
    growing –   105
Dost thou hear?
MIRANDA   Your Tale, Sir, would cure Deafness.
PROSPERO – To have no Screen between this part he
    play'd
And him he play'd it for, he needs will be
Absolute Millaine (me, poor man, my Library
Was Dukedom large enough: of temporal Roalties   110
He thinks me now incapable), confederates
(So dry he was for Sway) wi'th' King of Naples
To give him annual Tribute, do him Homage,
Subject his Coronet to his Crown, and bend
The Dukedom yet unbow'd (alas, poor Millaine)   115
To most ignoble Stooping.
MIRANDA   Oh the Heavens.
PROSPERO Mark his Condition, and th' Event, then
    tell me
If this might be a Brother.
MIRANDA   I should sin
To think but Nobly of my Grandmother:

120   **Good . . . Sons**   Miranda's generalization parallels what
          Prospero said about his 'Trust' as a 'Parent' (lines 93–97).
          Borne means both 'carried' and 'given birth to'; compare
          I.i.35.

122   **inveterate**   of long duration; literally, 'of old'.

122–   **hearkens . . . mine**   heeds Antonio's request, namely that the
25   King of Naples, in exchange for Milan's loyal obedience and
          for who knows how large an annual payment, should
          immediately remove me and everything belonging to me. The
          phrase *in lieu of the Premises* means 'in return for what
          Antonio pledged to grant him for his assistance'. *Suit* echoes
          lines 79–81.

127   **Honours**   prerogatives pertaining to that title.

128   **levied**   raised; conscripted, drafted.
          one Mid-night   during the middle of one night.

131   **Ministers . . . thence**   subordinates commissioned to do the job
          rushed away from Milan.

134   **Hint**   signal (here one that derives from a particular occasion).

136–   **the . . . upon's**   the urgent task that now calls for our full
37   concentration.

138   **Impertinent**   beside the point, irrelevant.
          Wherefore   why.

139   **demanded**   asked.

141–   **set . . . Business**   betray their treachery with an act that would
42   lead the people to rise up against men suspected of bloodshed.
          Mark so Bloody suggests the blood used to designate the
          hunters who have taken part in a kill (compare *Julius Caesar*,
          III.i.106–11, 120–22, 152–70, 205–11, where this ritual
          denotes the assassins as slaughterers of a 'brave Hart', 'a
          Deer, stroken by many Princes'). Prospero's repetition of *Dear*
          in lines 140–41 helps reinforce the association with
          game-hunting.

143   **Fairer**   (a) less dark, (b) less violent, (c) less 'Foul'-looking.

144   **In . . . Bark**   in short, they shoved us aboard a ship.

145   **some Leagues**   an unspecified number of three-mile lengths.

Good Wombs have borne Bad Sons.

PROSPERO   Now the Condition.   120
  This King of Naples, being an Enemy
  To me inveterate, hearkens my Brother's Suit,
  Which was that he in lieu o'th' Premises,
  Of Homage and I know not how much Tribute,
  Should presently extirpate me and mine   125
  Out of the Dukedom and confer fair Millaine,
  With all the Honours, on my Brother; whereon,
  A treacherous Army levied, one Mid-night
  Fated to th' Purpose, did Antonio open
  The Gates of Millaine and i'th' dead of
    Darkness   130
  The Ministers for th' Purpose hurried thence
  Me and thy crying self.

MIRANDA   Alack, for Pity:
  I, not rememb'ring how I cried out then,
  Will cry it o'er again. It is a Hint
  That wrings mine Eyes to't.

PROSPERO   Hear a little further,   135
  And then I'll bring thee to the present
    Business
  Which now's upon's, without the which this
    Story
  Were most Impertinent.

MIRANDA   Wherefore did they not
  That Hour destroy us?

PROSPERO   Well demanded, Wench:
  My Tale provokes that Question. Dear, they
    durst not,   140
  So dear the Love my People bore me, nor set
  A Mark so Bloody on the Business, but
  With Colours Fairer painted their Foul Ends.
  In few, they hurried us aboard a Bark,
  Bore us some Leagues to Sea, where they
    prepared   145

146 **Butt** a small boat (here a decayed tub without sailing gear).

148 **have quit it** had abandoned it [as a vessel likely to sink].

151 **Did ... Wrong** inflicted only the pains that manifest love.
Compare lines 59–63, and see *The Winter's Tale*, V.iii.75–76.

154 **Infused** filled (literally, 'in-poured').

155 **deck'd ... Salt** covered the sea with salty teardrops. *Full* recalls
line 20 and anticipates line 394.

156– **which ... ensue** which smile gave me the intestinal fortitude to
58 endure the labour-like trials that lay before us. Here *Stomach*
means 'courage', now denoted by the word *guts*; but it also
reinforces the suggestion that Prospero's 'Burthen' was
analogous to that of a woman in the advanced stages of
pregnancy. Compare the imagery in *The Comedy of Errors*,
V.i.398–404, and see Romans 8:18–28, where the Apostle
Paul says that 'the whole creation groaneth and travaileth in
pain' until it can be 'delivered from the bondage of corruption
into the glorious liberty of the children of God'. Paul notes
that 'we are saved by hope', and he maintains that 'all things
work together for good to them that love God, to them who
are called according to his purpose'.

159– **By ... Water** Most editors substitute a full stop (period) after
60 *Divine*. The Folio line arrangement suggests that a slight
pause for emphasis is in order.

161 **Noble Neapolitan** gentle (generous-spirited) Lord of Naples.

162 **Charity** Christian compassion, care (see I.i.10, 44, and I.ii.16,
174). *Charity* derives from *caritas*, the Latin word for the
kind of self-giving love known as *agape* in Greek.

164 **Stuffs** household goods.

165 **steeded much** stood us in good stead; sustained us well.

168 **prize above** treasure more than I do. *Prize* echoes lines 89–92.
The wish Miranda makes in lines 168–69 will soon be
fulfilled.

172 **made ... profit** caused you to benefit more.

A rotten Carcass of a Butt, not rigg'd,
Nor Tackle, Sail, nor Mast (the very Rats
Instinctively have quit it); there they hoist
    us
To cry to th' Sea, that roar'd to us, to sigh
To th' Winds, whose Pity sighing back again   150
Did us but loving Wrong.

MIRANDA   Alack, what Trouble
Was I then to you?

PROSPERO   O, a Cherubin
Thou wast, that did preserve me. Thou didst
    smile,
Infused with a Fortitude from Heaven,
When I have deck'd the Sea with Drops full
    Salt,   155
Under my Burthen groan'd, which rais'd in me
An undergoing Stomach, to bear up
Against what should ensue.

MIRANDA   How came we ashore?

PROSPERO   By Providence Divine,
Some Food we had, and some fresh Water, that   160
A Noble Neapolitan, Gonzalo,
Out of his Charity, who, being then appointed
Master of this Design, did give us, with
Rich Garments, Linens, Stuffs, and Necessaries
Which since have steeded much; so of his
    Gentleness,   165
Knowing I lov'd my Books, he furnish'd me
From mine own Library with Volumes that
I prize above my Dukedom.

MIRANDA   Would I might
But ever see that Man.

PROSPERO   Now I arise;
Sit still, and hear the last of our Sea-sorrow.   170
Here in this Island we arriv'd, and here
Have I, thy Schoolmaster, made thee more profit

173 **Princess** princesses.

174 **Vainer** emptier; more frivolous.
Careful care-full, conscientious. Compare line 16.

176 **beating** pounding (like a hammer on a forge). Compare *The Merry Wives of Windsor*, IV.ii.235, *Henry V*, V, Chorus, line 23, *The Winter's Tale*, IV.iv.17, and *Hamlet*, III.i.178–79. Also compare lines 8–9.
Reason This word was pronounced much like 'raising' (line 177). See *Coriolanus*, V.vi.58.

180 **Prescience** pre-science (ability to foresee the future).

181– **my ... Star** my rise to Fortune's height depends upon my
82 wooing the 'Influence' of a favourable ascendant 'Star'. Prospero compares the successful astrologer to an attentive courtier who must please his would-be sponsor the way Queen Elizabeth's ambitious suitors had sought to gratify her. See *The Winter's Tale*, IV.iv.51–52.

185 **inclin'd** disposed to 'droop' (line 184). Prospero's verb relates both to his own need to be 'inclin'd' upward if he hopes to win his 'dear Lady' and to the 'droop' he will experience if he should 'omit' (neglect) to pursue his 'Zenith' while 'bountiful Fortune' is receptive to his advance. Compare *Pericles*, IV.iii.104–6, 153–55. As Prospero speaks, his entranced daughter falls into a deep slumber.

190 **answer ... Pleasure** respond to whatever you ask of me.

192– **task ... Quality** give a task to Ariel and all his abilities and
93 subordinate spirits.

194 **to point** in every detail. Compare lines 180–84, 496–98.

197 **Waste** either (a) waist (middle), or (b) waste (uninhabited hold, hatches).
Deck poop (a raised deck at the stern – rear – of the ship).

Than other Princess can, that have more Time
For Vainer Hours, and Tutors not so Careful.
MIRANDA   Heavens thank you for't. And now I pray
    you, Sir,   175
For still 'tis beating in my Mind, your Reason
For raising this Sea-storm?
PROSPERO   Know thus far forth:
By Accident most strange, bountiful Fortune
(Now my dear Lady) hath mine Enemies
Brought to this Shore; and by my Prescience   180
I find my Zenith doth depend upon
A most auspicious Star, whose Influence,
If now I court not, but omit, my Fortunes
Will ever after droop. Here cease more
    Questions:
Thou art inclin'd to Sleep. 'Tis a good
    Dullness,   185
And give it way: I know thou canst not choose.
– Come away, Servant, come; I am ready now;
Approach, my Ariel, come.

Enter Ariel.

ARIEL   All hail, great Master, grave Sir, hail:
    I come
To answer thy best Pleasure, be't to Fly,   190
To Swim, to Dive into the Fire, to Ride
On the curl'd Clouds. To thy strong Bidding
    task
Ariel and all his Quality.
PROSPERO   Hast thou, Spirit,
Perform'd to point the Tempest that I bad
    thee?
ARIEL   To every Article.   195
I boorded the King's Ship: now on the Beak,
Now in the Waste, the Deck, in every Cabin,

198 **flam'd Amazement** drove them into a maze-like state with my
flame-like sizzling (the phenomenon known as St Elmo's Fire).
Compare line 14.

200 **Yards** horizontal spars across the mast to support the sails.
Boresprit bowsprit (tapered spar extending forward from the
bow – prow or 'Beak', line 196 – of a ship).

201 **Jove's Lightning** the lightning flashes generated by Jove himself
(that is, Nature unassisted by spirits such as Ariel);
'Precursors' (forerunners) of thunder, but too quick for 'Sight'
to keep up with them (line 203).

204 **Sulphurous Roaring** lightning followed by 'Cracks'
(explosions) of 'Thunderclaps'.

204–5 **the . . . besiege** seem to surround the God of the Ocean
himself.

206 **dread Trident** fearful three-pronged weapon.

207–8 **Who . . . Reason?** who could have been so unbending in
resolve that this turmoil would not affect his judgement?

209– **But . . . Desperation** who didn't experience fits of madness and
10 have tricks played on him like those that affect people in the
extremities of despair.

211 **quit** abandoned. This verb recalls lines 147–48.

212 **afire with me** covered with the flames I caused.

213 **up-staring** standing straight up (like stiff 'Reeds'). *Hair*
anticipates line 217; see the note to line 391.

217 **Not . . . perish'd** Ariel's phrasing echoes lines 28–31 and
alludes to Matthew 10:29–31 (see the notes to *The Merchant
of Venice*, III.ii.301, IV.i.334). It also evokes Acts 27:34,
where (in the midst of a nautical narrative that Shakespeare
drew upon for *The Tempest*), the Apostle Paul tells a crew of
mariners that 'there shall not an hair fall from the head of any
of you'. As in *Macbeth*, I.iii.133, *Hair* plays on *Heir*.
Compare *Cymbeline*, V.v.448, and *The Winter's Tale*,
IV.iv.758–59, V.i.127.

218 **sustaining** (a) wreck-enduring, (b) life-preserving, and (c)
stain-resisting.

I flam'd Amazement. Sometime I'd divide
And burn in many Places: on the Top-mast,
The Yards, and Boresprit would I flame
   distinctly,   200
Then meet and join. Jove's Lightning, the
   Precursors
O'th' dreadful Thunderclaps, more Momentary
And Sight-outrunning were not; the Fire and
   Cracks
Of Sulphurous Roaring the most mighty Neptune
Seem to beseige and make his bold Waves tremble,   205
Yea, his dread Trident shake.
PROSPERO   My brave Spirit,
   Who was so Firm, so Constant, that this Coil
   Would not infect his Reason?
ARIEL   Not a Soul
   But felt a Fever of the Mad, and play'd
   Some Tricks of Desperation. All but Mariners   210
   Plung'd in the foaming Brine and quit the
      Vessel;
   Then all afire with me, the King's Son
      Ferdinand,
   With Hair up-staring (then like Reeds, not
      Hair),
   Was the first Man that leapt, cried 'Hell is
      empty,
   And all the Divels are here.'
PROSPERO   Why that's my Spirit.   215
   But was not this nigh Shore?
ARIEL   Close by, my Master.
PROSPERO   But are they, Ariel, safe?
ARIEL   Not a Hair perish'd:
   On their sustaining Garments not a Blemish,
   But Fresher than before; and as thou badst me,
   In Troops I have dispers'd them 'bout the Isle.   220
   The King's Son have I landed by himself,

223   **odd Angle**   angular configuration. Compare *deep Nook*, line
        227, and see II.i.104–5.

224   **in . . . Knot**   enfolded in this manner [here, no doubt, imitated
        by Ariel].

225   **dispos'd**   taken care of. Prospero's verb can refer to a
        mischievous disposition to be merry at another's expense
        (compare *Julius Caesar*, I.iii.33), and that sense, pertinent to
        the context, colours Prospero's query.

229   **Still-vext Bermoothes**   ever-agitated Bermudas.

230   **under Hatches stowed**   secured in the chambers below the deck.
        Compare lines 26–32, where Prospero implies that the ship
        has sunk (or at least that Miranda saw it sink).

231   **Who . . . Labour**   who, with a magic spell to round off the
        agonizing trials they've endured. Ariel's words are a reminder
        that Prospero has just administered a similar 'Charm' to
        Miranda, who has 'suffered / With those that [she] saw suffer'
        (lines 5–6). Compare lines 153–58.

234   **Flote**   sea-waves, flood.

236   **wrack'd**   wrecked; put on the shelf (as in *The Merchant of
        Venice*, I.i.181). See the note to line 26.

237–   **thy . . . perform'd**   you have discharged your assigned role
38   perfectly.

239   **mid Season**   midpoint, high noon ('Zenith', line 181). Compare
        'Mid-night' in line 128.

240   **Glasses**   hourglasses. It is past two o'clock in the afternoon.
        'twixt Six and now   between now and six in the evening. For a
        similar treatment of time in reverse chronological order, see
        Julius Caesar, II.i.62–64; compare *Macbeth*, I.v.48–49.

241   **spent most preciously**   used with utmost efficiency (because
        every instant is of incalculable value). See lines 177–84.

242   **Pains**   (a) 'Toil', labour to do, and (b) trouble, effort.

243   **remember**   remind.

244   **perform'd me**   done for me.

246   **Before . . . out?**   Before the figurative hourglass that measures
        your servitude has emptied all the sand out of its upper half?
        See line 240. Compare the use of *out* in lines 40–41.

Whom I left cooling of the Air with Sighs
In an odd Angle of the Isle, and sitting
His Arms in this sad Knot.
PROSPERO   Of the King's Ship,
　The Mariners, say how thou hast dispos'd,   225
　And all the rest o'th' Fleet?
ARIEL   Safely in Harbour
　Is the King's Ship: in the deep Nook where once
　Thou call'dst me up at Midnight to fetch Dew
　From the still-vext Bermoothes, there she's
　　hid;
　The Mariners all under Hatches stowed,   230
　Who with a Charm join'd to their suff'red Labour
　I have left asleep; and for the rest o'th' Fleet
　(Which I dispers'd), they all have met again
　And are upon the Mediterranean Flote
　Bound sadly home for Naples,   235
　Supposing that they saw the King's Ship wrack'd
　And his great Person perish.
PROSPERO   Ariel, thy Charge
　Exactly is perform'd; but there's more Work.
　What is the Time o'th' Day?
ARIEL   Past the mid Season.
PROSPERO   At least two Glasses: the Time 'twixt
　Six and now   240
　Must by us both be spent most preciously.
ARIEL   Is there more Toil? Since thou dost give me
　　Pains,
　Let me remember thee what thou hast promis'd,
　Which is not yet perform'd me.
PROSPERO   How now? Moody?
　What is't thou canst demand?
ARIEL   My Liberty.   245
PROSPERO   Before the Time be out? No more.
ARIEL   I prethee,
　Remember I have done thee worthy Service,

248 **Mistakings** mistakes (literally, mis-takings). In *A Midsummer Night's Dream*, Puck, Ariel's counterpart, *does* make mistakes.

249 **or Grudge** either resentment.

250 **bate me** abate (reduce) my period of obligation to you. Prospero never acknowledges this 'promise' in his reply to Ariel.

253 **much** a great hardship.
Ooze slimy depths. Compare line 50 and III.iii.100.

255 **do ... Earth** serve me by venturing into the underground streams that function in the earth like veins in the human body.

256 **bak'd** solidified.

258 **fowl** Prospero probably means *foul* (see line 60, and compare II.i.124–25), but the name of Caliban's mother suggests that she may have been part fowl; see the note to the stage direction following III.iii.52.
Sycorax The name probably derives from the Greek words *sus* (sow) and *corax* (raven), with an echo of *Circe*, the seductive charmer in Homer's *Odyssey* who deformed men into beasts. Given its metrical position, *Sycorax* is probably to be syncopated to 'Sick-racks', a pronunciation that suggests her power to make her victims sick and rack them with pain; see the notes to lines 26, 236, 367.
Envy malice.

259 **grown ... Hoop** bent into a hoop-like (folded over) posture, like that of a perching vulture.

261 **Argier** Algiers.
Oh ... so either (a) oh, so she was! or (b) oh, was she so? (the usual interpretation).

264 **manifold** multiple; literally, many-fold. See the note to line 259.

265 **Humane** human (but with a reminder of the other modern word that derives from the same Renaissance root). So also in line 284.

266 **one ... did** Prospero implies that, notwithstanding her wickedness, Sycorax performed one deed or function that benefited the state of Argier. Compare lines 307–13.

Told thee no Lies, made thee no Mistakings,
   serv'd
Without or Grudge or Grumblings; thou did
   promise
To bate me a full Year.

PROSPERO   Dost thou forget   250
  From what a Torment I did free thee?

ARIEL   No.

PROSPERO   Thou dost; and think'st
  It much to tread the Ooze of the Salt Deep,
  To run upon the sharp Wind of the North,
  To do me Business in the Veins o'th' Earth   255
  When it is bak'd with Frost.

ARIEL   I do not, Sir.

PROSPERO   Thou liest, Malignant Thing. Hast thou
    forgot
  The fowl Witch Sycorax, who with Age and Envy
  Was grown into a Hoop? Hast thou forgot her?

ARIEL   No Sir.

PROSPERO   Thou hast. Where was she born? Speak;
    tell me.   260

ARIEL   Sir, in Argier.

PROSPERO   Oh, was she so: I must
  Once in a Month recount what thou hast been,
  Which thou forget'st. This damn'd Witch
    Sycorax,
  For Mischiefs manifold, and Sorceries terrible
  To enter Humane Hearing, from Argier   265
  Thou know'st was banish'd: for one thing she
    did
  They would not take her Life. Is this not true?

ARIEL   Ay Sir.

269   **blew**   blue. But the Folio spelling also suggests the possibility of wordplay on *blown* (in full bloom), here perhaps to mean 'swollen-lidded' or 'bulge-eyed'. Compare *The Winter's Tale*, II.i.13–15, and see *Hamlet*, V.i.267.
    with Child   pregnant (a condition associated with blue eyelids).

271   **As . . . self**   as you describe yourself (see lines 242–44). Prospero uses the term 'Slave' only for the base offspring of Sycorax (see line 308).

272   **for**   because.
    delicate   refined, elevated (unlike Circe's victims).

274   **grand Hests**   imperious behests, commands.

275   **Ministers**   agents; subordinate spirits.

276   **unmitigable**   incapable of being mitigrated (made milder).

277   **cloven**   split, rifted [and then re-shut].

280   **vent**   utter; give voice to. *Groans* echoes lines 153–58 and anticipates line 287.

281   **as . . . strike**   as the paddles on mill-wheels strike [the rushing water].

282   **Save . . . here**   except for the son that 'this Island' allowed to be born here as part of his 'litter' (assortment of offspring). Most editors emend *he* to *she*, assuming that the pronoun must apply to the 'Hag'.

283   **freckl'd Whelp**   dark, splotchy, subhuman infant.
    Hag-borne   both (a) carried, and (b) given birth to, by a hag.

285   **Dull**   slow-witted, stupid; subhuman. Compare line 185. *Thing* echoes line 257.

292   **made gape**   caused to open wide again. Compare I.i.60–62.

294   **If . . . murmur'st**   if you complain any further. Prospero's verb recalls Exodus 15:24, where the recently released children of Israel begin a series of murmurings against Moses, their deliverer from bondage to the Egyptians. See especially Exodus 16:9–12, 17:2–3.
    rend   tear open.

295   **peg**   drive, embed. *Knotty* echoes line 224. Prospero's phrasing in lines 295–96 evokes the howling of the winter wind. Compare *Measure for Measure*, III.i.72–75, where *Winters* also has the effect of emphasizing how long and harsh a specified number of years would be.

PROSPERO   This blew-ey'd Hag was hither brought
    with Child,
And here was left by th' Sailors. Thou, my
    Slave,   270
As thou report'st thy self, was then her
    Servant;
And, for thou wast a Spirit too delicate
To act her earthy and abhorr'd Commands,
Refusing her grand Hests, she did confine
    thee,
By help of her more potent Ministers,   275
And in her most unmitigable Rage,
Into a cloven Pine, within which Rift
Imprison'd thou didst painfully remain
A Dozen Years, within which Space she died
And left thee there, where thou didst vent thy
    Groans   280
As fast as Mill-wheels strike. Then was this
    Island
(Save for the Son that he did litter here,
A freckl'd Whelp, Hag-borne) not honour'd with
A Humane Shape.
ARIEL   Yes: Caliban her Son.
PROSPERO   Dull Thing, I say so: he, that Caliban   285
Whom now I keep in Service. Thou best know'st
What Torment I did find thee in; thy Groans
Did make Wolves howl, and penetrate the Breasts
Of ever-angry Bears; it was a Torment
To lay upon the Damn'd, which Sycorax   290
Could not again undo. It was mine Art,
When I arriv'd, and heard thee, that made gape
The Pine and let thee out.
ARIEL   I thank thee, Master.
PROSPERO   If thou more murmur'st, I will rend an
    Oak
And peg thee in his knotty Entrails till   295

297 **correspondent** responsive, cooperative. Recognizing that his fortunes depend upon Prospero's patronage, Ariel will now court his master's good will again. Compare lines 177–84.

298 **Spryting** sprightly spirit-work.
gently without resistance. Compare line 165.

299 **discharge thee** release you; remove your 'charge' (commission, burden of servitude). Compare lines 237–38. As things transpire, Ariel gets released well ahead of the promised date.

301-2 **subject / To** capable of being apprehended by.

304 **hither come in't** return here so attired.

307 **Heaviness** weariness, dullness.

309 **kind Answer** a reply in keeping with (a) normal courtesy, (b) the kind of request it responds to, and (c) the kind of person who makes the request. *Slave* echoes line 270.

311 **miss him** fail to continue looking on him [because we cannot manage without him]. Here *miss* does double duty as an aphetic form of *dismiss*.

312-13 **Offices ... us** jobs that help us. Compare I.i.39–40, I.ii.83–84. *Profit* echoes line 172.

314 **Earth** Prospero addresses Caliban by the name of the lowest of the four elements. By contrast, Ariel, who controls Fire and whose name associates him with Air, represents the two highest elements and takes the form of Water (line 301), the element between Air and Earth in the hierarchy of fundamental substances. *Earth* echoes lines 272–73. *Caliban* is probably to be read as an anagram of *Cannibal* (a word deriving from *Carib*).

315 **Business** work. Compare lines 141–42, 255–56.

316 **when?** How long must I wait? Compare *Richard II*, I.i.162.

Thou hast howl'd away twelve Winters.

ARIEL   Pardon, Master,
  I will be correspondent to Command
  And do my Spryting gently.

PROSPERO   Do so, and after two Days
  I will discharge thee.

ARIEL   That's my noble Master.
  What shall I do? Say what? What shall I do?   300

PROSPERO   Go make thy self like a Nymph o'th' Sea:
    be subject
  To no Sight but thine and mine, Invisible
  To every Eye-ball else. Go take this Shape
  And hither come in't; go; hence with Diligence.

                                        Exit [Ariel].

  – Awake, dear Heart, awake, thou hast slept well,   305
    Awake.

MIRANDA   The Strangeness of your Story put
  Heaviness in me.

PROSPERO   Shake it off. Come on,
  We'll visit Caliban, my Slave, who never
  Yields us kind Answer.

MIRANDA   'Tis a Villain, Sir,
  I do not love to look on.

PROSPERO   But as 'tis,   310
  We cannot miss him. He does make our Fire,
  Fetch in our Wood, and serves in Offices
  That profit us. – What ho; Slave; Caliban;
  Thou Earth, thou, speak.

CALIBAN   *within*   There's Wood enough within.

PROSPERO   Come forth, I say, there's other Business
    for thee: 315
  Come, thou Tortoise; when?

          Enter Ariel like a Water-Nymph.

                  – Fine Apparition:

317 **queint** quaint; dainty. Prospero takes delight in a servant who, unlike Caliban, is willing to do his bidding.
hark . . . Ear Prospero whispers a command.

319 **Got** begotten; conceived. Compare lines 55–59, 89–96, 281–84.

320 **Dam** mother.
ere both (a) before, and (b) e'er (ever).

322 **Fen** low-lying marshland, swamp. Compare *Coriolanus*, IV.i.30–31.
Southwest disease-carrying wind from the southwest.

324 **to night** tonight.

325 **Side-stitches** painful constrictions of the ribcage.
Urchins hedgehogs (small porcupine-like mammals).

327 **Exercise** do their will. Line 326 echoes *A Midsummer Night's Dream*, III.ii.382–93, *Macbeth*, II.i.48–55, and *Hamlet*, I.i.142–60, III.ii.419–23.

328 **As . . . Honeycomb** until your skin is honeycombed with stings and welts.

329 **Dinner** the main midday meal.

330 **by** as property I inherit from.

332 **strok'st** The proper verb grammatically would be *stroked'st*; but the Folio spelling is no doubt true to the way the word was here pronounced in Shakespeare's theatre.
made . . . me treated me with loving favour. *Much* echoes line 253.

333 **Water . . . in't** According to Sylvester Jourdain's *A Discovery of the Barmudas* (1610), drinks made from cedar berries were popular with the natives of Bermuda.

334 **Bigger . . . Less** Caliban refers here to the Sun and the Moon.

336 **Qualities** characteristics, features. Compare lines 192–93.

339 **light** alight.

341 **sty-me** both (a) sty me (keep me in an enclosure, as if I were a pig), and (b) stymie me (obstruct my movements). Compare *peg thee* (*peg-thee* in the Folio), line 295, and see lines 270–91.

My queint Ariel, hark in thine Ear.

ARIEL   My Lord, it shall be done.   *Exit.*

PROSPERO   — Thou poisonous Slave,
Got by the Divel himself upon thy Wicked
Dam, come forth.

Enter Caliban.

CALIBAN   As wicked Dew as ere   320
My Mother brush'd with Raven's Feather from
Unwholesome Fen drop on you both: a Southwest
Blow on ye, and blister you all o'er.

PROSPERO   For this, be sure, to night thou shalt
    have Cramps,
Side-stitches, that shall pen thy Breath up;
    Urchins   325
Shall, for that vast of Night that they may work,
All Exercise on thee; thou shalt be pinch'd
As thick as Honeycomb, each Pinch more
    stinging
Than Bees that made 'em.

CALIBAN   I must eat my Dinner.
This Island's mine by Sycorax my Mother,   330
Which thou tak'st from me. When thou cam'st first,
Thou strok'st me, and made much of me; would'st
    give me
Water with Berries in't, and teach me how
To name the Bigger Light, and how the Less,
That burn by Day and Night; and then I lov'd thee   335
And shew'd thee all the Qualities o'th' Isle,
The fresh Springs, Brine-pits, Barren Place and
    Fertile.
Curs'd be I that did so. All the Charms
Of Sycorax — Toads, Beetles, Bats — light on you:
For I am all the Subjects that you have,   340
Which first was mine own King, and here you
    sty-me

344 **Whom ... move** who may be motivated by lashings with a whip. *Kindness* echoes line 309. *Stripes* (whelps) echoes Isaiah 53:5.

345 **lodg'd** housed. But *lodg'd* can also mean 'pegged' or 'wedged' (a sense in keeping with lines 294–96 and 341–42); compare the ambiguity in *Othello*, III.iv.7–13, where *lodg'd* relates to the kind of activity that Caliban attempted with Miranda. *Humane* recalls lines 265, 284.

348 **had peopl'd else** would otherwise have populated. Compare *Much Ado About Nothing*, II.iii.257–58.

350 **Which ... take** who cannot be imprinted with any stamp of virtue.

351 **capable ... Ill** able to take and retain the impression of any evil and reproduce it. *Capable* can also mean 'capacious' or 'full' (as in *Othello*, III.iii.448), and here that sense is pertinent to Miranda's description of Caliban. *Pains* recalls lines 242–44.

354 **thine own Meaning** (a) what your 'gabble' conveyed, (b) what you intended to say, your 'Purpose', and (c) your own significance. Compare lines 17–18.

356 **vild Race** vile, 'Brutish' (line 355) strain. Here *Brutish* plays on the sense of brute inarticulation that Shakespeare associates with the name *Brutus* in *Julius Caesar*, III.ii.110, and *Hamlet*, III.ii.110–13. In lines 351–56 a semicolon could be substituted for a comma after either *other* (line 353) or *Brutish* (line 355).

358 **abide** bear. *Confin'd* (line 359) recalls lines 274–77.

361 **my Profit on't** what I have gained from it. Compare lines 172–73, 312–13.

362 **Red-plague** possibly the bubonic plague, which produces red sores. But see the note to III.ii.83.
rid remove, destroy. Compare *Julius Caesar*, III.ii.263.

363 **learning** teaching.
Hag-seed both (a) offspring of a witch, and (b) bag of hag-seed to reproduce Calibans. *Hag* echoes lines 269–70.

364 **thou'rt best** you're best advised.

365 **answer other Business** to obey other commands. *Answer* recalls line 309.

In this hard Rock, whiles you do keep from me
The rest o'th' Island.

PROSPERO　　　　　　Thou most lying Slave,
　Whom Stripes may move, not Kindness: I have
　　us'd thee,
　Filth as thou art, with Humane Care, and lodg'd
　　thee   345
　In mine own Cell, till thou didst seek to
　　violate
　The Honour of my Child.

CALIBAN　　　　　Oh ho, Oh ho, would't had been done.
　Thou didst prevent me; I had peopl'd else
　This Isle with Calibans.

MIRANDA　　　　　　Abhorred Slave,
　Which any Print of Goodness wilt not take,   350
　Being capable of all Ill: I pitied thee,
　Took Pains to make thee speak, taught thee each
　　Hour
　One thing or other, when thou didst not, Savage,
　Know thine own Meaning, but wouldst gabble like
　A Thing most Brutish, I endow'd thy Purposes   355
　With Words that made them known. But thy vild
　　Race
　(Though thou didst learn) had that in't which
　　Good Natures
　Could not abide to be with; therefore wast thou
　Deservedly confin'd into this Rock,
　Who hadst deserv'd more than a Prison.   360

CALIBAN　You taught me Language, and my Profit
　　on't
　Is I know how to curse: the Red-plague rid you
　For learning me your Language.

PROSPERO　　　　　　　　Hag-seed, hence:
　Fetch us in Fuel, and be quick, thou'rt best,
　To answer other Business. Shrug'st thou, Malice?   365
　If thou neglect'st or dost unwillingly

367   **rack ... Cramps**   curse you with the cramps that afflict the elderly. See the notes to lines 26, 236, 258.

368   **Aches**   here pronounced 'aitch-es'. *Roar* recalls I.i.18, 43, I.ii.2.

371   **Setebos**   a Patagonian god, about whom Shakespeare knew from Robert Eden's *History of Travail* (1577). *Vassail* (vassal, line 372) means 'serf'.

S.D.   **invisible**   This adjective applies only to Ariel. See lines 301–3.

375   **Curtsied ... kiss'd**   when you have curtsied and kissed.

376   **whist**   [now] being brought to a hush.

377   **Foot it featly**   step (dance) nimbly and gracefully. *Featly* recalls *The Winter's Tale*, IV.iv.176.

378   **And ... Burthen**   and now let the sweet Spirits carry the bass portion of the song.

S.D.   **Burthen dispersedly.**   Sing in voices that come from disparate directions. In all likelihood lines 379–82 are sung in alternating voices, perhaps from within (behind the stage façade), by the 'sweet Sprights' Ariel invokes in line 378. Then Ariel concludes the song by vocalizing lines 383–84. *Dispersedly* echoes lines 220, 232–35.

384   **Chanticleer**   a rooster's name that was already traditional when Chaucer used it in 'The Nun's Priest's Tale' of *The Canterbury Tales* in the late fourteenth century.

385   **should ... be**   can this music be coming from.

386   **waits upon**   (a) serves, pays its duty to, (b) is under the control and patronage of, and (c) awaits its reward from. Compare lines 177–84, and see the note to III.ii.148.

388   **Wrack**   death by shipwreck. Ferdinand's noun echoes lines 236, 367, (*rack*). Most editions revise the Folio punctuation (here retained) in lines 386–88, replacing the comma after *Island* with a full stop, and the full stop after *Wrack* with a comma. In the Folio version of the passage the 'God o'th' Island' is depicted as compassionate; thus its 'sweet Air' (line 391) is comforting to the mournful Ferdinand. In modern editions, it is usually Ferdinand, not the 'God', who is depicted as 'sitting on a Bank' grieving over his 'Father's Wrack'.

What I command, I'll rack thee with old Cramps,
Fill all thy Bones with Aches, make thee roar
That Beasts shall tremble at thy Din.
CALIBAN   No, 'pray thee.
— I must obey: his Art is of such Pow'r   370
It would control my Dam's God Setebos
And make a Vassail of him.
PROSPERO   So, Slave, hence.
                                        Exit Caliban.

*Enter Ferdinand and Ariel, invisible, playing
                and singing.*

SONG

ARIEL   *Come unto these Yellow Sands,*
                And then take Hands;
            Curtsied when you have, and kiss'd,   375
                The wild Waves whist,
            Foot it featly here, and there,
                And sweet Sprights bear
                    the Burthen.
Burthen   *Hark, hark,*
dispersedly. *Bowgh-wawgh:*   380
            The Watchdogs bark,
                Bough-wawgh.
ARIEL   *Hark, hark, I hear*
            The Strain of strutting Chanticleer
                cry Cockadiddle-dow.

FERDINAND   Where should this Music be? I'th' Air
    or th' Earth?   385
It sounds no more: and sure it waits upon
Some God o'th' Island, sitting on a Bank,
Weeping again the King my Father's Wrack.

390 **Allaying** lessening, alleviating. Lines 388–92 recall lines 1–2,
221–24, and I.i.22–25.
Passion grief. Compare *The Two Gentlemen of Verona*,
IV.iv.170–71, where Julia describes 'Ariadne, passioning / For
Theseus' Perjury', and see *Hamlet*, II.ii.587–603.

391 **Air** both (a) melody, and (b) atmosphere. As with *Hair*, *Air*
can play on *Heir*; see line 217, and compare lines 222–23,
419–20, and 442–44 (where *e'er* continues the pattern of *Heir*
echoes).

394 **Full . . . lies** your father lies five fathoms (thirty feet) deep at
sea. *Full* echoes lines 19–21, 155.

397– **Nothing . . . Strange** Nothing about him fades (decays and
99 loses its lustre) unless it metamorphoses into something more
vivid and wondrous. Ariel's evocative song recalls line 217
and I.i.40–42, 59–60, and it suggests that, in some sense as
yet 'Strange', a 'Drowning Mark' may be better than a 'dry
Death' (I.i.31, 69). *Suffer* recalls lines 5–6; *Change*, lines
81–83; *Strange*, lines 178, 306–7.

400 **Sea . . . Bell** Ariel refers to his own role (line 301), but the
'Burthen' that follows suggests that his attendant 'Sprights'
(line 378) intone the 'Ding dong' signifying the 'Bell'.

403 **remember** memorialize; call to my memory. Compare lines
38–52, 62–65, 132–35, 242–47, and I.i.20.

404 **This . . . Business** Ferdinand means (a) that this song is not the
doing of 'Mortal' beings; but his words can also signify (b)
that this song is not about mortality (death).

405 **That . . . owes** that is earthly in origin (owned by the Earth).

406 **fringed Curtains** lash-fringed eyelids.
advance uplift. Compare lines 80–81.

407 **What . . . Spirit?** This question can be spoken with a pause
after either *What* or *is't*; in the Folio, as here, it appears
without punctuation. Compare lines 351–56.

409 **brave** splendid, beauteous. Compare line 6.

412 **something** both (a) somewhat, and (b) something (some
object). *Stain'd* echoes *sustaining* (line 218).

413 **Beauty's Canker** the cankerworm (or the cancer) that eats
Beauty's bud before it blooms. *Wrack* (shipwreck) echoes line
388.

This Music crept by me upon the Waters,
Allaying both their Fury and my Passion   390
With its sweet Air: thence I have follow'd it
(Or it hath drawn me rather), but 'tis gone.
No, it begins again.

ARIEL   *Full Fadom five thy Father lies,*
         Of his Bones are Coral made.   395
      Those are Pearls that were his Eyes;
         Nothing of him that doth fade,
      But doth suffer a Sea-change
      Into something Rich, and Strange.
      Sea Nymphs hourly ring his Bell.   400
Burthen: *Ding dong.*
      Hark, now I hear them: Ding-dong Bell.

FERDINAND   The Ditty does remember my drown'd
    Father:
    This is no Mortal Business, nor no Sound
    That the Earth owes. I hear it now above me.   405
PROSPERO   The fringed Curtains of thine Eye
    advance,
    And say what thou seest yond.
MIRANDA   What is't a Spirit?
    Lord, how it looks about. Believe me, Sir,
    It carries a brave Form. But 'tis a Spirit.
PROSPERO   No, Wench, it eats, and sleeps, and hath
    such Senses   410
    As we have: such. This Gallant which thou seest
    Was in the Wrack; and but he's something
    Stain'd
    With Grief (that's Beauty's Canker), thou
    might'st call him

415   **strays**   wanders. Lines 387–93 and 417–18 make it clear that Ferdinand has been 'drawn' to this setting.

416   **Natural**   created by Nature alone. Compare lines 385–87, 404–5. *Thing Divine* echoes lines 257, 285, 355, and anticipates line 430.

417   **Noble**   This word echoes lines 114–16, 118–20, 161, 299.
        It goes on   (a) my charm works, and (b) Miranda responds.

419–   **Most . . . attend**   This has to be the Divinity these songs serve.
20   *Attend* recalls lines 38, 47, 78, 87, 385–87. See the note to I.i.7. *Airs* echoes line 391.

420   **Vouchsafe**   please grant that.

421   **remain**   permanently reside.

423   **bear me**   carry (conduct) myself.
        prime Request   foremost question. *Prime* recalls line 72.

424   **Wonder**   marvel, miracle. Compare line 430.

425   **Maid**   both (a) virgin, and (b) unmarried. See lines 445–47.

429   **wert thou**   would you be.

430   **Single**   Ferdinand means (a) solitary, and (b) weak, unassisted. But *Single* can also mean (c) unmarried, and (d) manly. Compare *Macbeth*, I.iii.138, I.vi.16, and *Coriolanus*, II.i.36.

432   **Naples**   the King of Naples. Ferdinand is amazed because he has yet to identify himself as a Neapolitan.

433   **at Ebb**   at low tide (without a full sea of tears). Compare II.i.203–10.

434   **wrack'd**   drowned in a shipwreck. Compare line 388, and see the note to *King Lear*, V.iii.311.

436   **his brave Son**   the son of Antonio, the usurping Duke of Milan. He is mentioned only here, to set up lines 436–38.

437   **control**   correct, overpower. Compare line 371 and *Titus Andronicus*, II.iii.60.

A Goodly Person. He hath lost his Fellows,
And strays about to find 'em.

MIRANDA   I might call him   415
A Thing Divine, for nothing Natural
I ever saw so Noble.

PROSPERO   — It goes on, I see,
As my Soul prompts it. — Spirit, fine Spirit,
   I'll free thee
Within two Days for this.

FERDINAND   Most sure the Goddess
On whom these Airs attend. Vouchsafe my Pray'r   420
May know if you remain upon this Island,
And that you will some good Instruction give
How I may bear me here. My prime Request,
Which I do last pronounce, is (O you Wonder)
If you be Maid, or no?

MIRANDA   No Wonder, Sir,   425
But certainly a Maid.

FERDINAND   My Language? Heavens,
I am the Best of them that speak this Speech,
Were I but where 'tis spoken.

PROSPERO   How? The Best?
What wert thou if the King of Naples heard thee?

FERDINAND   A Single Thing, as I am now, that
   wonders   430
To hear thee speak of Naples. He does hear me,
And that he does, I weep: my self am Naples,
Who with mine Eyes (never since at Ebb) beheld
The King my Father wrack'd.

MIRANDA   Alack, for Mercy.

FERDINAND   Yes faith, and all his Lords, the Duke
   of Millaine   435
And his brave Son being twain.

PROSPERO   — The Duke of Millaine
And his more braver Daughter could control thee
If now 'twere fit to do't. — At the first Sight

439   **They . . . Eyes** both (a) they have exchanged eyes (looked at each other and fallen in love), and (b) they possess transformed eyes (eyes that have suffered a 'see-change' with analogies to the 'Sea-change' described in line 398). *Chang'd* echoes line 82.

442   **ungently** both (a) uncivilly, without the manners of the gentle classes, and (b) unkindly, harshly. Compare lines 165, 298.

445   **inclin'd my way** (a) disposed the same way I am, and (b) inclined to favour my inclination. Compare line 185.

446   **gone forth** already committed (spent). See lines 62–63.

449– **least . . . light** lest its being obtained too easily make them
50   place too little value on the 'Prize'. Prospero plays on *light* as a word that can mean not only 'insubstantial', 'trivial', and 'fleeting', but 'wanton'; the second sense is reinforced by *Business*, a word that frequently relates to illicit transactions (as in *King Lear*, IV.v.18).

450– **I . . . me** both (a) I command you to mark my words, and (b) I
51   order you to attend me as my vassal. *Charge* recalls lines 237–38, and *attend* echoes lines 419–20.

452   **ow'st** ownest. Compare line 405.

455   **There's . . . Temple** no evil can reside in so 'Fair' (both good and beautiful) and holy a dwelling. *Temple* alludes to 1 Corinthians 3:16–17, 6:19, where the human body is called 'the temple of God'. Lines 456–57 recall Mark 3:22–27, where Jesus says that a house divided against itself cannot stand and implies that the stronger spirit (God) will bind and expel the weaker (Beelzebub). Compare Mark 1:23–26, 32–34, 5:1–20, where Jesus casts evil spirits out of the bodies they have striven to dwell within.

461   **fresh-book Mussels** Though freshwater mussels are collected for their shells, which are sometimes made into buttons, they are not valued as food.

461– **Husks . . . cradled** the empty shells, rather than the edible
62   meat, of acorns.

463   **Entertainment** treatment (as distinguished from 'hospitality', another sense of this word). Compare II.i.14–18.

They have chang'd Eyes. Delicate Ariel,
I'll set thee free for this. – A Word, good Sir,   440
I fear you have done your self some Wrong: a Word.
MIRANDA   Why speaks my Father so ungently? This
Is the third Man that e'er I saw, the first
That e'er I sigh'd for: Pity move my Father
To be inclin'd my way.
FERDINAND   O, if a Virgin,   445
And your Affection not gone forth, I'll make
    you
The Queen of Naples.
PROSPERO   Soft, Sir, one Word more.
– They are both in either's Pow'rs. But this
    swift Business
I must Uneasy make, least too light Winning
Make the Prize light. – One Word more: I charge
    thee   450
That thou attend me. Thou dost here usurp
The Name thou ow'st not, and hast put thy self
Upon this Island as a Spy, to win it
From me, the Lord on't.
FERDINAND   No, as I am a Man.
MIRANDA   There's nothing Ill can dwell in such a
    Temple: 455
If the Ill Spirit have so Fair a House,
Good Things will strive to dwell with't.
PROSPERO   – Follow me.
– Speak not you for him: he's a Traitor. – Come,
I'll manacle thy Neck and Feet together.
Sea-water shalt thou drink; thy Food shall be   460
The fresh-brook Mussels, wither'd Roots, and
    Husks
Wherein the Acorn cradled. Follow.
FERDINAND   No,
I will resist such Entertainment till
Mine Enemy has more Pow'r.

465 **rash** hasty, ill-advised. Miranda little suspects that what her father is doing is intended as a 'Trial' (a test of character), and is calculated only to appear 'rash'.

466 **Fearful** threatening. But Ferdinand's behaviour shows that he is 'not Fearful' in the other sense (afraid) either. *Gentle* echoes line 442.

467 **Foot** the basest part of my self.
Tutor instructor. Compare lines 171–74.

468 **Shew** show [of eschewing my command].

469 **from thy Ward** drop your defensive posture.

471 **Beseech** I beseech. So also in II.i.1 and frequently elsewhere.

473 **Surety** guarantor, bail [so that if he attempts anything untoward, you may arrest me in his stead]. Compare I.i.49, I.ii.44–46.

475 **An ... Impostor** one who defends and supports a man who pretends to be King of Naples and seeks to usurp the lordship of this island (lines 450–53). In a sense Prospero's epithet for Ferdinand is correct: though the young man doesn't yet know it, he *is* making a false claim when he refers to himself as 'Naples' (line 432). *Shapes* (line 476) echoes lines 284, 303, 409.

478 **To th' most** compared to the majority.

482 **Nerves** sinews; muscles. *Goodlier* (line 481) echoes lines 414, 457.

484 **My ... up** my vital spirits, like those of a person in a dream-state, are all shackled (line 459). *Bound* echoes lines 97, 235; and Ferdinand's captivity recalls such previous passages as lines 75–77, 88–92, 144–51, 203–6, 230–37, 272–81, 356–60, 370–72, 391–93.

486 **Wrack** destruction. Compare lines 388 and 411–12.
nor Here the best paraphrase is 'and'.

He draws, and is charmed from moving.

MIRANDA   O dear Father,
  Make not too rash a Trial of him, for   465
  He's Gentle, and not Fearful.
PROSPERO   What, I say,
  My Foot my Tutor? – Put thy Sword up, Traitor,
  Who mak'st a Shew but dar'st not strike, thy
    Conscience
  Is so possess'd with Guilt. Come, from thy
    Ward,
  For I can here disarm thee with this Stick   470
  And make thy Weapon drop.
MIRANDA   Beseech you, Father.
PROSPERO   Hence: hang not on my Garments.
MIRANDA   Sir, have Pity,
  I'll be his Surety.
PROSPERO   Silence: one Word more
  Shall make me chide thee, if not hate thee.
    What,
  An Advocate for an Impostor? Hush: 475
  Thou think'st there is no more such Shapes as
    he,
  Having seen but him and Caliban. Foolish Wench,
  To th' most of Men this is a Caliban,
  And they to him are Angels.
MIRANDA   My Affections
  Are then most Humble: I have no Ambition   480
  To see a Goodlier Man.
PROSPERO   – Come on, obey:
  Thy Nerves are in their Infancy again,
  And have no Vigour in them.
FERDINAND   So they are;
  My Spirits, as in a Dream, are all bound up;
  My Father's Loss, the Weakness which I feel,   485
  The Wrack of all my Friends, nor this Man's
    Threats,

487   **light** insignificant. Compare lines 152–58, 449–50.

488   **Might I** if I might.

490–   **Space . . . Prison** See *Hamlet*, II.ii.266–68, where the Prince,
91   having compared Denmark to a prison, says, 'I could be
bounded in a Nutshell and count my self a King of Infinite
Space, were it not that I have Bad Dreams.' *Corners* (line 489)
echoes line 223. Ferdinand's comments recall the situations of
Palamon and Arcite, once they've seen Emilia, in Chaucer's
'The Knight's Tale', a narrative that Shakespeare and his
colleague John Fletcher dramatized in *The Two Noble
Kinsmen* (see II.iii.1–23 of that play).

491   **It works** My scheme succeeds (see lines 448–50, and compare
lines 417–18). In line 491 'Come on' appears to be addressed
to Ferdinand (and perhaps to Miranda as well).

495   **unwonted** unlike his normal behaviour; ungentle (line 442).

497–   **but . . . Command** but to make that come to pass, follow every
98   one of my orders with the utmost precision. *Points* recalls
lines 193–94.

499   **Come follow** These words could be addressed to Ariel,
Ferdinand, or Miranda – or to any combination of the three.

To whom I am subdu'd, are but light to me,
Might I but through my Prison once a Day
Behold this Maid. All Corners else o'th' Earth
Let Liberty make use of; Space enough   490
Have I in such a Prison.

PROSPERO   – It works. – Come on.
– Thou hast done well, fine Ariel. Follow me:
Hark what thou else shalt do me.

MIRANDA   – Be of Comfort:
My Father's of a better Nature, Sir,
Than he appears by Speech. This is unwonted   495
Which now came from him.

PROSPERO   – Thou shalt be as Free
As Mountain Winds; but then exactly do
All Points of my Command.

ARIEL   To th' Syllable.

PROSPERO   Come follow: speak not for him.   *Exeunt.*

II.i   This scene takes place somewhere near the shore of the island.

1   **Beseech**   I beseech. Compare I.ii.471.
        Cause   reason; basis. This word occurs again with this sense in
        line 111 and in V.i.177–78.

2–3   **for ... Loss**   because what we have escaped with (including our
        own lives) is much more than the little we have lost.
        Gonzalo's remarks recall what Prospero has said about his
        and Miranda's 'Escape' in I.ii.151–68.

3   **Hint of**   cue (occasion) for. Compare I.ii.134–35.

5   **Masters ... Merchant**   either (a) chief ship's officers in the
        employ of some merchant, or (b) ranking officers of some
        merchant vessel. Lines 3–6 echo *Hamlet*, I.ii.68–74.

6   **Theme of Woe**   cause to grieve.

8–9   **weigh ... Comfort**   place our sorrow on the scales alongside
        that which should give us comfort [and you will see that
        comfort outweighs it overwhelmingly].

9   **Prethee peace**   I pray you please keep silent.

10   **He ... Porridge**   Sebastian plays on the proverbial expression
        'cold comfort'; compare *King John*, V.vii.42, and *The Taming
        of the Shrew*, IV.i.31–32.

11   **Visitor**   visitor (here a person, such as a minister or doctor, who
        visits the sick to comfort or relieve them).
        give ... so   surrender his body to death and his soul to despair.

13   **Tell**   Keep count.

14–15   **When ... Entertainer**   When every grief is admitted and given
        welcome that comes in search of lodging, then the one who
        receives it. Gonzalo's phrasing echoes I.ii.463–64.

15   **A Dollor**   A dollar (a unit of currency) for the professional
        'Entertainer' who provides music, jests, or dramatic diversions
        [rather than 'Dolour', sadness or 'Trouble' for a host, as in
        Macbeth, I.vi.11–14, *Much Ado About Nothing*, I.i.98–105,
        and *The Winter's Tale*, I.ii.26 and V.iii.9]. Compare
        I.ii.151–53.

ACT II

Scene 1

Enter Alonso, Sebastian, Antonio, Gonzalo, Adrian, Francisco, and Others.

GONZALO   Beseech you, Sir, be Merry; you have Cause,
So have we all, of Joy; for our Escape
Is much beyond our Loss. Our Hint of Woe
Is Common: every Day some Sailor's Wife,
The Masters of some Merchant, and the Merchant   5
Have just our Theme of Woe. But for the Miracle
(I mean our Preservation), few in Millions
Can speak like us: then wisely, good Sir, weigh
Our Sorrow with our Comfort.

ALONSO   Prethee peace.

SEBASTIAN   He receives Comfort like Cold Porridge.   10

ANTONIO   The Visitor will not give him o'er so.

SEBASTIAN   Look,
He's winding up the Watch of his Wit: by and by
It will strike.

GONZALO   Sir —

SEBASTIAN   One. Tell.

GONZALO   When every Grief is entertain'd that's offer'd,
Comes to th' Entertainer —

SEBASTIAN   A Dollor.

GONZALO   Dolour   15

17   **purpos'd** intended. Compare I.ii.353–56.

       Wiselier in a wiser sense. *Wiselier* can also mean 'more profitably' (more to the benefit of your character). Compare I.ii.361–2. Sebastian's point is that Gonzalo has 'taken' the ambiguous word *Dollor* to mean 'dolour' rather than 'dollar'; in the process Gonzalo has preserved his sense of *Entertainer* (host) rather than yield to Sebastian's (minstrel). For the pejorative connotations associated with *Entertainer* in Sebastian's sense, see *Romeo and Juliet*, III.i.47–52, IV.iii.187–235.

20   **spare** withhold further words.

21   **of . . . Adrian** choosing between him and Adrian.

22   **crow** speak (like a rooster sounding the arrival of dawn).

23   **Cock'rel** young cock (probably referring to Adrian).

       Done: the Wager? It's a bet. What do you stake on it?

24   **A Match** Agreed. The wager is based on the proverb 'He laughs that wins'. Compare *Othello*, IV.i.124, where the Moor believes his loss and humiliation to be the object of the laughter he hears from Cassio.

25   **Desert** deserted (empty of people).

26   **you're paid** you've had your laugh. If we are correct in assuming that Adrian, and not Gonzalo, is the 'Cock'rel', Sebastian has lost the wager; but since Sebastian laughs at himself, the morose Antonio doesn't need to collect his winnings with another laugh at the loser's expense.

       Uninhabitable incapable of sustaining human life.

27   **Inaccessible** unreachable. Compare *Cymbeline*, III.ii.84.

28   **miss't** (a) fail to hit it (this inaccessible island), and (b) fail to 'crow' first. Compare I.ii.310–11, and see line 39.

29   **delicate Temperance** temperate, fine (benign) climate. *Delicate* echoes I.ii.272, 439; compare *Macbeth*, I.vi.9–10, and *The Winter's Tale*, III.i.1–2. In the speech that follows, Antonio turns 'Temperance' into the name of a 'delicate [enticing] Wench'; compare *Othello*, I.iii.357–59, where *delicate* means 'appetizing' and 'refined'.

30   **subtle** both (a) moderate (Adrian's meaning), and (b) licentious (Sebastian's implication). Compare V.i.123–24.

Comes to him indeed: you have spoken Truer than
You purpos'd.
SEBASTIAN   You have taken it Wiselier than
I meant you should.
GONZALO   Therefore, my Lord –
ANTONIO   Fie, what
A Spendthrift is he of his Tongue.
ALONSO   I prethee spare.
GONZALO   Well, I have done. But yet –   20
SEBASTIAN   He will be talking.
ANTONIO   Which, of he or Adrian,
For a good Wager, first begins to crow?
SEBASTIAN   The Old Cock.
ANTONIO   The Cock'rel.
SEBASTIAN   Done: the Wager?
ANTONIO   A Laughter.
SEBASTIAN   A Match.
ADRIAN   Though this Island seem to be Desert –   25
SEBASTIAN   Ha, ha, ha.
ANTONIO   So: you're paid.
ADRIAN   Uninhabitable,
And almost Inaccessible –
SEBASTIAN   Yet –
ADRIAN   Yet –
ANTONIO   He could not miss't.
ADRIAN   It must needs be of subtle,
Tender, and delicate Temperance.
ANTONIO   Temperance was
A delicate Wench.
SEBASTIAN   Ay, and a subtle, as he   30
Most learnedly deliver'd.

32   **breathes upon us** wafts our way. Compare I.ii.385–93,
       414–20, where *Air* means both (a) atmosphere, and (b)
       melody. Here *Air* provides a reminder that the heir who now
       rules the island 'breathes upon' his adversaries 'most sweetly';
       compare lines 56–57, and see I.ii.15–17.

34   **Fen** putrid ('rotten') swamp. Compare I.ii.320–22.

35   **save the Means** except for the wherewithal.

38   **Tawny** (a) parched and brown, and (b) sunburnt and sensual
       (as in *Antony and Cleopatra*, I.i.6).
       Eye of Green Sebastian is probably playing on *Lusty*
       (luxuriant) as a word that could also mean 'lustful', a
       condition traditionally associated with *Green* (the colour of
       Venus) and with the female 'Eye' a male 'I' seeks when both
       are feeling wanton. See the notes to *King Lear*, I.i.73,
       I.iv.200–8, and compare *Love's Labour's Lost*, I.ii.85, 89,
       and II.i.185.

42   **Rariety** rarity. In line 43 *Credit* means 'credulity, belief', as in
       I.ii.102. And in line 44 *vouch'd* means 'sworn', avowed.
       Compare III.iii.21–27, where Sebastian and Antonio suspend
       their scepticism about travellers' tales of rare creatures.

46–47 **hold . . . Glosses** maintain nevertheless their fresh lustre.
       Compare I.ii.217–19, 394–99. *Stain'd* (line 48) echoes
       I.ii.411–14. *Glosses* can also be 'interpretations', especially
       flattering ones, as in *Timon of Athens*, I.ii.20.

51   **very . . . Report** pretend he didn't hear himself called a liar and
       thus 'pocket up' his grievance rather than valiantly maintain
       his honour in a duel.

55   **Tunis** capital of Tunisia, built near, if not on, the site of the
       original Carthage on the north coast of Africa.

56–57 **we . . . Return** Sebastian is being sarcastic, of course, but his
       verb is a reminder that, however he and his companions
       'prosper', they now do so under the auspices of a Prospero
       who also seeks to 'prosper well' in his 'Return'.

ADRIAN   The Air breathes upon us here most sweetly.

SEBASTIAN   As if it had Lungs, and rotten ones.

ANTONIO   Or as
'Twere perfum'd by a Fen.

GONZALO   Here is every thing
Advantageous to Life.

ANTONIO   True, save the Means   35
To live.

SEBASTIAN   Of that there's none, or little.

GONZALO   How Lush
And Lusty the Grass looks? How Green?

ANTONIO   The Ground
Indeed is Tawny.

SEBASTIAN   With an Eye of Green in't.

ANTONIO   He misses not much.

SEBASTIAN   No: he doth but mistake the Truth   40
totally.

GONZALO   But the Rariety of it is, which is indeed
almost beyond Credit –

SEBASTIAN   As many vouch'd Rarieties are.

GONZALO   That our Garments, being, as they were,   45
drench'd in the Sea, hold notwithstanding their
Freshness and Glosses, being rather new Dy'd
than Stain'd with Salt-water.

ANTONIO   If but one of his Pockets could speak,
would it not say he lies?   50

SEBASTIAN   Ay, or very falsely pocket up his Report.

GONZALO   Me thinks our Garments are now as Fresh
as when we put them on first in Afric, at the
Marriage of the King's fair Daughter Claribel
to the King of Tunis.   55

SEBASTIAN   'Twas a sweet Marriage, and we prosper
well in our Return.

ADRIAN   Tunis was never grac'd before with such a
Paragon to their Queen.

GONZALO   Not since Widow Dido's Time.

58

60 **Dido**   the Carthaginian queen who was loved and left by the
Trojan hero Aeneas when he visited her kingdom on his way
to found Latium (see Virgil's *Aeneid*, Books I–IV). Antonio
mocks Gonzalo for calling Dido a widow. In fact *Widow* and
Widower were apt terms for Aeneas and Dido when they met;
moreover, both words can mean 'bereft' (an applicable sense,
given that the forsaken Dido committed suicide). The courtly
Gonzalo apparently wishes to portray the lovers' brief liaison
as wedded bliss; unfortunately, it is 'Impossible' to make this
'easy' gloss fit the traditional 'Matter' of the story (lines
73–74).

64 **take it**   (a) construe it (if Sebastian refers to Gonzalo's
disposition to view everything in the best light), or (b) pocket
it up (if Sebastian refers to Gonzalo's meekness). Compare
lines 17–18.

69–70 **miraculous Harp**   the instrument wielded by Amphion, a
legendary Greek singer, to erect the walls of Thebes.

75–76 **carry . . . home**   Sebastian's jest would have amused playgoers
who had seen or heard about natives and goods brought back
to Europe by visitors to the Americas. The word *easy* recalls
I.ii.448–49.

78 **sowing**   planting. Lines 77–78 recall I.ii.343–49, 363.

79 **I**   either (a) 'ay' (if the sweet-natured Gonzalo is going along
with the jest), or (b) 'I –' (if Gonzalo has been interrupted).
Compare lines 30, 38, 51, 85.
in good Time   Antonio probably means that it's about time
Gonzalo admitted that he has been sowing kernels in the sea
(indulging in fantasies about 'I lands' that exist only in his
own imagination).

84 **Bate**   except. But *bate* can also mean 'pant and beat one's wings
excitedly'. Compare I.ii.249–50.

85 **I**   ay. In this line Antonio may be playing on *O* and *I*, both of
which could refer to the part of 'Widow Dido' that attracted
her 'Widow-er' [widow-maker] Aeneas. 'O' (nothing) relates
to the commonplace that a woman's 'I' ('eye', as noted in line
38) has 'no thing' and thus desires the upright I or 1 of a male
who is willing to become 'one flesh' with her (Genesis 2:24).

86 **Doublet**   a man's tight-fitting jacket.

ANTONIO   Widow?   60
  A Pox o' that: how came that Widow in?
  Widow Dido!
SEBASTIAN   What if he had said Widower Aeneas
      too? – Good Lord, how you take it?
ADRIAN   Widow Dido, said you? You make me study   65
  of that: she was of Carthage, not of Tunis.
GONZALO   This Tunis, Sir, was Carthage.
ADRIAN   Carthage?
GONZALO   I
  Assure you, Carthage.
ANTONIO   His Word is more than the miraculous
  Harp.   70
SEBASTIAN   He hath rais'd the Wall, and Houses
  too.
ANTONIO   What Impossible Matter will he make
  easy next?
SEBASTIAN   I think he will carry this Island   75
  home in his Pocket, and give it his Son for
  an Apple.
ANTONIO   And, sowing the Kernels of it in the
  Sea,
  Bring forth more Islands.
GONZALO   I.
ANTONIO   Why in good Time.
GONZALO   Sir, we were talking, that our Garments
  seem now   80
  As Fresh as when we were at Tunis at
  The Marriage of your Daughter, who is now
  Queen.
ANTONIO   And the Rarest that e'er came there.
SEBASTIAN   Bate, I beseech you, Widow Dido.
ANTONIO   O Widow Dido? I, Widow Dido.   85
GONZALO   Is not, Sir, my Doublet as Fresh as the

87   **in a sort** (a) relatively speaking (comparing the items in an assortment), or (b) in a manner (sort) of speaking.

88   **Sort** (a) lot (destiny), (b) choice, (c) portion, and (d) allotment (as in the 'lucky catch' of a fisherman who wasn't even angling).

90–91 **against . . . Sense** with no regard for my lack of appetite. *Stomach* recalls I.ii.153–58.

93   **in my Rate** as I assess matters. Compare I.ii.92. Lines 95–97 recall I.ii.426–44; see the note to I.ii.391.

98   **Surges** cresting waves.

100   **Enmity** hostility.

103   **lusty** vigorous. Francisco echoes lines 36–37. And his description of the swimming Ferdinand recalls *Twelfth Night*, I.ii.7–16, and *Julius Caesar*, I.ii.98–107.

104   **his Wave-worn Basis** its sea-eroded foundation (lower shoreline). Compare I.ii.223, 227.

105   **As . . . him** as if reaching down to help him. Compare line 16 of the Epilogue.

108   **bless** grace, favour.

109   **loose** both (a) release, and (b) lose. Compare *Hamlet*, II.ii.167.

110   **at least** at the very least [apart from any other calamities that may befall her or you]. Compare lines 91–95.

111   **wet . . . on't** water the sadness of it with your own tears.

112   **importun'd** urged.

first Day I wore it? I mean in a sort.

ANTONIO   That Sort was well fish'd for.

GONZALO   When I wore it at your Daughter's
   Marriage.

ALONSO   You cram these Words into mine Ears against   90
   The Stomach of my Sense. Would I had never
   Married my Daughter there: for coming thence
   My Son is lost, and (in my Rate) she too,
   Who is so far from Italy removed
   I ne'er again shall see her. — O thou mine Heir   95
   Of Naples and of Millaine, what strange Fish
   Hath made his Meal on thee?

FRANCISCO   Sir, he may live:
   I saw him beat the Surges under him
   And ride upon their Backs; he trod the Water,
   Whose Enmity he flung aside, and breasted   100
   The Surge most swoll'n that met him; his bold
      Head
   'Bove the contentious Waves he kept, and oared
   Himself with his good Arms in lusty Stroke
   To th' Shore, that o'er his Wave-worn Basis
      bowed
   As stooping to relieve him. I not doubt   105
   He came alive to Land.

ALONSO   No, no, he's gone.

SEBASTIAN   Sir, you may thank your self for this
   great Loss,
   That would not bless our Europe with your
      Daughter,
   But rather loose her to an African,
   Where she at least is banish'd from your Eye   110
   Who hath Cause to wet the Grief on't.

ALONSO   Prethee peace.

SEBASTIAN   You were kneel'd to and importun'd
   otherwise
   By all of us; and the fair Soul her self

114 **Waigh'd** (a) weighed [on the two sides of a set of scales], and (b) 'wayed' [caught at the parting of the ways]. Compare lines 8–9.
Loathness unwillingness [and temptation to disobedience].

117 **Moe . . . making** more widows in them because of this expedition. Here *Business* may be construed as a possessive (*Business'*); it recalls I.ii.315, 365, 404, 448–49.

119 **dear'st** (a) most precious, and thus (b) most grievous.

121 **Gentleness** both (a) nobility (gentility), and (b) kind tenderness. Compare I.ii.466. Compare the rebukes to Paulina in *The Winter's Tale*, III.ii.217–19, V.i.20–23.
Time . . . in timeliness (appropriateness, as in I.ii.438).

122 **Plaister** medicinal plaster [to protect and soothe the wound].

123 **Chirurgeonly** surgeon-like.

124–25 **It . . . Cloudy** None of us bears a sunny disposition, sir, when you are in a gloomy mood that hides your real self.

125 **Fowl** either (a) suitable for fowl (playing on the imagery in lines 21–29), or (b) defined by overhead fowl (such as the kites that hover in anticipation of carrion, or the harpies that befoul banquets, as noted in connection with the stage direction following III.iii.52). Compare I.ii.60–63, where the first occurrence of *Foul* is spelled *fowle* in the Folio.
Foul filthy (from bird droppings).

126 **Plantation of** the charter to begin colonies on. Antonio takes the word in its literal sense, with reference to planting.

127 **sow't . . . Mallows** plant English weeds in it. *Sow* recalls line 78. See the note to I.ii.319.

130 **by Contraries** in a manner contrary to what is normal today.

131 **Traffic** trade, commerce.

132 **Letters** writing and reading; documents and books.

133 **use of Service** master and servant relationships.

134 **Contract . . . Land** agreements, inheritances, boundaries, property. *Borne* (bourn, border, 'Bound of land') plays on the sense of bearing that relates to 'Succession', and specifically to primogeniture, the convention that the firstborn inherits an estate; see the note on *Heir* at I.ii.391. And for other instances of *Borne* and *Bourn*, see *Hamlet*, III.i.76–77, and *King Lear*, IV.vi.57.

Waigh'd between Loathness and Obedience, at
Which End o'th' Beam should bow. We have lost
   your Son,   115
I fear for ever. Millaine and Naples have
Moe Widows in them of this Business making
Than we bring Men to comfort them.
The Fault's your own.
ALONSO   So is the dear'st o'th' Loss.
GONZALO   My Lord Sebastian, the Truth you speak
   doth lack   120
Some Gentleness, and Time to speak it in.
You rub the Sore, when you should bring the
   Plaister.
SEBASTIAN   Very well.
ANTONIO   And most Chirurgeonly.
GONZALO   It is Foul Weather in us all, good Sir,
   When you are Cloudy.
SEBASTIAN   Fowl Weather?
ANTONIO   Very Foul.   125
GONZALO   Had I Plantation of this Isle, my Lord —
ANTONIO   He'd sow't with Nettle-seed.
SEBASTIAN   Or Docks, or Mallows.
GONZALO   And were the King on't, what would I do?
SEBASTIAN   'Scape
Being Drunk, for want of Wine.
GONZALO   I'th' Commonwealth
I would by Contraries execute all things: 130
For no kind of Traffic would I admit, no Name
Of Magistrate. Letters should not be known;
Riches, Poverty, and use of Service, none;
Contract, Succession, Borne, Bound of Land,

135 **Tilth** tilling of the land; agriculture.
    Corn grain (wheat or barley).

143 **Pike** weapon with a long wooden shaft and sharp metal
    spearhead. *Common* (line 141) echoes lines 3–6.
    Engine large war-making device.

145 **Of . . . Kind** of its own species (with no grafting or
    cross-breeding to improve on Nature). Compare *The Winter's
    Tale*, IV.iv.79–103.
    Foison harvest, 'Abundance'.

147 **idle** unproductive (living off the work of others). Antonio picks
    up on lines 136–37, where Gonzalo has described a utopian
    society in which there is no need for work in the usual sense.
    Antonio may also be alluding to the copulative sense of
    Occupation (line 136; see the note to *Measure for Measure*,
    IV.ii.40–41).

150 **Golden Age** the period in Greek and Roman mythology that
    corresponds to the unfallen Garden of Eden in Genesis.
    'Save God save.

152 **talk nothing** speak nonsense. Compare *Romeo and Juliet*,
    I.iv.95–103, and *King Lear*, I.iv.137–210, and see the note to
    Much Ado About Nothing, V.i.246–51.

154 **minister Occasion** provide an object of ridicule.

155– **sensible . . . nothing** ticklish lungs that they can't keep
56   themselves from laughing with little or no provocation.

162 **And . . . long** If only it hadn't fallen flat (rather than with its
    edge in a cutting position). *Blow* (retaliatory thrust) recalls the
    mockery in lines 49–51 (echoed in lines 75–77) and 64.

163 **Metal** mettle (manliness) with your metal (swords).

Tilth, Vineyard, none; no use of Metal, Corn,   135
Or Wine, or Oil; no Occupation, all
Men idle, all, and Women too,
But innocent and pure; no Sovereignty.

SEBASTIAN   Yet he would be King on't.

ANTONIO   The Latter End
Of his Commonwealth forgets the Beginning.   140

GONZALO   All things in common Nature should produce
Without Sweat or Endeavour. Treason, Felony,
Sword, Pike, Knife, Gun, or need of any Engine
Would I not have; but Nature should bring forth
Of it own Kind, all Foison, all Abundance   145
To feed my innocent People.

SEBASTIAN   No marrying 'mong
His Subjects?

ANTONIO   None, Man, all idle: Whores and Knaves.

GONZALO   I would with such Perfection govern, Sir,
T' excel the Golden Age.

SEBASTIAN   'Save his Majesty.   150

ANTONIO   Long live Gonzalo.

GONZALO   And do you mark me, Sir?

ALONSO   Prethee no more: thou dost talk nothing
    to me.

GONZALO   I do well believe your Highness, and did
it to minister Occasion to these Gentlemen,
who are of such sensible and nimble Lungs that   155
they always use to laugh at nothing.

ANTONIO   'Twas you we laugh'd at.

GONZALO   Who in this kind of merry Fooling am
nothing to you: so you may continue, and laugh
at nothing still.   160

ANTONIO   What a Blow was there given?

SEBASTIAN   And it had not fall'n flat-long.

GONZALO   You are Gentlemen of brave Metal: you
would lift the Moon out of her Sphere, if she

167   **Bat-fowling** hunting birds by moonlight with bats (sticks). This phrase often meant 'duping an innocent'. Here it probably also refers to 'fouling' in the sense, or senses, played upon in line 125 (including the implication that the puns on 'Foul' and 'Fowl' are themselves foul: indecorous and putrid).

169– **adventure . . . weakly** put my good judgement at risk by
70   getting upset at something so insignificant [as you two]. Gonzalo's good-natured optimism may seem naive, but he will turn out to be the true realist in the King's party. Like the Fool in another play that pits worldly wisdom against Christian folly, Gonzalo 'labours to out-jest' his sovereign's 'Heart-strook Injuries' (*King Lear*, III.i.16–17).

171   **Heavy** heavy-lidded; drowsy. *Heavy* recalls I.ii.306–7, and it anticipates lines 176 (where it means 'weighty') and 180.

175   **inclin'd** moved. Compare I.ii.185, 444–45.

176   **omit . . . it** fail to respond to this opportunity for the comfort that deep repose would give you. *Omit* recalls I.ii.180–84. Lines 177–78 echo *Julius Caesar*, II.i.4, 227–31. See the note to *The Winter's Tale*, II.iii.2.

178   **Comforter** Compare *Macbeth*, II.ii.32–37, III.iv.139, and 2 *Henry IV*, III.i.4–31. And see the note to II.ii.49.

181   **strange** mysterious. Compare I.ii.397–99.
       possesses them takes [demon-like] control of their bodies.

182   **Quality** peculiar nature. This word recalls I.ii.336.

185   **as by Consent** as if by common agreement. *Dispos'd* (line 184) recalls I.ii.225; *Nimble* echoes line 155.

would continue in it five Weeks without   165
changing.

Enter Ariel playing solemn Music.

SEBASTIAN   We would so, and then go a Bat-fowling.
ANTONIO   Nay, good my Lord, be not Angry.
GONZALO   No, I warrant you, I will not adventure
my Discretion so weakly. Will you laugh me   170
asleep, for I am very Heavy.
ANTONIO   Go sleep, and hear us.
ALONSO   What, all so soon asleep? I wish mine
    Eyes
Would, with themselves, shut up my Thoughts:
    I find
They are inclin'd to do so.
SEBASTIAN   Please you, Sir,   175
Do not omit the Heavy Offer of it.
It seldom visits Sorrow; when it doth,
It is a Comforter.
ANTONIO   We two, my Lord,
Will guard your Person while you take your Rest,
And watch your Safety.
ALONSO   Thank you. Wondrous Heavy.   180
SEBASTIAN   What a strange Drowsiness possesses
    them?
ANTONIO   It is the Quality o'th' Climate.
SEBASTIAN   Why
Doth it not then our Eyelids sink? I find not
My self dispos'd to Sleep.
ANTONIO   Nor I: my Spirits are Nimble.
They fell together all, as by Consent   185
They dropp'd, as by a Thunder-stroke. What
    might,
Worthy Sebastian? O what might? No more:
And yet me thinks I see it in thy Face,

189 **speaks thee** (a) speaks to you [urging you to act upon it now],
and (b) speaks through you [making your 'Face' its
mouthpiece]. *Occasion* echoes line 154; lines 189–91 and
197–99 recall I.ii.178–84, 296–98.

193 **sleepy Language** the kind of words one normally hears in
dreams. Compare *Julius Caesar*, II.i.60–68, and *Macbeth*,
II.i.30–55.

195 **Repose** sense of calm (here associated with consciences that are
being charmed to sleep by ambitious daydreams). Lines
195–96 echo the Sleepwalking Scene in *Macbeth*, especially
V.i.10–12, 28–29.

198 **Thou . . . sleep** you neglect to claim the fortune that waits for
you to arouse it. Compare *Julius Caesar*, II.i.45–57,
IV.iii.210–19.
winkst shuttest thine eyes.

199 **Waking** Antonio's phrasing echoes I.ii.88–93.

200 **Meaning** 'Matter' (line 212), significance. *Meaning* and
Purpose (line 206) recall I.ii.353–56.

201 **my Custom** is customary for me.

203 **Trebles thee o'er** makes you three times what you are now.
standing Water (a) a still or stagnant pond, waiting to be
stirred (as in V.i.33 and in *The Merchant of Venice*,
I.i.87–93), or (b) a tide that is neither waxing nor ebbing (as
in *Antony and Cleopatra*, I.iv.40–47, III.ii.47–50).

208 **invest it** clothe it [in your mind, by laying it bare and thus
calling attention to its need to be re-dressed].
Ebbing Men declining men, men who recede or sink to the
bottom. See I.ii.178–84, and compare *Julius Caesar*,
IV.ii.260–66, and *Antony and Cleopatra*, I.iv.41–44.

210 **Sloth** failure to act (see the notes to I.i.7, I.ii.178–84).

211 **Setting** fixed position. But *Setting* can also refer to the ebbing
(decline) of the Sun; compare III.i.21–23.

212 **A . . . thee** that you have something important to say.

What thou should'st be. Th' Occasion speaks
  thee, and
My strong Imagination sees a Crown   190
Dropping upon thy Head.

SEBASTIAN   What? Art thou Waking?

ANTONIO   Do not you hear me speak?

SEBASTIAN   I do, and surely
  It is a sleepy Language; and thou speak'st
  Out of thy Sleep. What is it thou didst say?
  This is a strange Repose, to be Asleep   195
  With Eyes wide open: standing, speaking,
    moving,
  And yet so fast Asleep.

ANTONIO   Noble Sebastian,
  Thou let'st thy Fortune sleep, die rather;
    wink'st
  Whiles thou art Waking.

SEBASTIAN   Thou dost snore distinctly;
  There's Meaning in thy Snores.   200

ANTONIO   I am more serious than my Custom; you
  Must be so too, if heed me, which to do
  Trebles thee o'er.

SEBASTIAN   Well: I am standing Water.

ANTONIO   I'll teach you how to flow.

SEBASTIAN   Do so: to ebb
  Hereditary Sloth instructs me.

ANTONIO   O!   205
  If you but knew how you the Purpose cherish
  Whiles thus you mock it, how in stripping it
  You more invest it. Ebbing Men indeed
  Most often do so near the Bottom run
  By their own Fear or Sloth.

SEBASTIAN   Prethee say on: 210
  The Setting of thine Eye and Cheek proclaim
  A Matter from thee; and a Birth indeed

213 **Which . . . yield** This phrase can mean (a) which puts you in the throes of labour until you have delivered it, (b) which will throw much benefit to you for yielding it up, and (c) which it will undo you thoroughly to bring forth. Compare I.i.14, I.ii.153–58, and see *Cymbeline*, V.iv.44, and *Antony and Cleopatra*, III.vii.80.

214 **this . . . Remembrance** this feeble-minded, senile lord (Gonzalo). *Remembrance* recalls I.ii.403, and it reminds us that Gonzalo's 'Remembrance' (care) of Prospero has garnered him a lasting 'Remembrance' (memory).

216 **earth'd** returned to his native element (Genesis 3:19).

217– **a . . . persuade** a persuasive personality, whose sole vocation is
18 to offer reliable, convincing counsel (I.i.22–25). *Onely* recalls I.ii.98.

222 **that way** (a) in that direction, and (b) of that kind.

223 **Another way** viewed differently. See I.ii.444–45.

223– **even . . . there** even steady-sighted (another sense of *even*)
25 Ambition cannot pierce a glimpse beyond the next hill, tempted to choose 'that way', without fear of 'Discovery' (detection as a traitor). *Wink* echoes lines 170–84.

229 **Ten . . . Life** thirty miles beyond a full lifetime's travel. Lines 228–32 echo what Alonso has said in lines 91–95.

230 **Note** notice; news of what has happened.
Post swift messenger.

231 **borne** both (a) born, and (b) carried, worn.

232 **Razorable** in need of a razor to shave them.
from whom coming from whom.

233 **cast again** (a) vomited up, (b) re-cast (assigned new roles in Destiny's drama), and (c) cast once more to begin a new dice game. Lines 232–33 echo I.ii.10–13.

235 **Whereof . . . Prologue** for which what has gone before [namely, my usurpation of Prospero's dukedom] is merely the Chorus' foreword to the primary action of the play. Compare lines 272–74. Ironically, Antonio's counsel is now memorialized on the exterior of the National Archives building in Washington, where observers are solemnly informed that 'What is Past is Prologue'.

Which throws thee much to yield.

ANTONIO   Thus Sir,
Although this Lord of weak Remembrance, this
Who shall be of as little Memory   215
When he is earth'd, hath here almost persuaded
(For he's a Spirit of Persuasion, onely
Professes to persuade) the King his Son's
    alive.
'Tis as impossible that he's undrown'd
As he that sleeps here swims.

SEBASTIAN   I have no hope   220
That he's undrown'd.

ANTONIO   O, out of that No Hope
What Great Hope have you? No Hope that way is
Another way so high a Hope that even
Ambition cannot pierce a Wink beyond
But doubt Discovery there. Will you grant with me   225
That Ferdinand is drown'd.

SEBASTIAN   He's gone.

ANTONIO   Then tell me,
Who's the next Heir of Naples?

SEBASTIAN   Claribel.

ANTONIO   She that is Queen of Tunis, she that
    dwells
Ten Leagues beyond Man's Life, she that from
    Naples
Can have no Note unless the Sun were Post   230
(The Man i'th' Moon's too slow), till new-borne
    Chins
Be Rough and Razorable; she that from whom
We all were Sea-swallow'd, though some cast
    again,
And by that Destiny to perform an Act
Whereof what's Past is Prologue, what to come   235

236 **In ... Discharge** in your hands and mine to carry out ('perform'). *Discharge* is another theatrical metaphor, and a word that can also refer to the unloading of a man's genital 'part' (see *Timon of Athens*, IV.iii.269–70, and *A Midsummer Night's Dream*, IV.ii.7–8, V.i.206–7, 364–65). Here it recalls I.ii.237–38, 298–99, 450–51.

239 **Cubit** 20-inch unit. *Space* (distance) recalls I.ii.279–80.

242 **let ... wake** let Sebastian's dreams become actualities.

244 **There be** there are those.

245– **prate ... unnecessarily** prattle as volubly and irrelevantly.
46

247– **make ... Chat** either (a) be as grave and wise as a jackdaw or
48 (b) teach a jackdaw to chatter as profoundly. Antonio is now tutoring Sebastian. See I.ii.467.

251– **And ... Fortune?** And in what way does your present
52 contentment (sloth) care for and advance your ambition? *Advancement* (line 250) recalls I.ii.406–7. *Tender* echoes lines 28–29.

253 **supplant** undermine, overthrow, and replace; graft yourself into the position of. Compare *Macbeth*, I.iv.28–29, V.iii.41, V.vii.94.

255 **Feater** fitter; with more ease and grace. Compare I.ii.377 and II.i.45–55, and see the note to *Macbeth*, V.ii.20–22.

256 **Fellows** equals.
Men subordinates, servants.

258 **I** both (a) ay, and (b) I. Compare lines 79, 85.

Kibe chilblain. Compare *King Lear*, I.v.8–12.

In yours and my Discharge.

SEBASTIAN   What Stuff is this? How say you?
  'Tis true my Brother's Daughter's Queen of
    Tunis;
  So is she Heir of Naples, 'twixt which Regions
  There is some Space.

ANTONIO   A Space whose ev'ry Cubit
  Seems to cry out 'How shall that Claribel   240
  Measure us back to Naples? Keep in Tunis,
  And let Sebastian wake.' Say this were Death
  That now hath seiz'd them, why they were no
    worse
  Than now they are. There be that can rule
    Naples
  As well as he that sleeps, Lords that can prate   245
  As amply and unnecessarily
  As this Gonzalo: I my self could make
  A Chough of as deep Chat. O, that you bore
  The Mind that I do: what a Sleep were this
  For your Advancement? Do you understand me?   250

SEBASTIAN   Me thinks I do.

ANTONIO   And how does your Content
  Tender your own good Fortune?

SEBASTIAN   I remember
  You did supplant your Brother Prospero.

ANTONIO   True:
  And look how well my Garments sit upon me,
  Much Feater than before: my Brother's Servants   255
  Were then my Fellows, now they are my Men.

SEBASTIAN   But for your Conscience.

ANTONIO   I Sir: where lies that? If 'twere a Kibe,
  'Twould put me to my Slipper; but I feel not
  This Deity in my Bosom. Twenty Consciences   260

261–   **candied . . . molest**   think of them as sugary flatterers who will
62   melt before they'll say anything to cross my will. *Candied*
      echoes *Julius Caesar*, III.i.35–43, *1 Henry IV*, I.iii.246–47,
      and *Hamlet*, III.ii.67.

264   **that . . . like**   a dead man. *Earth* recalls line 216 and I.ii.314.

266–   **whiles . . . Morsel**   while you performing the same deed might
68   put this old piece of flesh to sleep for ever (*aye*). *Wink* echoes
      line 224.

269   **Should . . . Course**   would then be prevented from condemning
      the course (action) we have taken.

270   **take Suggestion**   respond to our implication that they will be
      unwise to raise any questions about what has happened.

271–   **They'll . . . Hour**   They will submit as obediently as the tolling
72   mechanism on a clock to any story we tell them about what it
      was fitting and timely to do. *Business* recalls line 117.

272   **Case**   instance, example. Compare I.i.35–36, 56–57.

273   **President**   precedent, 'Prologue' (line 235).

276   **love thee**   treat you with all the love (and rewards) I will then
      owe you [because of the service you've done me].

277   **rear**   uprear; raise.

278   **fall it**   let it fall.

281   **Project**   plan. See I.ii.178–84. Precisely what Prospero's
      'Project' is remains indefinite at this point. But one part of it –
      what the erstwhile Duke of Milan hopes to achieve by
      wedding his daughter to Alonso's son – would be nullified if
      Alonso has been supplanted as King of Naples by his brother
      Sebastian.

That stand 'twixt me and Millaine, candied be
  they,
And melt ere they molest. Here lies your
  Brother,
No better than the Earth he lies upon,
If he were that which now he's like (that's
  Dead),
Whom I with this obedient Steel (three Inches
  of it)   265
Can lay to Bed for ever; whiles you doing thus
To the perpetual Wink for aye might put
This ancient Morsel, this Sir Prudence, who
Should not upbraid our Course. For all the rest,
They'll take Suggestion as a Cat laps Milk;   270
They'll tell the Clock to any Business that
We say befits the Hour.
SEBASTIAN   Thy Case, dear Friend,
  Shall be my President. As thou got'st Millaine,
  I'll come by Naples. Draw thy Sword: one Stroke
  Shall free thee from the Tribute which thou
    payest,   275
  And I the King shall love thee.
ANTONIO   Draw together,
  And when I rear my Hand, do you the like
  To fall it on Gonzalo.
SEBASTIAN   O, but one Word.

Enter Ariel with Music and Song.

ARIEL — My Master through his Art foresees the
  Danger
  That you, his Friend, are in, and sends me forth   280
  (For else his Project dies) to keep them living.
                              Sings in Gonzalo's Ear.

283 **Open-ey'd Conspiracy**   a plot that is now fully 'awake' (see lines 191–200, 239–50.

284 **His . . . take**   takes advantage of his offered opportunity. Compare lines 11–13, 20–26, 60, 79, 189–91, 234–36, 269–72.

285 **keep a Care**   retain any concern. *Care* recalls I.i.10, 44, I.ii.16. *Shake* (line 286) echoes I.ii.307.

288 **sudden**   (a) quick, and (b) violent.

291 **this Ghastly Looking**   these frightful, ghost-like looks.

292 **securing your Repose**   protecting you while you rested (see lines 178–80). If Sebastian had had his way, he and Antonio would have secured Alonso and Gonzalo's repose in a very different sense: making sure that neither man ever awoke from it (see lines 262–69). They would have taken what they regarded as steps toward 'securing' their own 'Repose'. See the note to lines 56–57.

293 **hollow**   deep.

295 **strook**   struck.
    terribly   terrifyingly.

297 **make an Earthquake**   cause the Earth itself to tremble. *Din* echoes I.ii.369; *Roar* echoes I.ii.368.

300 **strange**   weird. Compare line 181. *Shak'd* (line 301) echoes lines 285–86.

303 **verily**   truly [spoken].

304 **quit**   leave; flee. Compare I.ii.148, 211.

> *While you here do Snoring lie,*
> *Open-ey'd Conspiracy*
> *His Time doth take.*
> *If of Life you keep a Care,*   285
> *Shake off Slumber and beware:*
> *Awake, awake.*

ANTONIO   Then let us both be sudden.

GONZALO   Now good Angels,
Preserve the King.

ALONSO   Why how now, ho; awake? Why are you
drawn?   290
Wherefore this Ghastly Looking?

GONZALO   What's the matter?

SEBASTIAN   Whiles we stood here securing your
Repose,
Even now, we heard a hollow Burst of Bellowing
Like Bulls, or rather Lions. Did't not wake
you?
It strook mine Ear most terribly.

ALONSO   I heard nothing.   295

ANTONIO   O 'twas a Din to fright a Monster's Ear,
To make an Earthquake: sure it was the Roar
Of a whole Herd of Lions.

ALONSO   Heard you this, Gonzalo?

GONZALO   Upon mine Honour, Sir, I heard a Humming
(And that a strange one too), which did awake
me.   300
I shak'd you, Sir, and cried; as mine Eyes
open'd,
I saw their Weapons drawn; there was a Noise,
That's verily. 'Tis best we stand upon our
Guard,
Or that we quit this Place: let's draw our
Weapons.

307   **sure** Gonzalo means 'surely'. But in fact Ferdinand is 'sure'
(secure) as well. He is safely away from 'these Beasts', and he
is secured (shackled) by the charms Prospero has subjected
him to: (a) the magnetism of Miranda's beauty, (b) the spell
cast by Miranda's father to disarm her suitor, and (c) the
manacles that now restrict Ferdinand's movements. In several
senses Prospero has secured his future son-in-law's 'Repose'
(line 292), and in the process his own and his daughter's. If
Prospero has his way, he will 'recover' Ferdinand, 'and keep
him Tame, and get to Naples with him' (II.ii.74–75). See the
note to lines 56–57, 292.

309   **seek thy Son** The situation the King of Naples faces (finding his
lost son) parallels that of Cymbeline (whose sons have been
stolen away by an angry lord, and whose daughter has
subsequently fled the Court in search of the son-in-law the
King has refused to acknowledge), and that of both Leontes
and Polixenes in *The Winter's Tale* (who find their lost
daughter and son, respectively, at the same moment). *Son*
frequently plays on *Sun* (as in *Hamlet*, I.ii.67), and here it
reminds us that the despondent Alonso is also in desperate
need of spiritual light; see lines 124–25. By the time Alonso
finds Ferdinand, Prospero will have succeeded in his quest for
a 'Son' too.

II.ii   This scene takes place at a locale elsewhere in the island.

S.D.   **Burthen** burden, load.

1   **All . . . up** Caliban alludes to the Renaissance view that
infection-carrying fogs were drawn out of the earth by the
Sun. Compare I.ii.320–23, 362–63, II.i.32–34, and
Coriolanus, I.iv.31–35. *Sun* echoes the concluding line of the
preceding scene.

2   **Flats** low-lying flatlands; marshes. *Fens* recalls II.i.34. *Fall*
echoes II.i.278.

3   **By Inch-meal** inch by agonizing inch. Compare *Cymbeline*,
V.v.49–52.

5   **Urchin-shews** threats of attack by hedgehogs. See I.ii.325.

ALONSO   Lead off this Ground, and let's make
    further Search   305
For my poor Son.
GONZALO   Heavens keep him from these Beasts:
For he is sure i'th' Island.
ALONSO   Lead away.
ARIEL   Prospero, my Lord, shall know what I have
    done:
So, King, go safely on to seek thy Son.   *Exeunt.*

Scene 2

Enter Caliban, with a Burthen of Wood.
A Noise of Thunder heard.

CALIBAN   All the Infections that the Sun sucks up
From Bogs, Fens, Flats, on Prosper fall, and
    make him
By Inch-meal a Disease. His Spirits hear me,
And yet I needs must curse. But they'll nor
    pinch,
Fright me with Urchin-shews, pitch me i'th'
    Mire,   5

6   **Fire-brand** burning ember. Caliban refers to the will-o'-the-wisp or *ignis fatuus* (foolish fire or fool's fire), a flame floating at night over marshes and now thought to be caused by the spontaneous combustion of organic gases. In *A Midsummer Night's Dream*, II.i.39, its workings are attributed to Puck, who uses it to 'mislead night Wanderers, laughing at their Harm'. Compare I.ii.196–206, where Ariel delights in his deployment of similar special effects.

9   **moe** mow, make faces. Compare IV.i.46–47, and see *King Lear*, IV.i.60.

10   **after** afterwards.

11–12 **mount . . . Foot-fall** rear their prickly spines so that I will step on them with my bare feet.

13   **All wound** wound about; entwined.
      Adders small poisonous snakes.
      cloven divided. This word recalls I.ii.277.

17   **mind me** pay any mind to me; notice me.

18–19 **bear . . . Weather** shelter me from rain.

21–22 **foul Bumbard** rotting leather vessel. Originally a *bombard* was a heavy cannon used to attack besieged fortresses.

22   **Liquor** any liquid, but here wine and its 'Dregs' (line 44). Lines 20–22 echo II.i.124–25, 167, and anticipate lines 37–38.

24–25 **cannot choose** This phrase recalls I.ii.185–86. Lines 23–24 echo Matthew 8:20, where Jesus says that 'The foxes have holes, and the birds of the air have nests; but the Son of man hath not where to lay his head.'

27   **ancient** both (a) old (referring to the odour emitted by a fish that has been out of water for some time, line 28), and (b) time-honoured, venerable. Lines 25–29 recall II.i.88–97, 262–69.

29   **Poor-John** cheap dried hake. Compare *Romeo and Juliet*, I.i.33–34. *Strange Fish* echoes II.i.96.

31   **painted** represented with paint, as on a signboard hung outside a booth to exhibit the 'Monster' (line 33) at a fair.
      Holiday-Fool gullible holiday customer. The phrase *piece of Silver* would have reminded Shakespeare's audiences of the thirty pieces of silver Judas took as a bribe from the priests who paid him to betray his Lord; see Matthew 26:14–16, 48–49, 27:3–10.

Nor lead me like a Fire-brand in the Dark
Out of my way unless he bid 'em. But
For every Trifle are they set upon me:
Sometime like Apes, that moe and chatter at me,
And after bite me; then like Hedgehogs, which   10
Lie tumbling in my Bare-foot Way, and mount
Their Pricks at my Foot-fall. Sometime am I
All wound with Adders, who with cloven Tongues
Do hiss me into Madness.

Enter Trinculo.

          Lo, now lo,
Here comes a Spirit of his, and to torment me   15
For bringing Wood in slowly. I'll fall flat:
Perchance he will not mind me.
TRINCULO   Here's neither Bush nor Shrub to bear
off any Weather at all. And another Storm
brewing, I hear it sing i'th' Wind. Yond same   20
black Cloud, yond huge one, looks like a foul
Bumbard that would shed his Liquor. If it
should Thunder, as it did before, I know not
where to hide my Head. Yond same Cloud cannot
choose but fall by Pailfuls. What have we   25
here, a Man, or a Fish? Dead or Alive? A Fish,
he smells like a Fish: a very ancient and
Fish-like Smell, a kind of, not of the newest,
Poor-John. A Strange Fish. Were I in England
now, as once I was, and had but this Fish   30
painted, not a Holiday-Fool there but would
give a piece of Silver. There would this
Monster make a Man: any Strange Beast there

33   **make a Man**   make a man rich; make his fortune. But Trinculo's phrasing also suggests that in England 'any Strange Beast' can pass himself off as 'a Man'. Compare *A Midsummer Night's Dream*, IV.ii.17–24, *Hamlet*, V.i.155–64, *Measure for Measure*, V.i.349, and *The Winter's Tale*, III.iii.124.

34   **Doit**   a small Dutch coin worth half a farthing in England.

38   **let loose**   surrender; release (like foul air, excrement, urine, or vomit).

42   **Gaberdine**   long cloak. *Misery* (line 43) recalls I.i.35–36.

48   **scurvy**   vile, scurfy (covered with scaly, peeling skin).

49   **Comfort**   consolation. Compare II.i.175–78, where sleep is called 'a Comforter'. There, and perhaps here, Shakespeare alludes to John 14:16–17, where Jesus tells his disciples, 'I will pray the Father, and he shall give you another Comforter, . . . the Spirit of truth.'

50   **Swabber**   seaman whose job is to swab (scrub) the ship.

52   **Mall**   a nickname for 'Mary', one that often refers to a moll (whore).

54   **Tang**   sting; sharp, biting flavour ('Savour', line 56).

55   **hang**   hang yourself; beat it. See *Love's Labour's Lost*, V.ii.268, 600.

56   **Pitch**   another word for 'Tar'; compare I.ii.3.

57   **Tailor**   here, a man with a ready 'Tail' (*penis* in Latin). For wordplay on *Tail*, see *Romeo and Juliet*, II.iii.102–8; for *Tailor*, see *A Midsummer Night's Dream*, II.i.53–54, *The Merchant of Venice*, III.i.27–30, *2 Henry IV*, III.ii.160–72, *Coriolanus*, IV.vi.78–89, and *Henry VIII*, I.iii.19–20.

makes a Man. When they will not give a Doit
to relieve a lame Beggar, they will lay out   35
ten to see a dead Indian. Legg'd like a Man,
and his Fins like Arms. Warm, o' my troth. I
do now let loose my Opinion, hold it no longer:
this is no Fish, but an Islander, that hath
lately suffered by a Thunderbolt. Alas, the   40
Storm is come again. My Best Way is to creep
under his Gaberdine: there is no other Shelter
hereabout. Misery acquaints a Man with Strange
Bedfellows. I will here shroud till the Dregs
of the Storm be past.   45

Enter Stephano singing.

STEPHANO   *I shall no more to Sea, to Sea;*
    Here shall I die ashore.

This is a very scurvy Tune to sing at a Man's
Funeral. Well, here's my Comfort.   *Drinks. Sings.*

   The Master, the Swabber, the Boatswain,
     and I,   50
    The Gunner, and his Mate,
  Lov'd Mall, Meg, and Marian, and Margerie,
    But none of us car'd for Kate.
    For she had a Tongue with a Tang,
    Would cry to a Sailor 'Go hang.'   55
  She lov'd not the Savour of Tar nor of Pitch,
  Yet a Tailor might scratch her where e'er she
     did itch.
    Then to Sea, Boys, and let her go hang.

This is a scurvy Tune too; but here's my
Comfort.   *Drinks.*   60
CALIBAN   Do not torment me: oh.

62–63 **Do . . . Inde?** Are you trying to frighten us by taking the forms of (or possessing the bodies of) savages and Indians?

65 **Proper** fit, handsome. *Scap'd* echoes II.i.128–29.

66 **went** walked. Stephano alludes to a proverb referring to anyone who walks on two legs (that is, any normal mortal). His drunken variation on the original is apt for all three of the characters in this scene. *Ground* echoes II.i.305.

68 **at'** at his.

71 **who . . . Ague** who has caught, as I gather, a fever (a 'Fit', line 79) that causes him to shiver. See line 91. *As I take it* echoes II.i.64.

73–74 **I . . . that** I will give him some assistance (a drink), if only because he speaks 'our Language'. Compare I.ii.426–28.

74 **recover** revive, restore. *Relief* echoes line 35 and II.i.105.

76 **Neat's-leather** cowhide (shoe-leather). Compare *Julius Caesar*, I.i.27–31, where the Cobbler uses this phrase and puns on *recover* ('re-cover'), and *The Merchant of Venice*, I.i.111, where 'Neat's Tongue' appears to refer to a male member that has become 'dri'd' and thus unable to perform as a 'Tailor' to the Kates of the world.

80 **after the Wisest** in the most coherent fashion. Compare II.i.14–18.

84 **hath him** purchases him.

85 **soundly** thoroughly, completely. Compare Bottom's self-contradiction in *A Midsummer Night's Dream*, IV.ii.29–32.

90 **Here . . . Cat** Stephano alludes to the proverb 'Liquor will make a cat talk'. Compare *All's Well That Ends Well*, IV.iii.268–69. Lines 89–90 recall I.ii.349–63 and II.i.269–72.

91 **shake your Shaking** 'remove' your 'Fit' (line 82). *Shake* recalls I.ii.206, 307, and II.i.286, 301.

93 **Chaps** chops, jaws.

94 **should know** think I recognize.

STEPHANO   What's the matter?
  Have we Divels here? Do you put Tricks upon's
  with Salvages and Men of Inde? Ha? I have not
  scap'd Drowning to be afeard now of your four
  Legs. For it hath been said, as Proper a Man   65
  as ever went on Four Legs cannot make him give
  Ground; and it shall be said so again, while
  Stephano breathes at' Nostrils.
CALIBAN   The Spirit torments me: oh.
STEPHANO   This is some Monster of the Isle, with   70
  four Legs, who hath got, as I take it, an Ague.
  Where the Divel should he learn our Language?
  I will give him some Relief, if it be but for
  that. If I can recover him, and keep him Tame,
  and get to Naples with him, he's a Present for   75
  any Emperor that ever trod on Neat's-leather.
CALIBAN   Do not torment me, 'prethee: I'll bring my
  Wood home faster.
STEPHANO   He's in his Fit now, and does not talk
  after the Wisest. He shall taste of my Bottle;   80
  if he have never drunk Wine afore, it will go
  near to remove his Fit. If I can recover him,
  and keep him Tame, I will not take too much
  for him; he shall pay for him that hath him,
  and that soundly.   85
CALIBAN   Thou dost me yet but little Hurt; thou
  wilt anon, I know it by thy Trembling. Now
  Prosper works upon thee.
STEPHANO   Come on your ways; open your Mouth;
  here is that which will give Language to you, Cat.   90
  Open your Mouth: this will shake your Shaking,
  I can tell you, and that soundly. You cannot
  tell who's your Friend; open your Chaps again.
TRINCULO   I should know that Voice. It should be —
  but he is drown'd, and these are Divels. O   95
  defend me.

97   **Delicate**   special; exquisite, choice. This word recalls II.i.28–29.

99–   **utter Foul Speeches**   The literal meaning of *utter* is 'come out
100   with', or *vent* (line 115), and here Stephano's phrase suggests
       both flatulence and excretion. Compare lines 20–22 and 'let
       loose my Opinion' (line 38).

100   **detract**   insult; literally, 'draw away'.

102   **Amen**   there; so be it. Compare line 139.

107   **Long Spoon**   Stephano refers to the proverb 'He must have a
       long spoon that will eat with the devil.' See *Henry VIII*,
       V.iii.38, and *The Comedy of Errors*, IV.iii.60–63.

112   **lesser**   smaller, shorter. Compare I.ii.334.

115   **Siege**   stool, here meaning both (a) seat, and (b) excrement. See
       the note to lines 99–100. The more usual sense of *siege* is also
       applicable here, since Caliban believes himself to be besieged
       by Prospero's spirits (see lines 15–17, 69, 77–78).
       Moon-calf   a monster whose deformity was thought to be
       caused by a malign influence from the Moon.
       vent   void. Compare I.ii.280 and *Coriolanus*, I.i.229–30,
       IV.vii.119.

117   **not drown'd**   This phrase echoes such previous passages as
       I.i.30–32, 58–60; I.ii.394–403; II.i.95–106, 208–10, 213–26.
       Thunder-stroke (line 116) echoes II.i.186, II.ii.40.

124   **constant**   stable, able to withstand motion [because of nausea
       induced by excessive drinking]. This word recalls I.ii.206–8.
       Stomach echoes I.ii.156–58, II.i.90–91. Lines 120–24
       anticipate line 130 and recall I.ii.62, 75, 81, and II.i.109, 233.

125   **and if**   if.
       Sprights   spirits. Compare the reactions of Ferdinand and
       Miranda upon seeing each other in I.ii.407–9, 415–25. *Fine
       Things* recalls I.ii.355, 416, 430, 455–57, and anticipates
       III.ii.62.

126   **brave**   splendid. This word echoes I.ii.6, 206, 409, 436;
       II.i.163.
       Celestial Liquor   liquor as divine as the nectar of the Olympian
       Gods. Compare lines 20–22, and see I.ii.385–87, 407–9,
       415–17, 419–25.

STEPHANO   Four Legs and Two Voices: a most Delicate
Monster. His Forward Voice now is to speak well
of his Friend; his Backward Voice is to utter
Foul Speeches, and to detract. If all the Wine   100
in my Bottle will recover him, I will help his
Ague. Come: Amen, I will pour some in thy other
Mouth.

TRINCULO   Stephano.

STEPHANO   Doth thy other Mouth call me? Mercy,   105
mercy: this is a Divel, and no Monster. I will
leave him, I have no Long Spoon.

TRINCULO   Stephano, if thou beest Stephano, touch
me, and speak to me: for I am Trinculo. Be not
afeard, thy good Friend Trinculo.   110

STEPHANO   If thou beest Trinculo, come foorth.
I'll pull thee by the lesser Legs. If any be
Trinculo's Legs, these are they. Thou art very
Trinculo indeed: how cam'st thou to be the
Siege of this Moon-calf? Can he vent Trinculos?   115

TRINCULO   I took him to be kill'd with a Thunder-
stroke. But art thou not drown'd, Stephano? I
hope now thou art not drown'd. Is the Storm
over-blown? I hid me under the dead Moon-calf's
Gaberdine, for fear of the Storm. And art thou   120
living, Stephano? O Stephano, two Neapolitans
scap'd?

STEPHANO   'Prethee do not turn me about: my Stomach
is not constant.

CALIBAN   – These be Fine Things, and if they be not
Sprights.   125
That's a brave God, and bears Celestial Liquor:
I will kneel to him.

STEPHANO   How didst thou scape? How cam'st thou
hither? Swear by this Bottle how thou cam'st

130 **Butt of Sack** cask of Spanish wine. *Butt* echoes lines 20–22 and recalls I.ii.146. *Heav'd o'erboard* recalls lines 20–22, 44–45, 123–24; compare I.i.64, I.ii.62, 75, 81, 114–16, 153–58, 250–51, 280, 291–93.

131 **by this Bottle** I swear by this bottle.

133 **cast ashore** vented (line 115). Compare lines 130–31.

139 **kiss the Book** Stephano's 'Book' (Bible) is the bottle Caliban has vowed to 'swear upon' (line 134, echoed in line 138). See lines 102–3.

140 **Goose** (a) silly fool, and (b) wanton. See *Love's Labour's Lost*, III.i.96–128, and *Romeo and Juliet*, II.iii.78–94.

145 **dropp'd from Heaven** descended from the sky (compare lines 20–22). Caliban's question recalls the stories Shakespeare's contemporaries would have heard about the way European explorers were regarded by the first New World natives to see them. Meanwhile it alludes to the 'dew' (manna) provided by God for the children of Israel during their wanderings from Egypt to the Promised Land; see Exodus 16:12–18. Compare I.ii.294, 320–23.

147 **when Time was** at one time. Lines 146–47 recall II.i.230–31.

149 **My ... thee** See I.ii.349–60, where Miranda reminds Caliban of all she taught him. The Dog and Bush accompanying the Man in the Moon derive from a legend that he had been a peasant who disobeyed the Sabbath laws by gathering firewood on a Sunday; he and his dog were banished to the Moon, along with the bush he had in his hand.

151 **Contents** Stephano means liquid contents, of course, but he likens them to (a) the matter a book contains, and (b) the table of contents enumerating the headings under which that matter is arranged.

153 **shallow** ignorant, foolish.

155 **creadulous** credulous, with a Folio spelling to remind us that Caliban now has a new creed (religion). See lines 193–94.

158 **By this Light** an oath that can refer to (a) the Sun, (b) the speaker's eyes, or (c) the speaker's intellect. *Foot* (line 157) recalls I.ii.467.
perfidious untrustworthy. Compare I.ii.67–68.

hither. I escap'd upon a Butt of Sack, which   130
the Sailors heaved o'erboard; by this Bottle,
which I made of the Bark of a Tree, with mine
own Hands, since I was cast ashore.

CALIBAN   I'll swear upon that Bottle to be thy
    true Subject:
For the Liquor is not Earthly.   135

STEPHANO   Here. – Swear then how thou escap'dst.

TRINCULO   Swom ashore, Man, like a Duck: I can
    swim like a Duck, I'll be sworn.

STEPHANO   Here, kiss the Book. Though thou canst
    swim like a Duck, thou art made like a Goose.   140

TRINCULO   O Stephano, hast any more of this?

STEPHANO   The whole Butt, Man; my Cellar is in a
    Rock by th' Seaside, where my Wine is hid.
    – How now, Moon-calf, how does thine Ague?

CALIBAN   Hast thou not dropp'd from Heaven?   145

STEPHANO   Out o'th' Moon, I do assure thee. I was
    the Man i'th' Moon, when Time was.

CALIBAN   I have seen thee in her; and I do adore
    thee.
My Mistress shew'd me thee, and thy Dog, and
    thy Bush.

STEPHANO   Come, swear to that: kiss the Book. I   150
    will furnish it anon with new Contents. Swear.

TRINCULO   By this good Light, this is a very
    shallow Monster: I afeard of him? A very weak
    Monster. The Man i'th' Moon? A most poor
    creadulous Monster, in good sooth.   155

CALIBAN   I'll shew thee every fertile Inch o'th'
    Island,
And I will kiss thy Foot. I prethee be my God.

TRINCULO   By this Light, a most perfidious and
    drunken Monster: when's God's asleep he'll rob
    his Bottle.   160

162 **down**   both (a) kneel down, and (b) down the hatch.

164 **Puppy-headed**   simple-minded. Compare *The Winter's Tale*,
IV.iv.728. Trinculo is probably thinking of the practice of
drowning unwanted kittens and puppies; see *The Two
Gentlemen of Verona*, IV.iv.3–5, *The Merry Wives of
Windsor*, III.v.10–14, and *Othello*, I.iii.339.
scurvy   scaly-skinned (line 48). See lines 25–40.

168 **abhominable**   nonhuman. In Shakespeare's time this word was
thought to derive from the Latin *ab* (away from) plus *homine*
(mankind). Compare *Hamlet*, III.ii.41.

172 **follow thee**   be your disciple. Caliban's phrasing echoes such
New Testament passages as Matthew 4:19 ('Follow me, and I
will make you fishers of men'), 8:22 ('Follow me; and let the
dead bury their dead'), 16:24 ('If any man will come after me,
let him deny himself, and take up his cross, and follow me'),
and 19:21 ('If thou wilt be perfect, go and sell that thou hast,
and give to the poor, and thou shalt have treasure in heaven:
and come and follow me').

174 **rediculous**   ridiculous (the Folio spelling plays on *red* and
reminds us that Caliban is flush with drink).

175 **Wonder**   marvel; object of adoration. Compare I.ii.423–26,
II.i.180. Among the amusing ironies of this scene is the fact
that while Caliban talks in dignified verse, the clown he
idolizes as a 'God' speaks prose; so does Trinculo.

176 **Crabs**   crab apples.

177 **Pig-nuts**   groundnuts (similar to, or identical with, peanuts).

179 **Marmazet**   marmoset (a small species of monkey). *Nimble*
recalls II.i.184.

180 **Philbirts**   filberts; hazelnuts.

181 **Scamels**   According to one source, scamels are godwits (wading
snipes). Others believe that Caliban is referring to (a) some
type of shellfish, or (b) *seamells* (sea-mews, sea birds).

CALIBAN   I'll kiss thy Foot. I'll swear my self
   thy Subject.
STEPHANO   Come on then: down and swear.
TRINCULO   I shall laugh my self to death at this
   Puppy-headed Monster. A most scurvy Monster:
   I could find in my Heart to beat him.   165
STEPHANO   Come, kiss.
TRINCULO   But that the poor Monster's in Drink,
   an abhominable Monster.
CALIBAN   I'll shew thee the best Springs; I'll
   pluck thee Berries;
   I'll fish for thee, and get thee Wood enough.   170
   A Plague upon the Tyrant that I serve:
   I'll bear him no more Sticks, but follow thee,
   Thou Wondrous Man.
TRINCULO   A most rediculous Monster, to make a
   Wonder of a poor Drunkard.   175
CALIBAN   I prethee let me bring thee where Crabs
   grow,
   And I with my long Nails will dig thee Pig-nuts,
   Show thee a Jay's Nest, and instruct thee how
   To snare the nimble Marmazet. I'll bring thee
   To clust'ring Philbirts, and sometimes I'll get
   thee   180
   Young Scamels from the Rock. Wilt thou go with
   me?

184– **inherit here** assume possession of this island. Compare lines
85   183–85 with I.ii.427–38, 450–54. Since Caliban, who has
    earlier spoken of the island as his kingdom (I.ii.330–31,
    340–41), has sworn himself to be Stephano's 'Subject' (lines
    161–62), Stephano can claim to have inherited it from the
    'Monster' who pays tribute to him as a newly arrived god. See
    I.ii.331–38 for Caliban's description of an initial response to
    Prospero that strongly parallels the way the shallow 'Monster'
    now adores and serves Stephano. The discussion of rulership
    in this passage offers a comic parody of other remarks about
    authority, rule, and possession in I.i.22–28; I.ii.53–132,
    286–93, 432–34, 451–54; II.i.126–53, 186–278.

190 **Firing** firewood.

191 **At requiring** upon demand.

192 **Trenchering** trenchers; wooden serving platters.

193 **Ban Ban Cacalyban** Caliban appears to be so inebriated that
    he cannot even pronounce his own name without slurring and
    hiccuping his way through it. In other contexts *Ban* means
    'curse', 'prohibit', or 'poison' (bane). See *The Merchant of
    Venice*, IV.i.46, *Hamlet*, III.ii.283, and *2 Henry VI*, II.iv.25,
    III.iii.305, 319.

195 **Freedom** Like Ariel, Caliban can hardly wait until he is
    emancipated from Prospero; compare I.ii.242–50. But we
    should remember that Prospero too is anxious to seize his
    'high-day' and be liberated from the constraints of an
    unforgiving, largely barren island; see I.ii.178–84. Like most
    of Shakespeare's comedies and romances, *The Tempest* is an
    action whose final cause is release from bondage, wandering,
    confusion, or loss. *Man* (line 194) recalls II.i.256.

197 **brave** admirable; bold-spirited. Compare line 126.

STEPHANO   I prethee now lead the way without any
   more talking. – Trinculo, the King and all our
   Company else being drown'd, we will inherit
   here. Here, bear my Bottle. Fellow Trinculo,   185
   we'll fill him by and by again.
CALIBAN *sings drunkenly*
         Farewell, Master; farewell, farewell.

TRINCULO   A howling Monster, a drunken Monster.
CALIBAN   *No more Dams I'll make for Fish,*
               Nor fetching in Firing   190
                  At requiring,
            Nor scrape Trenchering, nor wash Dish;
               Ban Ban Cacalyban
               Has a new Master, get a new Man.

   Freedom, high-day, high-day Freedom, Freedom   195
   high-day, Freedom.
STEPHANO   O brave Monster; lead the way.   *Exeunt.*

III.i   This scene takes place near Prospero's cell. It commences in a
        way that parallels the opening of the preceding scene.

1–2   **There . . . off**   It is not clear whether Ferdinand is saying (a)
        some sports are so strenuous that the effort to engage in them
        offsets any pleasure they bring us, or (b) some games are so
        arduous as to be painful, but the pleasure we take in them
        compensates for the effort they require, or (c) some
        recreations bring us pain, but we appreciate the delightful
        fruits of them all the more because of the labour required to
        deliver (give birth to) those fruits. Compare *1 Henry IV*,
        I.ii.229–36, where Prince Hal says that his bad reputation as a
        youth will be a 'Foil' (a contrasting backing) that sets off the
        'Bright Metal' of his 'Reformation' and makes it seem extra
        'glitt'ring' by contrast. The conclusion of the preceding scene
        serves as a foil for the meditation that commences this one; by
        contrast with a gleeful, dancing Caliban, and his exuberance
        over 'high-day Freedom', we now see a log-laden Fordinand
        who is delighted to have exchanged his freedom for the
        servitude imposed upon him by a master whose slave is now
        celebrating the liberation he thinks he's about to win.

2   **Baseness**   abasement, servitude; hardship. Consider lines 2–4 in
        the light of Matthew 5:3, 5, 10–11, and Philippians 2:5–9.
        Undergone recalls I.ii.151–58.

4   **Mean**   menial; humbling; more fit for a slave than for a prince.

5   **Odious**   detestable. *Heavy* recalls II.i.171, and reminds us why
        Prospero has imposed this 'Uneasy' labour on Ferdinand
        (I.ii.448–50).

6   **quickens**   restores, resurrects. Compare II.i.80–83, 97–106.

8   **crabb'd**   sour and shrivelled in disposition, like a crab apple.
        See II.ii.176. *Gentle* recalls II.i.121.

11   **Upon . . . Injunction**   in response to orders that are both severe
        and 'painful' (line 1). *Sore* recalls II.i.122; see the note to
        IV.i.20.

13   **Had . . . Executor**   was never done (a) by someone like me, and
        (b) with the kind of 'work' I put into it. Miranda has seen
        only Caliban in the role that Ferdinand now bears. The phrase
        'never like Executor' can also refer to Prospero, whom
        Miranda has never seen executing his will like this before (see
        I.ii.442, 494–96).

ACT III

Scene 1

Enter Ferdinand, bearing a Log.

FERDINAND There be some Sports are painful, and
  their Labour
  Delight in them set off. Some kinds of Baseness
  Are nobly undergone; and most Poor Matters
  Point to Rich Ends. This my Mean Task
  Would be as Heavy to me as Odious, but   5
  The Mistress which I serve quickens what's Dead
  And makes my Labours Pleasures. O she is
  Ten times more gentle than her Father's
    crabb'd;
  And he's compos'd of Harshness. I must remove
  Some thousands of these Logs, and pile them up,   10
  Upon a sore Injunction. My sweet Mistress
  Weeps when she sees me work, and says such
    Baseness
  Had never like Executor. I forget:

14   **refresh**   revivify (line 6); 'recover' (II.ii.74, 82, 100–2).

15   **Most . . . it**   which make me feel both most and least busy when I work [because Miranda's 'sweet Thoughts', and my sweet thoughts about her, make my otherwise painful exertions seem like sports]. Here *lest* appears to mean 'least' (just as *least* in Shakespeare often means 'lest', as is illustrated by I.ii.449 and IV.i.169); but there may also be wordplay on *busilest* (busiest). *Busy* recalls II.i.117. In this passage (lines 13–15) the Everyman text adheres to the punctuation in the Folio.

17   **enjoin'd**   ordered. Miranda's verb is a reminder that Ferdinand enjoys his labour because it makes him feel more 'enjoin'd' to his 'sweet Mistress'.

19   **weep**   release its oozing sap. Compare lines 11–12, and see I.ii.132–35, 153–58, 430–34, II.i.14–17.

21   **safe**   securely away [so that we can speak 'safely', II.i.309]. See the note to II.i.307.

22   **discharge**   literally, unload what I must 'undergo' (line 27). Compare I.ii.153–58, 299, and II.i.235–36. *Sun* recalls II.i.309; *set* echoes II.i.211–12, and anticipates III.ii.10.

26   **crack my Sinews**   rupture my tendons and muscles.

28   **Lazy**   slothfully. Compare I.i.7, II.i.147, 208–10.

30   **my . . . it**   my willing consent is disposed to it. *Ease* recalls I.ii.448–50, II.1.73–74.

31–32 **Poor . . . it**   My poor weak dear, you have caught a disease; your coming here and offering to do Ferdinand's work proves it. *Infected* often means 'infatuated with love' (as in *Richard III*, I.ii.151). But an infection can also be the consequence of a divine 'Visitation', a plague (see *Love's Labour's Lost*, V.ii.179, 419–22). *Worm* carries biblical echoes; see Job 25:4–6, where one of Job's friends asks how man can 'be justified with God'. Even 'the stars', he says, 'are not pure in his sight. How much less man, that is a worm?' Compare *Measure for Measure*, III.i.15–17, and *King Lear*, IV.i.32–37.

35   **set**   insert. This word echoes lines 2, 18 and 22.

But these sweet Thoughts do even refresh my
   Labours,
Most busy lest, when I do it.

   Enter Miranda and Prospero [unobserved].

MIRANDA   Alas, now pray you   15
   Work not so hard. I would the Lightning had
   Burnt up those Logs that you are enjoin'd to
      pile.
   Pray set it down, and rest you. When this burns,
   'Twill weep for having wearied you. My Father
   Is hard at Study; pray now rest your self,   20
   He's safe for these three Hours.
FERDINAND   O most dear Mistress,
   The Sun will set before I shall discharge
   What I must strive to do.
MIRANDA   If you'll sit down,
   I'll bear your Logs the while: pray give me
      that,
   I'll carry it to the Pile.
FERDINAND   No, precious Creature,   25
   I had rather crack my Sinews, break my Back,
   Than you should such Dishonour undergo
   While I sit Lazy by.
MIRANDA   It would become me
   As well as it does you; and I should do it
   With much more Ease, for my Good Will is to it   30
   And yours it is against.
PROSPERO   — Poor Worm, thou art Infected:
   This Visitation shews it.
MIRANDA   You look wearily.
FERDINAND   No, noble Mistress, 'tis fresh Morning
      with me
   When you are by at Night. I do beseech you,
   Chiefly that I might set it in my Prayers,   35

37 **Hest** behest; command. Compare I.ii.274.
Admir'd marvellous. Ferdinand plays on the Latin meaning of *Miranda* (in the original sense, 'wondered at').

39 **What's Dearest** whatever is most precious. See II.i.119.

40 **best Regard** (a) noblest vision; (b) highest approbation. The phrase 'I have ey'd' echoes Sonnet 104, line 2.

42 **several** different.

45 **ow'd** both (a) owned, and (b) owed to Nature. Compare I.ii.405.

46 **put . . . Foil** (a) fence with it (using 'foils', bated swords), (b) defeat it (as does a wrestler who 'foils', overthrows, his opponent), and (c) set it off as one bright jewel against a duller background. See the note to lines 1–2, and compare *Hamlet*, V.ii.267–69.

47 **Peetless** Most editions emend to 'Peerless'. But *Peetless* could mean either (a) peat-less (without the petulance of a spoiled pet), or (b) repeat-less (unduplicable, unique). For the first sense see *The Taming of the Shrew*, I.i.78–79.

50 **Glass** mirror. Lines 48–57 recall I.ii.476–81.

52 **abroad** elsewhere.

53 **skilless of** unable to judge [with no foil for comparison].

57 **like of** be enamoured of; favour. *Prattle* echoes II.i.245–47. *Shape* echoes I.ii.475–77.

58 **something too wildly** somewhat too unrestrainedly.
Precepts instructions (here, prohibitions).

59 **Condition** situation; position, rank. Compare I.ii.117, 120.

61 **I . . . so** though I wish that were not so.

62 **wodden Slavery** woeful, wood-bearing servitude. *Wodden* can also mean 'mad' (see *A Midsummer Night's Dream* II.i.192, and *King Lear*, II.ii.184, 199).

62–63 **suffer . . . Mouth** permit flies to take up residence and lay their eggs in my mouth as if I were a putrefying corpse.

65 **there** there it.

67 **patient** (a) submissive, (b) long-suffering, and (c) uncomplaining. *Slave* recalls I.ii.270–71, 308.

What is your Name?

MIRANDA   Miranda. – O my Father.
I have broke your Hest to say so.

FERDINAND   Admir'd Miranda,
  Indeed the top of Admiration, worth
  What's Dearest to the World. Full many a Lady
  I have ey'd with best Regard, and many a Time   40
  Th' Harmony of their Tongues hath into Bondage
  Brought my too diligent Ear: for several Virtues
  Have I lik'd several Women, never any
  With so full Soul but some Defect in her
  Did quarrel with the Noblest Grace she ow'd   45
  And put it to the Foil. But you, O you,
  So Perfect and so Peetless, are created
  Of every Creature's Best.

MIRANDA   I do not know
  One of my Sex; no Woman's Face remember,
  Save, from my Glass, mine own. Nor have I seen   50
  More that I may call Men than you, good Friend,
  And my dear Father. How Features are abroad
  I am skilless of; but by my Modesty
  (The Jewel in my Dower), I would not wish
  Any Companion in the World but you.   55
  Nor can Imagination form a Shape
  Besides your self to like of. But I prattle
  Something too wildly, and my Father's Precepts
  I therein do forget.

FERDINAND   I am in my Condition
  A Prince, Miranda, I do think a King   60
  (I would not so), and would no more endure
  This wodden Slavery than to suffer
  The Flesh-fly blow my Mouth. Hear my Soul speak:
  The very Instant that I saw you did
  My Heart fly to your Service; there resides   65
  To make me Slave to it, and for your sake
  Am I this patient Log-man.

69   **crown . . . Event** ratify and reward what I avow with fittingly happy consequences ('Rich Ends', line 4). *Crown* is a reminder of what Ferdinand has said in lines 59–61, and it reinforces our awareness that a union between him and Miranda would produce a 'kind Event' for a new queen. *Sound* (line 68) recalls I.ii.386, 404–5.

70   **Hollowly** emptily (with no substance behind my words). Compare *Julius Caesar*, IV.ii.22.

70–71 **invert . . . Mischief** reverse the best fortune destined for me and turn it to calamity. *Mischief* recalls I.ii.264.

72   **all . . . else** the boundaries that apply to anything else. Ferdinand's phrasing echoes *King Lear*, I.i.55–59.

76   **Wherefore** why. *Breeds* recalls I.ii.319, II.i.127. *Weep* echoes line 19.

78–79 **much . . . want** even less dare to take what I will die without.

79   **Trifling** foolish coyness (because my feelings are too obvious to hide). Line 81 echoes *Romeo and Juliet*, II.i.131.

81   **shews** shows (even as it attempts to eschew it). Compare I.ii.468, where Prospero uses *shew* in a way that hints at an aphetic form of *eschew*.

82   **prompt** guide and correct. Miranda dismisses one of her performance coaches ('bashful Cunning', a 'Modesty' that only pretends to be unmoved by affection), and puts herself at the disposal of another, 'holy Innocence' (a simple directness that expresses true chastity). Compare *Romeo and Juliet*, II.i.121–22, 131, 140–43, III.ii.14–16.

84   **your Maid** your virginal but no less loving adorer, and 'Servant'.
    Fellow equal; here, Queen. Compare line 47, and see II.i.255–56.

86   **My Mistress** the Lady who rules my actions. Compare lines 6, 11.

87   **thus Humble** in this way reduced to '*your* Servant' (line 85). See the note to line 47, and compare I.ii.479–81.

88   **I** both (a) I, and (b) ay. Compare II.i.258.

MIRANDA   Do you love me?
FERDINAND   — O Heaven, O Earth, bear witness to
    this Sound,
  And crown what I profess with kind Event
  If I speak True; if Hollowly, invert   70
  What best is boded me to Mischief. — I,
  Beyond all Limit of what else i'th' World,
  Do love, prize, honour you.
MIRANDA   I am a Fool
  To weep at what I am glad of.
PROSPERO   Fair Encounter
  Of two most Rare Affections: Heavens rain Grace   75
  On that which breeds between 'em.
FERDINAND   Wherefore weep you?
MIRANDA   At mine Unworthiness, that dare not offer
  What I desire to give, and much less take
  What I shall die to want. But this is Trifling;
  And all the more it seeks to hide it self,   80
  The bigger Bulk it shews. — Hence, bashful
    Cunning,
  And prompt me, plain and holy Innocence.
  — I am your Wife, if you will marry me;
  If not, I'll die your Maid. To be your Fellow
  You may deny me, but I'll be your Servant   85
  Whether you will or no.
FERDINAND   My Mistress, Dearest,
  And I thus Humble ever.
MIRANDA   My Husband then?
FERDINAND   I, with a Heart as willing

89 **As ... Freedom** as bondage ever was to be offered liberty. For Ferdinand the marriage bond will be a devoutly wished 'Freedom'. Compare II.ii.195–96. Here *ere* can mean both (a) before, and (b) ever (e'er). Compare I.ii.320.

91 **A thousand thousand** A million hours, you mean. Compare line 10, and see *As You Like It*, III.ii.332–37, and *Romeo and Juliet*, III.v.44–47.

93 **surpris'd with all** (a) taken by surprise by all that I have stage-managed, and (b) captured withal (therewith).

94 **to my Book** return to my book of magic (here a volume with lore on such arts as astrology, divination, and conjuration).

96 **appertaining** pertaining hereto. *Business* recalls II.i.271–72, and anticipates III.iii.69.

III.ii This scene appears to take us to the seaside rock where Stephano has hidden his butt of sack (see II.ii.141–43).

1 **Tell not me** Don't bother me with requests for water.
out out of wine; empty. Compare I.ii.246.

3 **bear ... 'em** stand tall, and drink as bravely as if you were carrying cargo aboard or boarding an enemy ship. *Bear* echoes the stage directions (and visual images) that open the two previous scenes (II.ii and III.i).

8 **brain'd like us** with brains in the brained state ours are in.

10 **set** Stephano means 'fixed in a glazed stare'; but in lines 11–13 Trinculo takes *set* to mean 'placed'. Line 10 is an amusing echo of II.i.211–12 and III.i.22–23.

13 **Tail** rear. But since Trinculo is speaking of 'Eyes' (see the note to II.ii.38), *Tail* is coloured by the implications enumerated in II.ii.57.

14 **Man-Monster** Stephano probably means both (a) 'Servant Monster', line 5 (compare II.i.255–56, III.i.83–85), and (b) half-human monster (compare lines 33–34).

16 **recover** attain. See II.i.97–106, II.ii.74–76, III.i.14.

16–17 **five ... Leagues** 105 miles.

As Bondage ere of Freedom: here's my Hand.
MIRANDA   And mine, with my Heart in't; and now
    farewell   90
Till half an Hour hence.
FERDINAND   A thousand thousand.
                                   Exeunt.

PROSPERO   So glad of this as they I cannot be,
Who are surpris'd with all; but my Rejoicing
At nothing can be more. I'll to my Book,
For yet ere Supper Time must I perform   95
Much Business appertaining.   *Exit.*

Scene 2

Enter Caliban, Stephano, and Trinculo.

STEPHANO   Tell not me; when the Butt is out we
will drink Water, not a Drop before. Therefore
bear up, and boord 'em, Servant Monster; drink
to me.
TRINCULO   Servant Monster? The Folly of this   5
Island. They say there's but five upon this
Isle. We are three of them; if the other two
be brain'd like us, the State totters.
STEPHANO   Drink, Servant Monster, when I bid thee:
thy Eyes are almost set in thy Head.   10
TRINCULO   Where should they be set else? He were
a brave Monster indeed if they were set in his
Tail.
STEPHANO   My Man-Monster hath drown'd his Tongue
in Sack. For my part, the Sea cannot drown me;   15
I swam, ere I could recover the Shore, five and
thirty Leagues off and on. – By this Light,

19   **Standard** Stephano means 'standard-bearer' (ensign); but the primary meaning of *Standard* (the pole that supports the 'standard', the banner) is a reminder that none of these characters can now do much valiant standing. They all 'list' (line 20) so severely that their 'State totters' (line 8).

20   **list** wish (but with unintended wordplay on 'lean, sway'). Compare *The Winter's Tale*, IV.iv.555. Also see *Hamlet*, I.v.21–22.

22   **run** run away. Stephano insists that he and Caliban will stand their ground. Trinculo says that they won't even 'go' (walk), perhaps with play on the sense of *go* that relates to ejaculation.

23   **lie** (a) lye (urinate, a sense of *run* and *go* that accords with *Standard* as a word for 'conduit'), (b) lie low, and (c) tell lies.

30   **in . . . Constable** in a fit condition to jostle a policeman. *Case* recalls I.i.35–36, 56–57, and II.i.272–73. In line 29 *Ignorant* means both (a) unlearned, dull-witted, and (b) wilfully ignoring or denying the truth. Compare *King Lear*, IV.v.9, and see the note to *Macbeth*, I.v.60.

31   **debosh'd** debauched, dissolute. Trinculo defends his 'Honour' (line 27). *Fish* recalls II.ii.25–40.

32   **to day** today. But here the context also permits *to* to serve as a preposition and *day* to function as a noun. Compare I.ii.324.

33–34 **half . . . Monster** Trinculo's phrasing implies that it is the non-fish half of Caliban that is monstrous.

37   **Natural** Trinculo uses this word in the sense that means 'idiot' (a natural fool, as opposed to a professional fool). Here the unintended humour drives from the fact that a 'Monster' is by definition a deviation from the 'Natural'.

39–40 **keep . . . Head** watch what you say; no more insolence.

40   **if . . . Tree** If you try to raise an insurrection against the king of this island, you'll hang on the next tree we see. Compare *Macbeth*, V.v.37–39.

44–45 **hearken . . . Suit** listen once more to my plea. Caliban's words recall I.ii.79–87, 121–32.

thou shalt be my Lieutenant Monster, or my
Standard.

TRINCULO   Your Lieutenant, if you list; he's no   20
Standard.

STEPHANO   We'll not run, Monsieur Monster.

TRINCULO   Nor go, neither; but you'll lie like
Dogs, and yet say nothing neither.

STEPHANO   Moon-calf, speak once in thy Life, if   25
thou beest a good Moon-calf.

CALIBAN   How does thy Honour? Let me lick thy Shoe;
I'll not serve him, he is not Valiant.

TRINCULO   Thou liest, most ignorant Monster: I
am in Case to justle a Constable. Why, thou   30
debosh'd Fish, thou, was ever man a Coward
that hath drunk so much Sack as I to day? Wilt
thou tell a Monstrous Lie, being but half a
Fish and half a Monster?

CALIBAN   Lo, how he mocks me; wilt thou let
him, my Lord?   35

TRINCULO   'Lord,' quoth he? That a Monster should
be such a Natural?

CALIBAN   Lo, lo again: bite him to death, I
prethee.

STEPHANO   Trinculo, keep a good Tongue in your
Head: if you prove a Mutineer, the next Tree.   40
The poor Monster's my Subject, and he shall
not suffer Indignity.

CALIBAN   I thank my noble Lord. Wilt thou be
pleas'd
To hearken once again to the Suit I made
To thee?   45

46 **Marry** truly. *Marry* evolved from an oath referring to the Virgin Mary. Shakespeare frequently embeds it in a context that permits ironic play on the usual sense of the word. Here Stephano's phrase offers a subtle link to the previous scene, where Ferdinand and Miranda have said 'Marry will I' in vows of their own (III.i.83–90); meanwhile it anticipates the notion Caliban will plant in Stephano's head in lines 99–110.

49 **Tyrant** Compare I.ii.451–54.
    Cunning (a) knowledge, expertise (the original sense), and (b) trickery. See III.i.81. In line 50 the invisible Ariel adopts Trinculo's voice.

55 **in's Tale** as he tries to tell us what is on his mind. Stephano's phrasing suggests that Trinculo is trying to 'trouble' Caliban's 'tail'. See the note to line 13, and compare *The Taming of the Shrew*, II.i.212–17. *Supplant* (remove) recalls II.i.252–53.

60 **thy Greatness** Caliban's honorific for Stephano (whose name derives from the Greek word for 'crown') is a reminder that *greatness* can refer to anything that is 'enlarged', whether or not it is *great* ('large') in the usual positive sense. Compare 'bigger' in III.i.79–81, and see the note to *Twelfth Night*, III.iv.49. Stephano's 'Greatness' (his grossly over-extended ego) is a consequence of two factors: (a) the liquor that has dulled his normal sense of fear and made him even more 'Valiant' than Trinculo (see lines 28–30), and (b) the adoration he receives from a Caliban whose eagerness for a god to champion his cause prevents him from perceiving inadequacies that will eventually become apparent to even a 'shallow Monster' (II.ii.153). *Thing* (line 62) recalls II.ii.125.

64 **compass'd** accomplished (literally, encircled).

68 **pied Ninny** mottled simpleton. *Patch* (referring to the particoloured patchwork of the court jester's professional attire) conveys much the same idea. See the note to line 37. *Scurvy* recalls II.ii.164.

69 **Blows** Caliban's phrasing (compare II.i.161) hints comically at the kinds of 'Blow' alluded to in *Troilus and Cressida*, I.ii.287–90. In the process it colours *Greatness* with a suggestion of tumescence; compare line 60.

STEPHANO   Marry will I; Kneel, and repeat it.
I will stand, and so shall Trinculo.

Enter Ariel invisible.

CALIBAN   As I told thee before, I am subject to
A Tyrant, a Sorcerer, that by his Cunning
Hath cheated me of the Island.   50
ARIEL   Thou liest.
CALIBAN   Thou liest, thou jesting Monkey, thou:
I would my valiant Master would destroy thee.
I do not lie.
STEPHANO   Trinculo, if you trouble him any more
in's Tale, by this Hand I will supplant some   55
of your Teeth.
TRINCULO   Why, I said nothing.
STEPHANO   Mum then, and no more. – Proceed.
CALIBAN   I say by Sorcery he got this Isle;
From me he got it. If thy Greatness will   60
Revenge it on him (for I know thou dar'st,
But this thing dare not) –
STEPHANO   That's most certain.
CALIBAN   Thou
Shalt be Lord of it, and I'll serve thee.
STEPHANO   How now
Shall this be compass'd? Canst thou bring me to
The party?
CALIBAN   Yea, yea, my Lord, I'll yield him thee   65
Asleep, where thou mayst knock a Nail into
His Head.
ARIEL   Thou liest, thou canst not.
CALIBAN   What a pied Ninny's this? – Thou scurvy
Patch.
– I do beseech thy Greatness give him Blows,
And take his Bottle from him. When that's gone,   70

71 **nought but Brine** nothing but salt water from the sea.

72 **quick Freshes** springs and streams of fresh water.

75 **turn . . . Doors** banish my mercy [and give you the beating you justly deserve].

76 **Stockfish** dried cod or hake, called *stockfish* because it must be softened with pounding (with 'Blows', line 69) before it can be cooked and eaten. See the note to II.ii.29.

79–80 **give . . . Lie** call me a liar. Compare *The Winter's Tale*, IV.iv.745–54.

82 **Pox o'** pox on. Here *Pox* is more or less synonymous with *Plague*, a generic word for any loathsome disease, from smallpox to leprosy to syphilis to bubonic plague. Compare I.i.39, 43, and II.ii.171.

83 **Murren** murrain (possibly the 'Red-plague' of I.ii.362, a disease common in cattle).

89 **brain him** knock his brains out. Compare lines 7–8. *Beat* (lines 86–87) echoes II.ii.165.

91 **paunch** punch; stab. Compare lines 65–67.

92 **Wezand** windpipe.

93 **possess** seize.

94 **Sot** ignoramus, dolt.

He shall drink nought but Brine, for I'll not
  shew him
Where the quick Freshes are.

STEPHANO   Trinculo, run
  Into no further Danger: interrupt
  The Monster one word further, and by this Hand
  I'll turn my Mercy out o' Doors and make   75
  A Stockfish of thee.

TRINCULO   Why, what did I? I
  Did nothing: I'll go farther off.

STEPHANO   Didst thou
  Not say he lied?

ARIEL   Thou liest.

STEPHANO   Do I so?
  Take thou that; as you like this, give me
  The Lie another Time.

TRINCULO   I did not give   80
  The Lie. Out o' your Wits and Hearing too?
  A Pox o' your Bottle; this can Sack and Drinking
  Do. A Murren on your Monster, and
  The Divel take your Fingers.

CALIBAN   Ha, ha, ha.

STEPHANO Now forward with your Tale. – Prethee
  stand further off.   85

CALIBAN Beat him enough; after a little Time
  I'll beat him too.

STEPHANO   – Stand farther. – Come proceed.

CALIBAN Why, as I told thee, 'tis a Custom with
  him
  I'th' Afternoon to sleep. There thou mayst
  brain him,
  Having first seiz'd his Books, or with a Log   90
  Batter his Skull, or paunch him with a Stake,
  Or cut his Wezand with thy Knife. Remember
  First to possess his Books, for without them
  He's but a Sot, as I am, nor hath not

96   **rootedly** deeply (all the way to the roots). Lines 95–96 echo *Macbeth*, V.ii.19–20, V.iii.22–28, 40–41.

97   **brave** splendid; impressive. *Utensils* is here to be accented on the first and third syllables.

98   **deck withal** adorn it with them. *Deck* recalls I.ii.155.

99   **that . . . consider** what we must chiefly bear in mind.

101   **a Non-pareil** a peerless beauty. Compare III.i.47. Lines 101–2 ('I . . . she') echo I.ii.475–79 and III.i.37–57.

102   **Dam** mother. *Onely* recalls II.i.217.

104   **brave** beautiful. Compare lines 12, 97, 106, 148. *Great'st* echoes lines 60, 69; *Least* recalls III.i.15.

106   **brave Brood** offspring of the finest breeding. Compare III.i.74–76.

108–9   **save our Graces** God save our graces. Stephano's expression provides an amusing perspective on how far removed he is from the 'Graces' that normally accompany either royalty or redemption.

113   **while thou liv'st** for as long as you live; for the rest of your life.

115   **asleep** This word draws our memories back to what almost happened in II.i. while Alonso and Gonzalo were asleep.

116   **I** both (a) I, and (b) ay. Here the Folio spelling calls attention to the unruliness Shakespeare frequently associates with *I* and *1*; see the notes to II.i.38, 51, 85, and compare III.i.88.

119   **Jocund** jolly, 'Merry'. Compare II.i.157–60.
    troule the Catch troll (sing) the round.

120   **while-ere** a short while ago.

121–22   **do Reason** do anything within reason. See the second note to I.ii.176.

124   **Flout** mock.
    cout colt, gibe.

125   **scout** sneer at. *Free* recalls III.i.89.

One Spirit to command: they all do hate him   95
As rootedly as I. Burn but his Books;
He has brave Utensils (for so he calls them),
Which, when he has a House, he'll deck withal.
And that most deeply to consider is
The Beauty of his Daughter: he himself   100
Calls her a Non-pareil. I never saw a Woman
But onely Sycorax my Dam and she;
But she as far surpasseth Sycorax
As Great'st does Least.

STEPHANO   Is it so brave a Lass?

CALIBAN   Ay, Lord, she will become thy Bed, I
    warrant,   105
And bring thee forth brave Brood.

STEPHANO   Monster, I will kill this Man. His
Daughter and I will be King and Queen, save
our Graces, and Trinculo and thy self shall be
Vice-roys. – Dost thou like the Plot, Trinculo?   110

TRINCULO   Excellent.

STEPHANO   Give me thy Hand, I am sorry I beat thee;
but while thou liv'st keep a good Tongue in
thy Head.

CALIBAN   Within this half Hour will he be asleep: 115
Wilt thou destroy him then?

STEPHANO   I, on mine Honour.

ARIEL   This will I tell my Master.

CALIBAN   Thou mak'st me Merry: I am full of
    Pleasure.
Let us be Jocund. Will you troule the Catch
You taught me but while-ere?   120

STEPHANO   At thy Request, Monster, I will do
Reason, any Reason. – Come on, Trinculo, let
us sing.   *Sings.*

        Flout 'em, and cout 'em;
        And scout 'em, and flout 'em;   125
            Thought is free.

S.D. **Tabor** small drum.

130 **Picture of Nobody** Trinculo means either (a) an image of a
non-person, or (b) a person whose image we cannot see. The
phrase may allude to the shop sign of John Trundle, a London
bookseller, which featured 'Nobody' (compare II.ii.30–31,
where Trinculo refers to a 'Fish painted' signboard). 'Nobody'
may have been a conventional image; if so, it was no doubt
reflected in the 1606 title-page of a comedy, *No-body and
Some-body*, which depicted a figure with arms, legs, and a
head, but no body (trunk).

132– **take't . . . list** take my challenge as you please. Stephano's
33   words echo an oath, 'The Devil take it.' *List* echoes line 20.

135 **He . . . Debts** whichever of us dies is acquitted of further
obligations. Stephano quotes a proverb; Edgar alludes to the
same expression in *King Lear*, V.i.42–44.

140 **sweet Airs** pleasing melodies. But Caliban's phrase can also
mean 'fragrant scents'; compare I.ii.389–91, II.i.32. *Sounds*
recalls III.i.68, and anticipates line 153.

141 **twangling** evidently Shakespeare's coinage for 'strumming'. See
The Taming of the Shrew, II.i.160.

147 **cried** cried out; begged. This speech portrays Caliban as a far
more sensitive, if not noble, savage than we would infer from
what Prospero and his daughter say about him. Caliban's
reference to sleep and dreaming echoes I.ii.44–46, 185–86,
305–7, II.i.170–200, 262–72, 282–92, 298–301, II.ii.43–44.
Meanwhile lines 145–46 recall II.ii.18–25.

148 **brave** magnificent. Stephano likes the idea of a 'Kingdom' in
which musicians perform free. Compare I.ii.385–87,
II.i.14–18.

152 **the Story** your 'Tale' (lines 55, 85). *Sound* (line 153) recalls
I.ii.386, 404–5, and line 140.

157 **follow Stephano** Most editions insert a comma after *follow*;
but it is not clear that Trinculo is addressing Stephano. 'Wilt
[thou] come?' seems at least as likely to be spoken to Caliban,
who is probably holding back out of a reluctance to 'follow'
the 'Sound' and risk being diverted from the mission foremost
in his mind. Like Prospero, Caliban knows that if he doesn't
seize the present moment, his 'Fortunes / Will ever after
droop' (I.ii.183–84). *Follow* (lines 153–57) echoes II.ii.172.

CALIBAN   That's not the Tune.
    Ariel plays the Tune on a Tabor and Pipe.
STEPHANO   What is this same?
TRINCULO   This is the Tune of our Catch, play'd
  by the Picture of Nobody.   130
STEPHANO   — If thou beest a Man, shew thy self in
  thy Likeness; if thou beest a Divel, take't as
  thou list.
TRINCULO   O forgive me my Sins.
STEPHANO   He that dies pays all Debts: I defy thee.   135
  Mercy upon us.
CALIBAN   Art thou afeard?
STEPHANO   No, Monster, not I.
CALIBAN   Be not afeard, the Isle is full of
    Noises,
  Sounds, and sweet Airs, that give Delight and
    hurt not;   140
  Sometimes a thousand twangling Instruments
  Will hum about mine Ears; and sometime Voices,
  That if I then had wak'd after long Sleep,
  Will make me sleep again; and then in Dreaming,
  The Clouds methought would open, and shew
    Riches   145
  Ready to drop upon me, that when I wak'd
  I cried to dream again.
STEPHANO   This will prove a brave Kingdom to me,
  where I shall have my Music for nothing.
CALIBAN   When Prospero is destroy'd.   150
STEPHANO   That shall be by and by: I remember
  the Story.
TRINCULO   The Sound is going away: let's follow
  it, and after do our Work.
STEPHANO   Lead, Monster, we'll follow. I would I   155
  could see this Taborer, he lays it on.
TRINCULO   Wilt come? I'll follow Stephano.   *Exeunt.*

III.iii   This scene returns us to the wanderings of Alonso and his party.

1   **By'r Lakin**   by our Ladykin (the Virgin Mary).

3   **Forth-rights and Meanders**   straight paths and winding ones.

5   **attach'd**   arrested, apprehended (a reminder of Ferdinand's attachment). *Dulling* (line 6) recalls I.ii.185.
      Weariness   Alonso's weariness is as much of the soul as of the body. He is on the verge of despair; and though he doesn't realize it, his Exodus-like travails signify his need for the 'rest' promised those who 'labour and are heavy laden' (Matthew 11:28). Compare I.ii.294, III.i.1–15.

8   **for my Flatterer**   as a worthless counsellor who merely flatters me. *Drown'd* recalls II.ii.117–18, III.ii.14–17.

9   **stray**   tread and stumble aimlessly. Compare I.ii.414–15.

10   **frustrate**   frustrated; thwarted at every turn.

12   **for one Repulse**   because of one chance rebuff.
      forgo   surrender. *Purpose* recalls I.ii.128–32, II.i.206–7. *Advantage* (line 13) echoes I.i.33–35.

14   **throughly**   thoroughly [to carry our purpose through to its conclusion].
      to night   tonight. So also in line 17. Compare I.ii.324, III.ii.32.

15   **Travail**   both (a) travel, and (b) hardship, affliction, 'Weariness' (line 5). Compare Job 15:20 ('The wicked man travaileth with pain all his days, and the number of years is hidden to the oppressor'), Isaiah 12:8 ('And they shall be afraid: pangs and sorrows shall take hold of them; they shall be in pain as a woman that travaileth: they shall be amazed one at another; their faces shall be as flames'), and Romans 8:22 ('For we know that the whole creation groaneth and travaileth in pain together until now', echoed in I.ii.156).

S.D.   **strange**   mysterious. This word recalls II.i.300 and II.ii.29, 33–34, 43–44, and anticipates lines 87, 94–95.
      on the Top   in the highest alcove above the stage. *Prosper* (Prospero) is the only spelling to be found in the Folio text.

Scene 3

Enter Alonso, Sebastian, Antonio, Gonzalo,
Adrian, Francisco, &c.

GONZALO   By'r Lakin, I can go no further, Sir:
My old Bones aches. Here's a Maze trod indeed
Through Forthrights and Meanders: by your
   patience,
I needs must rest me.
ALONSO   Old Lord, I cannot blame thee,
Who am my self attach'd with Weariness   5
To th' Dulling of my Spirits. Sit down and rest.
Even here I will put off my Hope, and keep it
No longer for my Flatterer. He is drown'd
Whom thus we stray to find, and the Sea mocks
Our frustrate Search on Land. Well, let him go.   10
ANTONIO   — I am right glad that he's so out of
      Hope:
Do not for one Repulse forgo the Purpose
That you resolv'd t' effect.
SEBASTIAN   The next Advantage
Will we take throughly.
ANTONIO   Let it be to night;
For now they are oppress'd with Travail, they   15
Will not, nor cannot, use such Vigilance
As when they are Fresh.
SEBASTIAN   I say to night: no more.

Solemn and strange Music; and Prosper on the Top,
invisible.

20 **kind Keepers** benevolent protectors and providers. Alonso is probably praying for guardian angels. But his words could also apply to the 'strange Shapes' that have just served a 'Banket' (banquet, a light repast of delicacies).

21 **living Drollery** puppet-like show with living forms enacting it.

23 **the Phoenix' Throne** the seat of the fabled Phoenix, an Arabian bird that was said to live for half a millennium, then expire in a flame that gave birth to a new Phoenix from its predecessor's ashes. Lines 21–27 recall II.i.39–44.

25–27 **what . . . 'em** anything else that lacks for believers in its authenticity, however far-fetched travellers' tales about it may seem to sceptical 'Fools' (line 27) back home. *Credit* (credibility) recalls I.ii.102, II.i.43, and II.ii.155. The phrase *be sworn* echoes II.ii.134–40, 150–51, 161–62.

29 **such Islands** islands on which such things occur. Most editions emend to *islanders*. Compare II.i.75–79, II.ii.29–36.

30 **certes** certainly: to be sure.

31 **Monstrous** hideous, frightful. See the note to III.ii.37. *Shape* recalls III.i.56–57.

32 **Gentle** (a) noble, (b) 'Kind' (humane). See III.i.7–8.

32–33 **of . . . Generation** among those (whether humane or not) who have been generated from the loins of human beings. Compare I.ii.265, 345.

36 **muse** wonder at; be amazed by.

37 **Sound expressing** both (a) completeness of expression (compare II.ii.84–92), and (b) expression of sound. But lines 39–40 suggest that the 'Shapes' who enter after the music express themselves through 'Gesture' rather than through audible 'Sound'. Compare III.i.68, III.ii.140, 153.

ALONSO   What Harmony is this? My good Friends,
   hark.

GONZALO   Marvellous sweet Music.

    *Enter several strange Shapes, bringing
    in a Banket; and dance about it with gentle
    actions of Salutations; and, inviting the
    King &c to eat, they depart.*

ALONSO   Give us kind Keepers, Heavens. What were
   these?   20

SEBASTIAN   A living Drollery. Now I will believe
  That there are Unicorns, that in Arabia
  There is one Tree, the Phoenix' Throne, one
    Phoenix
  At this Hour reigning there.

ANTONIO   I'll believe both;
  And what does else want Credit, come to me   25
  And I'll be sworn 'tis True. Travellers ne'er
  Did lie, though Fools at Home condemn 'em.

GONZALO   If
  In Naples I should report this now, would they
  Believe me? If I should say I saw such Islands;
  For certes, these are People of the Island,   30
  Who, though they are of Monstrous Shape, yet
    note
  Their Manners are more Gentle, Kind, than of
  Our Humane Generation you shall find
  Many, nay, almost any.

PROSPERO   – Honest Lord,
  Thou hast said well: for some of you there
    present   35
  Are worse than Divels.

ALONSO   I cannot too much muse
  Such Shapes, such Gesture, and such Sound
    expressing

38 **want** lack. Compare II.i.129, III.i.79, III.iii.25.

39 **dumb Discourse** mute speech.
Praise in departing Prospero alludes to a proverb advising guests to praise their host's entertainment only when they are safely on the way out (see *The Winter's Tale*, I.ii.9–10, and compare *Cymbeline*, V.iv.162–63).

41 **Stomachs** appetites for these 'Viands' (footstuffs), and the boldness to take what we wish. Compare II.ii.123–24.

45 **Dew-lapp'd** with fat, hanging jowls (owing to goitre). Compare *A Midsummer Night's Dream*, II.i.50, IV.i.125.

46–47 **such . . . Breasts** The title character refers to 'such Men' in *Othello*, I.iii.142–43.

48–49 **Each . . . of** every traveller who visits the Swiss Alps (where men as described in lines 46–47 were said to have been sighted) can verify. Gonzalo alludes to a form of pawning in which a departing traveller deposited with a speculator a sum of money to be kept if the traveller failed to return but to be repaid fivefold if he completed his trip successfully.

49 **stand to** take my chances (wager that it's safe to eat this food).

50 **Although my last** if it should turn out to be my last meal. *Last* alludes to the Last Supper (Luke 22:14–38).

S.D. **Harpy** a monstrous bird of prey with an angelic face. In Book III of Virgil's *Aeneid* harpies defile a feast and issue a dreadful prophecy. See the note to II.i.125.
a quient Device a clever trick (a theatrical special effect).

54–55 **That . . . in't** which has as its means of operation everything that constitutes 'this Lower World' (below the Moon).

55 **never surfeited** never-sated. Ariel implies that the insatiable Sea disgorged these 'Men of Sin', not because it had overeaten ('surfeited'), but because it would not digest anything so 'unfit' (line 58) as they. Compare II.i.232–36, II.ii.130, 133, 232–36.

59 **such . . . Valour** such seeming 'Valour' (rash frenzy). *Valour* recalls III.ii.28. For other Shakespearean treatments of the self-endangering 'valour' that derives from desperation, see *Antony and Cleopatra*, IV.i.9–10, *Romeo and Juliet*, IV.i.68–70, *Hamlet*, I.iv.86, *King Lear*, V.iii.161, and *1 Henry VI*, I.ii.25–26, II.i.44–45, IV.ii.46–52, IV.iii.55–60.

(Although they want the use of Tongue), a kind
Of excellent dumb Discourse.
PROSPERO   – Praise in departing.
FRANCISCO   They vanish'd strangely.
SEBASTIAN   No matter, since they have   40
   Left their Viands behind: for we have Stomachs.
   Will't please you taste of what is here?
ALONSO   Not I.
GONZALO   Faith Sir, you need not fear. When we were
      Boys,
   Who would believe that there were Mountaineers
   Dew-lapp'd like Bulls, whose Throats had
      hanging at 'em   45
   Wallets of Flesh? Or that there were such Men
   Whose Heads stood in their Breasts? Which now
      we find
   Each Putter-out of Five for One will bring us
   Good Warrant of.
ALONSO   I will stand to, and feed:
   Although my last, no matter, since I feel   50
   The Best is past. – Brother, my Lord the Duke,
   Stand to, and do as we.

   Thunder and Lightning. Enter Ariel, like a Harpy;
      claps his Wings upon the Table, and with a
         quient Device the Banquet vanishes.

ARIEL   You are three Men of Sin, whom Destiny,
   That hath to Instrument this Lower World
   And what is in't, the never surfeited Sea   55
   Hath caus'd to belch up you; and on this
      Island,
   Where Man doth not inhabit (you 'mongst Men
   Being most unfit to live), I have made you Mad;
   And even with such like Valour Men hang and
      drown

60   **proper** own.

62   **temper'd** composed and hardened (by extremes of heat and
        cold). Compare II.i.28–30. *Ministers* (line 61) recalls I.ii.131,
        275, II.i.153–56. The dialogue suggests that by line 60
        Prospero's adversaries have drawn their swords in defiance of
        him. The withdrawal of the banquet echoes Job 20, especially
        verses 4–8, 11–25, 27–29. See the note to line 85.

64   **still-closing** 'Invulnerable' (line 66); ever re-sealing.

65   **One . . . Plumbe** both (a) one feather (dowle) that's in my
        plume, and (b) one dowel (peg or pin) that's in my plumb
        [plumb-line to measure depth]. Compare line 101.

69   **my . . . you** my purpose in bringing you here (and my message
        to you). Compare III.i.94–96.

70   **supplant** displace. This verb recalls II.i.253, III.ii.55–56.

71   **requit** repaid (avenged); returned (as in lines 55–56). Compare
        I.ii.147–48, 210–11, II.i.303–4.

73   **The Powres** 'the higher powers' that ordain 'the powers that
        be' (Romans 13:1) in 'this Lower World' (line 54); here, the
        'Ministers of Fate' who determine human 'Destiny' (lines 61,
        53). *Powres* recalls I.ii.3 and anticipates line 90.

74   **Incens'd** infuriated; literally, enflamed. See I.ii.193–215.

76   **bereft** both (a) deprived, and (b) left bereaved (mournful).

77   **Ling'ring Perdition** protracted retribution; 'Inch-meal' torture
        (II.ii.3) until your 'Death' is final. *Perdition* recalls I.ii.30.

78   **attend** follow; wait upon. Compare I.ii.419–20, 450–51.

80   **desolate** forsaken; uninhabited (because largely barren).

81   **is . . . Sorrow** can be effected only by heartfelt repentance.

82   **a . . . ensuing** a pure (spotless) life thereafter.

S.D.   **Mows** scornful grimaces (as with *moe* in II.ii.9). Compare
        IV.i.46–47.

Their proper selves. You Fools, I and my
 Fellows   60
Are Ministers of Fate: the Elements,
Of whom your Swords are temper'd, may as well
Wound the loud Winds, or with bemock'd-at Stabs
Kill the still-closing Waters, as diminish
One Dowle that's in my Plumbe. My fellow
 Ministers   65
Are like Invulnerable: if you could hurt,
Your Swords are now too massy for your
 Strengths,
And will not be uplifted. But remember
(For that's my Business to you) that you three
From Millaine did supplant good Prospero,   70
Expos'd unto the Sea (which hath requit it)
Him and his innocent Child, for which Foul Deed
The Powres (delaying, not forgetting) have
Incens'd the Seas and Shores, yea all the
 Creatures,
Against your Peace. Thee of thy Son, Alonso, 75
They have bereft, and do pronounce by me
Ling'ring Perdition (worse than any Death
Can be at once) shall Step by Step attend
You and your Ways, whose Wraths to guard you
 from
(Which here in this most desolate Isle else
 falls   80
Upon your Heads) is nothing but Heart's Sorrow
And a Clear Life ensuing.

  He vanishes in Thunder; then, to soft Music,
   enter the Shapes again and daunce (with
  Mocks and Mows) and carrying out the Table.

PROSPERO Bravely the Figure of this Harpy hast
 thou

85   **bated**   omitted or neglected. Compare I.ii.249–50 and II.i.84.
      Prospero's verb is a reminder that Ariel and his attendant
      spirits have baited (pursued and snapped menacingly at) the
      'Men of Sin' they threatened with 'devouring' (line 84).
      Meanwhile line 84 evokes 1 Corinthians 11:27, where the
      Apostle Paul warns that 'Whosoever shall eat this bread or
      drink this cup of the Lord unworthily, shall be guilty of the
      body and blood of the Lord'. See the note to line 62.

86–88 **so . . . done**   likewise (just as 'Bravely', superbly), with lifelike
      performances and superhuman observance of my dictates,
      have my humbler spirits played their magical roles. *Ministers*
      echoes line 61. *Strange* recalls the stage direction following
      line 19 and anticipates lines 94–95.

89–90 **knit . . . Distractions**   entangled in their seizures ('Fits', line 91)
      of 'Ecstasy' (line 109), which drive them temporarily out of
      their minds (the root meaning of *ecstasy*). *Powre* (power)
      recalls line 73.

95   **In . . . Stare**   with this frenzied expression in your eyes.
      monstrous   terrifyingly ominous. Here *monstrous* carries
      something of its original sense, from the Latin *monstrare*: 'to
      show' or 'to warn'. Compare line 31. The phrase *something
      holy* (line 94) recalls I.ii.416 and echoes III.ii.62.

98   **dreadful Organ-pipe**   awesome voice of divine wrath. Line 97
      echoes II.ii.20.

99   **base my Trespass**   utter bass notes that evoked my basest sins.

100   **Therefore . . . bedded**   because of 'my Trespass' I have been
      punished with the drowning of my son.

101   **Plummet sounded**   plumb-line reached. Compare line 65 and
      I.ii.50. *Sounded* echoes line 37. Here, as in I.ii.320 and
      III.i.89, *ere* can mean both (a) before, and (b) e'er (ever).

102   **mudded**   'bedded' in the 'Ooze' (compare I.ii.253). But *mudded*
      is also a term for the 'muddy' (unsettled, unseeing) spirit of a
      man who has yet to find his way beyond the 'Sorrow' (line 81)
      that convinces him he's lost forever. Compare *The Winter's
      Tale*, I.ii.322–23.

Perform'd, my Ariel: a Grace it had devouring.
Of my Instruction hast thou nothing bated   85
In what thou had'st to say: so with Good Life
And Observation Strange, my meaner Ministers
Their several kinds have done. My high Charms
    work,
And these mine Enemies are all knit up
In their Distractions. They now are in my
    Powre,   90
And in these Fits I leave them, while I visit
Young Ferdinand (whom they suppose is drown'd)
And his and mine lov'd Darling.   *Exit above.*

GONZALO   I'th' name of something holy, Sir, why
    stand you
In this strange Stare?

ALONSO   O, it is monstrous, monstrous: 95
Me thought the Billows spoke, and told me of it,
The Winds did sing it to me, and the Thunder
(That deep and dreadful Organ-pipe) pronounc'd
The name of Prosper. It did base my Trespass:
Therefore my Son i'th' Ooze is bedded, and   100
I'll seek him deeper than ere Plummet sounded
And with him there lie mudded.   *Exit.*

102–3 **But . . . o'er**   If the fiends will merely come at me one at a time,
I'll fight a whole legion of them. Sebastian alludes to Mark
5:1–20, where Jesus exorcises a demon-possessed madman in
'the country of the Gadarenes'. When Jesus says, 'Come out
of the man, thou unclean spirit,' and asks, 'What is thy
name?' the spirit replies, 'My name is Legion; for we are
many.' Compare I.ii.286–93, 455–57.

104 **Second**   support (as in duelling or boxing).

105 **Poison . . . after**   Gonzalo describes a 'Ling'ring Perdition' (line
77) that now begins to 'bite' them with remorse (line 107) but
will eventually turn out to be 'a Grace' in its 'devouring' (line
84). See *Macbeth*, I.v.45–48.

108 **That . . . Joints**   whose limbs are nimble and swift. Compare
II.i.184.

SEBASTIAN   But one Fiend at
  A Time, I'll fight their Legions o'er.
ANTONIO   I'll be
  Thy Second.   *Exeunt.*
GONZALO   All three of them are desperate. Their
      great Guilt   105
  (Like Poison given to work a great Time after)
  Now gins to bite the Spirits. I do beseech you
  That are of suppler Joints, follow them swiftly,
  And hinder them from what this Ecstasy
  May now provoke them to.
ADRIAN   Follow, I pray you.   110
                              Exeunt omnes.

IV.i   This scene returns us to Prospero's cell.

1   **austerely punish'd**   severely tested. Compare lines 5–7 and I.ii.448–50. Prospero's words are a reminder that in the previous scene he has even more 'austerely punish'd' the 'Men of Sin' (III.iii.53) who have done him wrong in reality. Through his 'Ministers' Prospero has led them through a desolate, maze-like wilderness (see the notes to I.ii.294, II.i.309, II.ii.145, 195, III.iii.5, 15), taunted them by proffering a 'Banquet' analogous to the Eucharist (the bread and wine of the Lord's Supper), and then driven them to the verge of despair by withdrawing it in a way that appears to excommunicate them as reprobates 'unfit to live', let alone to partake of anything 'holy' (III.iii.58, 94).

2   **Your . . . Amends**   the reward you've received evens the balance.

3   **a . . . Life**   Prospero may be referring to the fifteen years he has devoted to rearing Miranda (see I.ii.38–41, 53–55). Or he may be thinking of Miranda's, her late mother's, and his own life as equal thirds.

5   **tender**   bestow, offer. Compare II.i.251–52. Lines 5–7 echo *A Midsummer Night's Dream*, IV.i.71–72, where Oberon says that once the lovers return to Athens from their experience in the Wood, they will 'think no more of this Night's Accidents / But as the fierce Vexation of a Dream'.

7   **strangely**   marvellously. Compare III.iii.87, 94–95.

9   **her of**   about her. *Out-strip* (line 10) recalls II.i.206–8. Compare III.i.79–81.

11   **halt . . . her**   pull up lame in its effort to keep pace with her. Compare *The Merchant of Venice*, III.ii.126–29.

12   **Against an Oracle**   even if a divine oracle pronounced otherwise. Ferdinand's words recall *The Winter's Tale*, III.ii.141–42, where Leontes sets his own opinion against the pronouncements of an oracle.

13–14 **and . . . purchas'd**   and as one who has acquired a new possession by virtue of his own worth. *Guest* recalls III.iii.39; compare I.ii.463–64 and II.i.11–17.

15   **Virgin-knot**   hymen, maidenhead. *Knot* echoes III.iii.89–90.

16   **sanctimonious**   sanctified, religious.

ACT IV

Scene 1

Enter Prospero, Ferdinand, and Miranda.

PROSPERO   If I have too austerely punish'd you,
Your Compensation makes Amends, for I
Have given you here a third of mine own Life,
Or that for which I live: who, once again,
I tender to thy Hand. All thy Vexations   5
Were but my Trials of thy Love, and thou
Hast strangely stood the Test. Here, afore
   Heaven,
I ratify this my rich Gift. O Ferdinand,
Do not smile at me that I boast her of,
For thou shalt find she will out-strip all
   Praise   10
And make it halt behind her.

FERDINAND   I do believe it
Against an Oracle.

PROSPERO   Then as my Guest, and thine own
   Acquisition
Worthily purchas'd, take my Daughter. But
If thou dost break her Virgin-knot before   15
All sanctimonious Ceremonies may

17   **Right**   both (a) right (legality), and (b) rite (ritual).

18   **sweet Aspersion**   shower ('sprinkling') of blessing. The adjective *sweet* is frequently associated with grace (divine beneficence) in Shakespeare; compare I.ii.378, 391, II.i.56, III.i.11, 14, III.ii.140, III.iii.19.

19   **Contract**   commitment ('drawing together') to wed.
      barrain   barren (with wordplay on *bare* and *brain*, as in *Love's Labour's Lost*, I.i.47, IV.ii.33, IV.iii.326), and on *rain*, as in *The Merchant of Venice*, I.iii.135.

20   **Sower**   sour, with wordplay on *sore* (as in II.i.122 and III.i.9–11) and on *sower* (one who sows, as in II.i.78 and in Galatians 6:7, 'whatsoever a man soweth, that shall he also reap'). Compare *Macbeth*, II.i.55, *Romeo and Juliet*, II.iv.24, III.ii.116, *Cymbeline*, V.v.26, and *Love's Labour's Lost*, I.i.318. Here *ey'd* picks up on the implications noted in II.i.38, 85.

21   **loathly**   loathsome. *Weeds* continues the *sower* imagery of line 20.

23   **As ... you**   as Hymen guides you till the torch of the Marriage God is lit (line 97).

24   **Quiet ... Issue**   harmonious days, blessed offspring.

27   **Our ... can**   our less spiritual impulses can try us with.

30–31 **When ... below**   when I'll be so eager for bedtime that I'll swear that either the Sun God's horses are crippled [so that the Sun can't set] or Night is being retained in a dungeon. Compare *Romeo and Juliet*, III.ii.1–31. *Edge* (line 29) echoes *Hamlet*, III.ii.269–75.

37   **Rabble**   'meaner Fellows', lowlier spirits (as in III.iii.87).

39   **Incite ... Motion**   both (a) spur them to move quickly, and (b) direct them to perform a 'quick Motion' (puppet show with live performers, as in the 'living Drollery' of III.iii.21). See *The Two Gentlemen of Verona*, II.i.98–99, *The Winter's Tale*, IV.iii.101–2, and compare *Hamlet*, III.ii.270–71.

41   **Vanity ... Art**   idle nothing of my devising. Compare II.i.152–60.

With full and holy Right be minist'red,
No sweet Aspersion shall the Heavens let fall
To make this Contract grow; but barrain Hate,
Sower-ey'd Disdain, and Discord shall bestrew   20
The Union of your Bed, with Weeds so loathly
That you shall hate it both. Therefore take
    Heed
As Hymen's Lamps shall light you.
FERDINAND   As I hope
For Quiet Days, Fair Issue, and Long Life,
With such Love as 'tis now, the murkiest Den,   25
The most opportune Place, the strong'st
    Suggestion
Our worser Genius can, shall never melt
Mine Honour into Lust, to take away
The Edge of that Day's Celebration,
When I shall think or Phoebus' Steeds are
    founder'd   30
Or Night kept chain'd below.
PROSPERO   Fairly spoke.
Sit then, and talk with her, she is thine own.
– What, Ariel; my industrious Servant Ariel.

Enter Ariel.

ARIEL   What would my potent Master? Here I am.
PROSPERO   Thou and thy meaner Fellows your last
    Service   35
Did worthily perform: and I must use you
In such another Trick. Go bring the Rabble
(O'er whom I give thee Powre) here to this
    Place;
Incite them to quick Motion, for I must
Bestow upon the Eyes of this young Couple   40
Some Vanity of mine Art. It is my Promise,
And they expect it from me.

42 **Presently?** Right now?

43 **Ay . . . Twink** Yes, as quickly as you can twinkle your eye. *Ay* is *I* in the Folio. Compare III.ii.105, 116.

47 **Mop and Mow** grin and grimace mockingly (as in II.ii.9 and in the stage direction following III.iii.82). Line 48 echoes III.i.67.

49 **delicate** exquisite, refined. This word recalls II.ii.97–98.

50 **conceive** understand (literally, 'take in'). But *conceive* can also mean 'generate', and that sense applies to Ariel's creativity too.

51 **Look thou** take heed that you.
   Dalliance flirtation with the 'Blood' (sensual desire), line 53. Compare *The Winter's Tale*, IV.iii.4–7.

52 **Raign** both (a) reign (sway), and (b) rein (liberty to run at will), with a hint at *rain* as well (compare lines 18–22).

53 **Be more Abstenious** abstain from (avoid) situations that prompt the 'Ardour' (fire) of the 'Liver' (seat of the passions), line 56.

54 **warrant** assure you. This word recalls I.i.49, II.i.169.

56 **Abates** suppresses ('beats down'). Compare *bated*, III.iii.85.

57–58 **bring . . . Spirit** bring an extra performer ('Corollary') or two rather than be caught with too few spirits for the occasion. *Want* (lack) recalls III.iii.38.

S.D. **Iris** Goddess of the Rainbow ('wat'ry Arch', line 71) and Messenger of Juno, 'Queen o'th' Sky' (line 70), the Goddess of Marriage and the 'Wife of Jupiter' (line 77).

60 **Ceres** Goddess of Bounty ('Foison plenty', line 110).
   rich Leas abundant fields.

61 **Fetches** vetches (a fodder crop).
   Pease peas.

63 **Meads** meadows.
   thetch'd with Stover thatched (thickly covered) with fodder-grass.

64 **Banks . . . Brims** stream banks furrowed ('pioned') and ridged to the brim. *Pioned* may mean 'peonied' (laced with peonies) as well as 'dug out' or 'sloped'.

ARIEL   Presently?
PROSPERO   Ay: with a Twink.
ARIEL   Before you can say 'come and go',
   And breathe twice, and cry 'so, so',   45
   Each one, tripping on his Toe,
   Will be here with Mop and Mow.
   Do you love me, Master? No?
PROSPERO   Dearly, my delicate Ariel. Do not
   approach
   Till thou dost hear me call.
ARIEL   Well: I conceive.   *Exit.*   50
PROSPERO   Look thou be True. Do not give Dalliance
   Too much the Raign: the strongest Oaths are
      Straw
   To th' Fire i'th' Blood. Be more Abstenious,
   Or else good night your Vow.
FERDINAND   I warrant you, Sir,
   The white cold Virgin Snow upon my Heart   55
   Abates the Ardour of my Liver.
PROSPERO   Well.
   – Now come, my Ariel; bring a Corollary,
   Rather than want a Spirit: appear, and pertly.

                    Soft Music. Enter Iris.

   – No Tongue; all Eyes; be Silent.
IRIS   Ceres, most bounteous Lady, thy rich Leas   60
   Of Wheat, Rye, Barley, Fetches, Oats, and
      Pease,
   Thy turfy Mountains, where live nibbling Sheep,
   And flat Meads thetch'd with Stover, them to
      keep,
   Thy Banks with pioned and twilled Brims,

65 **spungy** spongy, soggy. *Hest* recalls III.i.37.
    at . . . betrims at your command bedecks with blossoms.

66 **cold** virtuous, unmoved by the flames of passion.
    chast chaste; modest, faithful.
    Broom shrub with yellow flowers.

67 **dismissed** rejected; 'lorn' (forlorn), line 68.

68 **clipt** both (a) embraced, and (b) clipped, pruned. Here *Pole*
    may mean *poll* ('head', 'top').

69 **Sea-marge stirrile** seacoast sterile (barren, 'rocky-hard'). *Stirrile*
    echoes *King Lear*, I.iv.292.

74 **Peacocks fly amain** Juno's sacred birds fly in force, drawing her
    chariot. Many editions emend *Here* to *Her*; if *Here* is correct,
    Iris may be construed as giving a command to the 'Peacocks'.

78 **Saffron** orange-yellow (from the stigmas of the crocus).

80 **blew Bow** full blue rainbow. See the note to I.ii.269. *Bow*
    (rainbow) can also mean 'bow' in other senses (the archer's
    bow and the courtier's bow, or curtsy), and in V.i.94 it means
    'bough'.

81 **My . . . Down** my wooded lands and my shrubless hills.

83 **gras'd** both (a) grazed and (b) grassed. There may also be
    wordplay on *graced*; compare lines 72–73.

85 **Donation . . . estate** wedding gift generously to bestow. *Estate*
    (bequeath) parallels *A Midsummer Night's Dream*, I.i.98.

87 **her Son** Cupid, the 'Blind-boy' of line 90.

89 **dusky Dis** Pluto, dark God of the 'dusky' Underworld. He stole
    Ceres' daughter Proserpina to make her his Queen.

91 **forsworn** sworn off. *Society* means 'company'.

Which spungy April at thy Hest betrims   65
To make cold Nymphs chast Crowns, and thy
    Broom-groves,
Whose Shadow the dismissed Bachelor loves,
Being Lass-lorn, thy Pole-clipt Vineyard,
And thy Sea-marge stirrile and rocky-hard,
Where thou thy self dost air, the Queen o'th'
    Sky,   70
Whose wat'ry Arch and Messenger am I,
Bids thee leave these, and with her sovereign
    Grace,   *Juno descends.*
Here on this Grass-plot, in this very Place,
To come and sport. Here Peacocks fly amain.
Approach, rich Ceres, her to entertain.   75

Enter Ceres.

CERES   Hail, many-coloured Messenger, that ne'er
    Dost disobey the Wife of Jupiter,
    Who with thy Saffron Wings upon my Flow'rs
    Diffusest Honey Drops, refreshing Show'rs,
    And with each end of thy blew Bow dost crown   80
    My bosky Acres and my unshrubb'd Down,
    Rich Scarf to my proud Earth, why hath thy
        Queen
    Summon'd me hither to this short-gras'd Green?
IRIS   A Contract of true Love to celebrate,
    And some Donation freely to estate   85
    On the bless'd Lovers.
CERES   Tell me, Heavenly Bow,
    If Venus or her Son, as thou dost know,
    Do now attend the Queen? Since they did plot
    The Means that dusky Dis my Daughter got,
    Her and her Blind-boy's scandall'd Company   90
    I have forsworn.
IRIS   Of her Society

93   **Paphos**   a locale in Cyprus consecrated to Venus.

94   **Dove-drawn**   Doves, sacred to Venus, pull her chariot.

94–95 **thought . . . Maid**   they aimed to spur this couple to rush
       things. *Charm* (spell) recalls I.ii.231, 338–39, III.iii.88.

96   **Bed-right**   consummation of the marriage rite (line 17).

98   **Mars's hot Minion**   Iris refers to Venus' adulterous liaison with
       the God of War. It was publicly exposed by Venus' cuckolded
       husband Vulcan.

99   **waspish-headed**   mischievous and peevish.

101   **a . . . out**   an ordinary boy. But since 'Sparrows' (also sacred to
       Venus) are proverbially lustful, it is not clear that 'a Boy right
       out' will necessarily 'shoot no more'. See *Love's Labour's
       Lost*, III.i.180–210.

102   **Gate**   gait (here spelled to reinforce the rhyme with *State).*

103   **bounteous**   generous, prospering (since Ceres presides over the
       harvest).

104   **Twain**   pair.
       prosperous   fortunate in all things (not just material wealth).
       Compare II.i.56–57, II.ii.1–2, 87–88, III.iii.95–99.

107   **Long . . . increasing**   longevity and prolific, healthy offspring.

108   **still**   always.

110   **Increase**   'Foison', harvest abundance. Here *Foison* is probably
       to be pronounced 'fo-eē-son'. Compare II.i.145.

111   **Garners**   granaries.

112   **clust'ring Bunches**   grape clusters. Compare II.ii.180.

113   **with . . . bowing**   bending with ample fruit. Compare III.i.1–15
       for another kind of 'goodly Burthen' that bows (humbles) the
       spirit. *Burthen* recalls I.ii.156, 379, and the stage direction
       that commences II.ii.

114–   **at . . . Harvest**   at the latest, just as 'Harvest' ends. Here
  15   *Harvest* may refer to either (a) harvest-time (so that there will
       be no winter), or (b) the 'Foison' harvested (so that there will
       be no 'Want', 'Scarcity'). *Want* echoes lines 57–58.

Be not afraid. I met her Deity
Cutting the Clouds towards Paphos, and her Son
Dove-drawn with her. Here thought they to have
   done
Some wanton Charm upon this Man and Maid,   95
Whose Vows are that no Bed-right shall be paid
Till Hymen's Torch be lighted; but in Vain,
Mars's hot Minion is return'd again;
Her waspish-headed Son has broke his Arrows,
Swears he will shoot no more, but play with
   Sparrows   100
And be a Boy right out.
CERES   Highest Queen of State,
Great Juno comes: I know her by her Gate.
JUNO   How does my bounteous Sister? Go with me
To bless this Twain, that they may prosperous be,
And honour'd in their Issue.   *They sing.*   105

JUNO   *Honour, Riches, Marriage, Blessing,*
             Long continuance, and increasing;
             Hourly Joys be still upon you,
             Juno sings her Blessings on you.
[CERES]   *Earth's Increase, Foison plenty;*   110
             Barns and Garners never empty.
             Vines, with clust'ring Bunches growing,
             Plants, with goodly Burthen bowing;
             Spring come to you at the farthest
             In the very end of Harvest.   115
             Scarcity and Want shall shun you,
             Ceres' Blessing so is on you.

FERDINAND   This is a most majestic Vision, and

119 **charmingly** both (a) magically (with reference to the means by which it is produced), and (b) enchantingly (with reference to its effect on the audience). See lines 94–95.

123 **wond'red** wondrous (compare *Admir'd* in III.i.37); to be marvelled at for the wonders he performs. Lines 122–24 echo III.ii.148–49. *Confines* (line 121) recalls I.ii.274–75, 358–60.

S.D. **on employment** off to perform some further task. Compare *Much Ado About Nothing*, II.i.282–83, and *King Lear*, II.ii.126–27, V.iii.32–33.

127 **our ... marr'd** the spell will be broken. Lines 126–27 echo line 59.

128 **Naiades** water nymphs.
windring evidently a Shakespearean coinage to combine *winding* and *wandering*.

129 **sedg'd Crowns** coronets composed of sedge (a river plant).

130 **crisp** ripple-filled (literally, 'curled', as in I.ii.192). Compare line 64.

131 **Answer your Summons** appear in court as ordered by an official summons.

132 **temperate** (self-controlled); 'ever-harmless' (line 129). Iris' adjective recalls II.i.29 and III.iii.62 and anticipates line 145.

134 **Sicklemen** harvesters, reapers. *Weary* recalls III.iii.4–6.

135 **hether** hither; to here.

136 **Holly Day** holiday.

137 **fresh** young, unspoiled.
encounter meet, embrace. Compare III.i.74–75, and see the note on the erotic implications of this word in *Romeo and Juliet*, II.v.29.

138 **Country Footing** rustic dancing. Iris' phrasing hints at the fertility and lustiness of 'Country Copulatives' (*As You Like It*, V.iv.58). Compare *Hamlet*, III.ii.122, where 'Country Matters' plays on an English derivative of the Latin word *cunnus* (female pudendum). *Encounter* (line 137) plays on the same word.

S.D. **heavily** regretfully, sombrely.

Harmonious charmingly: may I be bold
To think these Spirits?
PROSPERO   Spirits, which by mine Art   120
I have from their Confines call'd to enact
My present Fancies.
FERDINAND   Let me live here ever:
So rare a wond'red Father, and a Wise,
Makes this place Paradise.

Juno and Ceres whisper, and send Iris on employment.

PROSPERO   Sweet now, silence:
Juno and Ceres whisper seriously,   125
There's something else to do. Hush and be Mute
Or else our Spell is marr'd.
IRIS   You Nymphs call'd Naiades of the windring
     Brooks,
With your sedg'd Crowns and ever-harmless Looks,
Leave your crisp Channels, and on this green
     Land   130
Answer your Summons. Juno does command.
Come, temperate Nymphs, and help to celebrate
A Contract of true Love; be not too late.

Enter certain Nymphs.

You Sun-burn'd Sicklemen of August weary,
Come hether from the Furrow, and be Merry;   135
Make Holly Day, your Rye-straw Hats put on,
And these fresh Nymphs encounter every one
In Country Footing.

*Enter certain Reapers, properly habited; they
join with the Nymphs in a graceful Dance, towards
the end whereof Prospero starts suddenly and
speaks, after which, to a strange, hollow,*

139   **Conspiracy**   This word recalls II.i.283.

140   **Confederates**   fellow conspirators. Compare I.ii.111.

142   **avoid**   clear out; begone.

143   **strange**   This adjective recalls lines 6–7. *Passion* recalls
       I.ii.389–91.

144   **works**   affects; works upon. Compare I.ii.491, II.ii.87–88,
       III.iii.88.

145   **distemper'd**   lacking in temper (self-control); his mind not
       governing his humours. Compare line 132.

146   **in . . . sort**   as if you are under the sway of some emotion. *Sort*
       recalls II.i.87–88.

147–   **be . . . ended**   take heart and don't trouble yourself further, sir,
48   because our entertainment is now concluded. Most editions
       substitute a full stop for the Folio's comma after *Sir*. If the
       original punctuation is correct, Prospero would appear to be
       reassuring Ferdinand that it is the proper time for the 'Revels'
       to end. *Dismay'd* anticipates V.i.14.

150   **melted**   dissolved (see line 154). Compare line 27 and
       II.i.260–62, V.i.66. *Air* echoes line 70 and recalls III.ii.140.

151   **baseless Fabric**   foundation-less structure. See II.i.101–5,
       III.iii.99–102.

153   **the great Globe**   both (a) the Earth, and (b) the Globe
       playhouse [and all who own or will inherit it].

156   **Rack**   (a) drifting cloud (as in Sonnet 33, line 6), and (b)
       supporting frame. But *Rack* can also mean (c) wrack (wreck),
       (d) shelf, and (e) instrument of torture. Compare I.ii.26–27,
       388, 412, 486, and see the notes to *The Merchant of Venice*,
       I.i.181, and *King Lear*, V.iii.311.

157   **made on**   both (a) built upon, and (b) composed of.

160   **Infirmity**   'Weakness', lack of firmness; insubstantiality. *Vext*
       (vexed, line 158) echoes lines 5–7.

163   **beating**   throbbing, disturbed. Compare I.ii.176. *Cleave* echoes
       cloven, I.ii.277.

and confused Noise, they heavily vanish.

PROSPERO   — I had forgot that foul Conspiracy
Of the beast Caliban and his Confederates   140
Against my Life. The Minute of their Plot
Is almost come. — Well done, avoid; no more.
FERDINAND   This is strange: your Father's in some
   Passion
That works him strongly.
MIRANDA   Never till this Day
Saw I him touch'd with Anger, so distemper'd.   145
PROSPERO   You do look, my Son, in a mov'd sort,
As if you were dismay'd; be cheerful, Sir,
Our Revels now are ended. These our Actors,
As I foretold you, were all Spirits, and
Are melted into Air, into thin Air,   150
And like the baseless Fabric of this Vision,
The Cloud-capp'd Tow'rs, the gorgeous Palaces,
The solemn Temples, the great Globe it self,
Yea, all which it inherit, shall dissolve,
And like this insubstantial Pageant faded   155
Leave not a Rack behind. We are such Stuff
As Dreams are made on; and our little Life
Is rounded with a Sleep. Sir, I am vext;
Bear with my Weakness, my old Brain is
   troubled;
Be not disturb'd with my Infirmity;   160
If you be pleas'd, retire into my Cell,
And there repose; a Turn or two I'll walk
To still my beating Mind.
FERDINAND, MIRANDA   We wish you Peace.
                    Exeunt Ferdinand, Miranda.

164 **Come ... come** Some editions specify that 'I thank thee' is addressed, not to Ariel, but to the exiting Ferdinand and Miranda. But the Folio text places no punctuation (not even a comma) after *thee*, which would suggest that 'I thank thee' is part of the speech Prospero directs to Ariel.

167 **I** ay (yes, I am ready). Compare lines 43, 209.

169 **Least** lest. Ariel reminds us that Prospero is testy. Compare I.ii.449, III.i.15.

170 **Varlots** varlets, rough villains.

171 **red-hot** (a) red-faced (see the note to II.ii.174), and (b) 'full of Valour' (heated with rash courage). Compare III.ii.28–32, III.iii.57–60.

174 **For ... Feet** either (a) for presuming to touch their feet, or (b) to make it kiss their feet in reverence. Compare II.ii.10–12.
bending directing themselves. These drunks were also 'bending' because of their inability to stand upright (III.ii.17–24).

175 **Project** objective. Compare II.i.281, V.i.1, and Epilogue, line 12, and see the notes to *Troilus and Cressida*, II.ii.130–35, 189, 200.

176 **unback'd Colts** colts that have borne, or will tolerate, no riders; unbroken, free-spirited horses. Here *prick'd* means 'lifted up in a state of alertness'; compare line 180, where *pricking* means 'sticking' or 'stinging' and echoes III.iii.105–7.

177 **Advanc'd** raised. Compare I.ii.80–81, 406, II.i.248–50.

178 **As they smelt** as if they sensed. Compare III.ii.139–47, and see *The Merchant of Venice*, V.i.70–88.

179 **Calf-like** obediently, meekly. Lines 175–81 recall III.ii.127–57.

180 **Furzes, Gosse** prickly evergreen shrubs. *Gosse* is gorse. *Furzes* echoes I.i.68.

182 **mantled** scum-covered. See lines 199–200. In lines 183–84, *foul* and *Bird* recall II.i.124–25, 167.

186 **Trumpery** gaudy regalia to use as a decoy (*Stale*, line 187). *Stale* is a word that can also refer to 'Horse-piss' (line 199); compare *Antony and Cleopatra*, I.iv.61–63.

PROSPERO — Come with a Thought, I thank thee, Ariel;
   come.

Enter Ariel.

ARIEL Thy Thoughts I cleave to: what's thy
   Pleasure?
PROSPERO Spirit,   165
   We must prepare to meet with Caliban.
ARIEL I, my Commander. When I presented Ceres,
   I thought to have told thee of it, but I fear'd
   Least I might anger thee.
PROSPERO Say again, where didst thou leave these
   Varlots?   170
ARIEL I told you, Sir, they were red-hot with
   Drinking,
   So full of Valour that they smote the Air
   For breathing in their Faces, beat the Ground
   For kissing of their Feet, yet always bending
   Towards their Project. Then I beat my Tabor,   175
   At which like unback'd Colts they prick'd their
   Ears,
   Advanc'd their Eye-lids, lifted up their Noses
   As they smelt Music; so I charm'd their Ears
   That Calf-like they my Lowing follow'd, through
   Tooth'd Briars, sharp Furzes, pricking Gosse,
   and Thorns,   180
   Which ent'red their frail Shins. At last I left
   them
   I'th' filthy mantled Pool beyond your Cell,
   There dancing up to th' Chins, that the foul
   Lake
   O'er-stunk their Feet.
PROSPERO   This was well done, my Bird.
   Thy Shape Invisible retain thou still;   185
   The Trumpery in my House, go bring it hither

188   **borne**   both (a) carried by, and (b) given birth to as. Compare
          I.i.35, I.ii.283, II.i.231.

189   **Nurture . . . stick**   attempts to cultivate can never take hold.
          Compare I.ii.349–51.
          Pains   efforts. Compare I.ii.242, III.i.1. Lines 188–90 recall
          I.ii.349–63.

190   **Humanely taken**   both (a) humanely undertaken, and (b)
          undertaken in an effort to turn a 'Devil' into a human.
          Compare III.iii.33.
          all   are all [unless *Pains* is to be read as *Pain's*].

192   **cankers**   becomes more (a) cancerous (malignant), and (b) eaten
          away (as by a cankerworm devouring the bud of a flower).
          Compare I.ii.413.
          plague   afflict. See the note to III.ii.82.

193   **Roaring**   screaming in terror; crying for mercy. This word
          recalls II.i.297.
          hang . . . Line   lay this assortment of 'glistering Apparel' on
          them [or on a clothes line for them]. In all likelihood, after
          Prospero speaks this line he steps aside with the invisible Ariel
          to observe as Caliban, Stephano, and Trinculo enter.

194   **the blind Mole**   either (a) even the mole beneath the soil (whose
          sense of hearing is especially acute to compensate for his
          blindness), or (b) Prospero reposing in his cell. *Mole* may be
          Caliban's euphemism for 'devil'; compare *Hamlet*, I.v.154.

198   **play'd the Jack**   performed the role of (a) a knave, and (b) a
          'jack-o'-lantern' or will-o'-the-wisp (see II.ii.6).

200   **Indignation**   anger over the indignity. Compare III.ii.41–42.

204   **lost**   dead. Compare 'quite lost' (totally wasted), line 190.

207   **Should . . . Mischance**   will place a blindfold over this mishap
          (so that your awareness of it will be hoodwinked).

209   **Ay . . . loose**   yes, but to be separated from. Here as elsewhere,
          loose can mean either 'loose' (release) or 'lose'. Compare line
          249.

210   **onely**   only. Compare III.ii.102.

212   **my Wetting**   my getting marinated in 'Horse-piss'. *Loss* (line
          211) echoes lines 204, 209.

For Stale to catch these Thieves.

ARIEL   I go, I go.   *Exit.*

PROSPERO   – A Devil, a borne Devil, on whose Nature
Nurture can never stick, on whom my Pains
Humanely taken, all, all lost, quite lost;   190
And as with Age his Body uglier grows,
So his Mind cankers. I will plague them all,
Even to Roaring.

Enter Ariel, loaden with glistering Apparel, &c.

– Come, hang on them this Line.

Enter Caliban, Stephano, and Trinculo, all wet.

CALIBAN   Pray you tread softly, that the blind Mole
   may not
Hear a Foot fall. We now are near his Cell.   195
STEPHANO   Monster, your Fairy, which you say is a
   harmless Fairy, has done little better than
   play'd the Jack with us.
TRINCULO   Monster, I do smell all Horse-piss, at
   which my Nose is in great Indignation.   200
STEPHANO   So is mine. Do you hear, Monster? If I
   should take a Displeasure against you, look
   you –
TRINCULO   Thou wert but a lost Monster.
CALIBAN   Good my Lord, give me thy Favour still.   205
   Be Patient, for the Prize I'll bring thee to
   Should hudwink this Mischance: therefore speak
      softly,
   All's hush'd as Midnight yet.
TRINCULO   Ay, but to loose our Bottles in the Pool.
STEPHANO   There is not onely Disgrace and Dishonour   210
   in that, Monster, but an infinite Loss.
TRINCULO   That's more to me than my Wetting. Yet

214 **fetch off** retrieve. Compare *All's Well That Ends Well*,
III.vi.19–23, where a plot is laid to force the braggart Parolles
to make good on his threat to 'fetch off' the drum his
company has lost in battle.

215 **o'er Ears** in the 'mantled Pool' (line 182) over my ears.
Compare lines 183–84.

218 **good Mischief** worthy misdeed. *Mischief* echoes III.i.70–71.
Lines 218–20 recall the promptings in II.i.186–278.

220 **aye** ever. *Bloody* (line 221) echoes I.ii.140–43.

222 **Peer** nobleman. But Trinculo's name for 'King Stephano' is a
comic reminder that he smells like the first among pee-ers; see
Othello, II.iii.89–96, where Iago sings a drinking song about
how King Stephen was 'a worthy Peer'.

227 **Frippery** used clothes shop. For Trinculo, a frippery of regal
garments is anything but 'Trash' (line 225). What he doesn't
realize is that Caliban's master has now learned how to 'trash
for over-topping' (I.ii.81).

231 **Dropsy** a disease in which the body becomes bloated with
fluids. Poor Caliban is becoming disillusioned with his 'God'
(II.ii.157). *Drown* recalls III.ii.14–17, III.iii.8–10.

232 **Luggage** loads of glittering but worthless knick-knacks.
Prospero's device for outwitting Caliban and his companions
recalls Autolicus' use of a pedlar's wares to fleece the just as
easily distracted attendees at a sheep-shearing feast in IV.iv of
The Winter's Tale.
Let's alone let's proceed unencumbered by all these travelling
companions (garments). Most editors emend *Let's* to *Let't*.

234 **Crown** head. Caliban's phrase is a reminder of the crown he'd
like to supplant from Prospero to 'King Stephano'. *Crown*
recalls I.ii.114, II.i.189–91, III.i.68–70, IV.i.66, 80–81,
128–29, and anticipates V.i.201.

235 **Strange Stuff** deformed creatures. *Strange* recalls line 143. *Stuff*
echoes I.ii.164, II.i.236.

this is your harmless Fairy, Monster.

STEPHANO   I will fetch off my Bottle, though I
be o'er Ears for my Labour.   215

CALIBAN   Prethee, my King, be quiet. Seest thou
here:

This is the Mouth o'th' Cell. No Noise, and
enter.

Do that good Mischief which may make this
Island

Thine own for ever, and I thy Caliban

For aye thy Foot-licker.

STEPHANO   Give me thy Hand.   220
I do begin to have Bloody Thoughts.

TRINCULO   O King Stephano, O Peer; O worthy
Stephano. Look what a Wardrobe here is for
thee.

CALIBAN   Let it alone, thou Fool, it is but Trash.   225

TRINCULO   Oh ho, Monster: we know what belongs to
a Frippery. – O King Stephano.

STEPHANO   Put off that Gown, Trinculo; by this
Hand, I'll have that Gown.

TRINCULO   Thy Grace shall have it.   230

CALIBAN   – The Dropsy drown this Fool. – What do
you mean

To dote thus on such Luggage? Let's alone

And do the Murther first. If he awake,

From Toe to Crown he'll fill our Skins with
Pinches,

Make us Strange Stuff.   235

236 **Mistress Line** either (a) a line tree (a lime or a linden), or (b) a garment-laden clothes line between two trees.

237 **Jerkin** a jacket trimmed with fur ('Hair', line 239).

237– **under the Line** under the line it was hanging from. But
38 Stephano puns on other senses: (a) south of the Equator (where voyagers were said to lose their hair because of tropical fevers), and (b) in the 'South' sexually (and losing one's hair to venereal disease). See I.ii.322–23, and compare *Henry VIII*, V.iii.42–43, and *Troilus and Cressida*, V.i.19–27.

240 **Do, do** yes, well said.
  by . . . Level with professional tools such as a mariner's plumb-line, a draughtsman's rule, and a carpenter's level.

241 **and't like** if it please.

245 **Pass of Pate** stroke from a witty head. *Pass* (from the Italian *passado*, thrust) is a term from fencing; compare *Romeo and Juliet*, II.iii.28, III.i.88, and *Hamlet*, V.ii.60–62, 310–12.

247 **Lime** birdlime. Trinculo tells Caliban to make his fingers sticky (thief-like). But the garments are Prospero's own 'Lime' ('Stale', line 187) to catch these gullible woodcocks.

249 **loose our Time** forfeit our opportunity. Compare I.ii.178–84. *Loose* echoes lines 209, 211, 238.

250 **Barnacles** either (a) shellfish that attach themselves to rocks, wharves and ships' bottoms, or (b) barnacle geese (so called because they were thought to have metamorphosed from barnacles). See the note to II.ii.140.

253 **Hogshead** 'Butt' (II.ii.130), barrel. In line 257 (as in lines 43, 167, and 209), the Folio prints *I* for 'Ay'.

254 **Go to** come now, jump to it.

260 **Tyrant** Like *Mountain* and *Silver* (lines 258–59), the name of a dog-like spirit. *Silver* recalls II.ii.29–32.

261– **charge . . . Convulsions** order my spirits to seize the leg joints
62 of the mischief-makers with convulsions. Prospero probably addresses Ariel, who presides over his 'Goblins' as the 'Rabble' (line 37) who have 'to Instrument this lower World' (III.iii.54). Compare the imagery in III.iii.105–7. *Charge* recalls I.ii.450–51 and III.i.22–23; here it means both (a) order, and (b) command to charge into battle.

STEPHANO Be you quiet, Monster. – Mistress Line,
is not this my Jerkin? Now is the Jerkin under
the Line. – Now Jerkin, you are like to lose
your Hair, and prove a bald Jerkin.

TRINCULO Do, do; we steal by Line and Level,   240
and't like your Grace.

STEPHANO I thank thee for that Jest: here's a
Garment for't. Wit shall not go unrewarded
while I am King of this Country. 'Steal by
Line and Level' is an excellent Pass of Pate: 245
there's another Garment for't.

TRINCULO Monster, come put some Lime upon your
Fingers, and away with the rest.

CALIBAN I will have none on't: we shall loose our
Time
And all be turn'd to Barnacles, or to Apes   250
With Foreheads villainous low.

STEPHANO Monster, lay to your Fingers. Help to
bear this away, where my Hogshead of Wine is,
or I'll turn you out of my Kingdom. Go to,
carry this.   255

TRINCULO And this.

STEPHANO Ay, and this.

A Noise of Hunters heard. Enter divers Spirits
in shape of Dogs and Hounds, hunting them
about: Prospero and Ariel setting them on.

PROSPERO Hey, Mountain, hey.

ARIEL Silver: there it goes, Silver.

PROSPERO Fury, Fury: there, Tyrant, there. Hark,
hark.   260
– Go, charge my Goblins that they grind their Joints

262 **Sinews** nerves, muscles. Compare I.ii.482, III.i.26.

263 **aged Cramps** the cramps that afflict the elderly. Compare lines 191–92.

264 **Pard** leopard.
 Cat o' Mountain lynx, catamount; wildcat.

265 **soundly** thoroughly (till they are all 'at my Mercy', line 266). Compare II.ii.85, 92, and see III.iii.37 and V.i.56.

267 **Labours** This word recalls lines 214–15 and I.i.14, I.ii.231–32, III.i.1–7, 14–15. Meanwhile it echoes such additional passages as I.ii.156–58, II.i.212–13, and III.iii.5.

268 **little** little while longer. *Air* recalls I.ii.222, 385, 390–91, II.i.32, IV.i.70, 148–50, 172–73, and anticipates V.i.21, 58, 102–3. *Freedom* echoes II.ii.195–96 and III.i.88–89; compare I.ii.250–51, 418–19, 440, 496–97, II.i.274–75, III.ii.126.

269 **Follow** continue to 'do me Service' as one of my followers. *Follow* echoes I.ii.457, 462, 492, 499, II.ii.172, III.ii.153–57, and III.iii.107–10, and anticipates V.i.7, 70.

With dry Convulsions, shorten up their Sinews
With aged Cramps, and more Pinch-spotted make
  them
Than Pard or Cat o' Mountain.

ARIEL   Hark, they roar.

PROSPERO   Let them be hunted soundly. At this Hour   265
Lies at my Mercy all mine Enemies.
Shortly shall all my Labours end, and thou
Shalt have the Air at Freedom. For a little
Follow, and do me Service.   *Exeunt.*

V.i   This scene takes place before Prospero's cell.

1   **Project**   undertaking, 'Purpose' (line 29, echoing III.iii.12). Prospero's phrasing alludes to the early scientific sense of *Project*: a 'projection' is the final stage of an alchemist's experiment, when everything must 'gather to a Head' (come to a boil or culmination). But *Project* can also refer to other undertakings (see the note to IV.i.175), including the types of political insurrection that Prospero has now counteracted.

2   **crack**   break; fail. Compare I.ii.203–4 and III.i.26. *Charms* echoes III.iii.88 and IV.i.95 and anticipates lines 17, 31, 54.

3   **Goes . . . Carriage**   (a) bears his load with an erect posture, not 'bending' (IV.i.174) like Prospero's abject 'Enemies' (IV.i.266), and (b) ascends to the 'Zenith' in his chariot, carrying Prospero's 'bountiful Fortune' with him (I.ii.178–84). Prospero has risen above the 'Infirmity' that disturbed him briefly in IV.i.160.

4   **Hower**   hour (here a two-syllable word).

7   **Confin'd**   This verb echoes I.ii.274–75, 358–60, and IV.i.120–22, and anticipates line 122.

8   **gave in Charge**   ordered in your instructions. *Charge* recalls I.ii.237–38, 298–99, 450–51; II.i.235–36; III.i.22–23; IV.i.261–62.

10   **Line-grove**   line of trees (probably either lime or linden, as noted at IV.i.236).
     Weather-fends your Cell   provides a wind-break to fend (keep back) rough weather from your cell.

11   **boudge**   budge.
     your Release   Ariel means 'you release them'; but Prospero himself must experience 'Release' before the action can conclude. See lines 30–31.

12   **abide . . . Distracted**   all remain crazed (pulled apart). Compare III.iii.89–90.

14   **Dismay**   paralysis (literally, 'lack of might or power'). This word echoes IV.i.147.

ACT V

Scene 1

Enter Prospero, in his Magic Robes, and Ariel.

PROSPERO   Now does my Project gather to a Head:
My Charms crack not, my Spirits obey, and Time
Goes upright with his Carriage. How's the
    Day?
ARIEL   On the Sixt Hower, at which Time, my Lord,
You said our Work should cease.
PROSPERO   I did say so,   5
When first I rais'd the Tempest. Say, my
    Spirit,
How fares the King and's Followers?
ARIEL   Confin'd together
In the same fashion as you gave in Charge,
Just as you left them: all Prisoners, Sir,
In the Line-grove which Weather-fends your
    Cell,   10
They cannot boudge till your Release. The King,
His Brother, and yours abide all three
    Distracted,
And the remainder mourning over them,
Brim full of Sorrow and Dismay; but chiefly
Him that you term'd, Sir, the good old Lord
    Gonzalo,   15
His Tears runs down his Beard like Winter's
    Drops

17   **Eaves of Reeds** the edges of thatched roofs. See II.ii.18–19.
        works 'em works upon them (compare IV.i.143–44); eats
        away at their 'Senses' (line 31, minds) and consciences (see the
        note to III.iii.105). Compare I.ii.491, III.iii.88, IV.i.143–44,
        V.i.5.

19   **Tender** soft, compassionate. Compare II.i.28–29.

20   **Humane** both (a) human, and (b) humane. Compare
        I.ii.263–65, 281–84, 344–47; III.iii.30–34; IV.i.188–90.

21   **but Air** a spirit (one whose names derives from 'Air'), without
        flesh and its ability to 'relish' (taste, feel) 'Passion'. *Air* echoes
        IV.i.268 and anticipates lines 54, 58, 102.

24   **Passion** feel passion. Most editions delete the Folio's comma
        after *sharply* (line 23); the effect is to turn *all* from a noun to
        an adverb, and *Passion* from a verb to a noun. See the second
        note to I.ii.390. *Passion* echoes IV.i.143.
        kindlier in keeping (kinship), with 'their Kind'; more
        sympathetically. See I.ii.309, III.iii.32.

27   **take part** take sides; join myself. *Rarer* means 'more choice'.

28   **Virtue** both (a) goodness, and (b) manliness (from Latin *vir*),
        here expressed not in irrational, vengeful 'Fury' but in gentle
        restraint ('Reason'). *Fury* recalls I.ii.390, IV.i.260.

31   **My . . . break** both (a) I'll cancel the spell that binds them, and
        (b) I'll destroy my own means of casting further charms. Here
        Senses means both (a) perceptive faculties, and (b) reasoning
        powers. *Release* echoes line 11.

32   **themselves** their true selves (not merely their former selves if
        they are genuinely 'Penitent', pent up with guilt).

33   **Elves** tiny, harmless earth-spirits, 'demi-Puppets' (line 36);
        'Weak Masters' (line 41), 'meaner Ministers' (III.iii.87). Many
        editions insert a stage direction before this speech, to indicate
        that Prospero takes his staff and draws a charmed circle; see
        the stage direction following line 57.

35   **ebbing Neptune** retreating surf. Compare I.ii.178–84,
        II.i.203–10.

37–38 **By . . . bites** make extra-green but sour-tasting 'fairy rings' in
        the grass while the Moon shines ('Ringlets' that female sheep
        won't eat). *Sowre* (line 37) recalls IV.i.20, and *bites* recalls
        III.iii.105–7.

From Eaves of Reeds. Your Charm so strongly
   works 'em
That if you now beheld them, your Affections
Would become Tender.
PROSPERO   Dost thou think so, Spirit?
ARIEL   Mine would, Sir, were I Humane.
PROSPERO   And mine shall.   20
   Hast thou, which art but Air, a Touch, a
      Feeling,
Of their Afflictions, and shall not my self,
One of their Kind, that relish all as sharply,
Passion as they, be kindlier mov'd than thou
   art?
Though with their high Wrongs I am strook to
   th' Quick,   25
Yet, with my nobler Reason, 'gainst my Fury
Do I take part. The rarer Action is
In Virtue than in Vengeance: they being
   Penitent,
The sole Drift of my Purpose doth extend
Not a Frown further. Go, release them, Ariel;   30
My Charms I'll break, their Senses I'll restore,
And they shall be themselves.
ARIEL   I'll fetch them, Sir.   *Exit*.
PROSPERO   — Ye Elves of Hills, Brooks, standing
      Lakes, and Groves,
And ye that on the Sands with printless Foot
Do chase the ebbing Neptune, and do fly him   35
When he comes back; you demi-Puppets that
By Moonshine do the green sowre Ringlets make,
Whereof the Ewe not bites; and you whose
   Pastime

39   **Mushrumps** mushrooms.

40   **Curfew** the ringing of a bell at nine o'clock to signal that fires
      are to be covered and that spirits are now emerging in 'that
      vast of Night that they may work' (I.ii.326).

45   **rifted** split open. Compare I.ii.277–79. *Roaring* (line 44)
      recalls II.i.297 and IV.i.264, and anticipates line 232.

46   **Promontory** jutting peak (compare II.i.104–5). *Bas'd* echoes
      III.iii.99–102 and IV.i.151–56.

51   **abjure** renounce, forswear (literally, 'swear away').
      requir'd both (a) requested, and (b) demanded.

53   **mine End** my 'Purpose' (line 29). But see the note to line 11.
      Work echoes line 17.

56   **Plummet sound** (a) plumb-line measure (compare III.iii.101),
      but also (b) plummet Sound (noise plunge downwards). See
      III.iii.37. The Folio capitalizes *Plummet*.

58   **Comforter** medicinal salve; compare II.ii.49.

59   **unsettled Fancy** muddied mind. See III.iii.102.

60   **useless Boil** either (a) an unproductive boil (turmoil, assuming
      that the Folio's *boil* is a noun), or (b) unavailingly aboil (if
      boil is an adverb and the Folio's *Braines* is a plural rather
      than a possessive, as indicated here). For similar syntactic
      ambiguities, see lines 23–24, 56. Compare line 1.

61   **Spell-stopp'd** (a) halted by my charm, and (b) dismayed (line
      14). Here the truncated half-line helps make the point.

63   **ev'n . . . thine** moved to feel a sense of society (fellowship, line
      64) with you when they see the look in your eyes. Compare
      IV.i.91–92.

Is to make Midnight Mushrumps, that rejoice
To hear the solemn Curfew (by whose Aid,   40
Weak Masters though ye be, I have bedimm'd
The Noontide Sun, call'd forth the mutinous
    Winds,
And 'twixt the green Sea and the azur'd Vault
Set roaring War); to the dread rattling Thunder
Have I given Fire, and rifted Jove's stout Oak   45
With his own Bolt; the strong bas'd Promontory
Have I made shake, and by the Spurs pluck'd up
The Pine and Cedar. Graves at my Command
Have wak'd their Sleepers, op'd, and let 'em
    forth
By my so potent Art. But this rough Magic   50
I here abjure; and when I have requir'd
Some Heavenly Music (which even now I do)
To work mine End upon their Senses that
This Airy Charm is for, I'll break my Staff,
Bury it certain Fadoms in the Earth,   55
And deeper than did ever Plummet sound
I'll drown my Book.   *Solemn Music.*

Here enters Ariel before; then Alonso with a
frantic Gesture, attended by Gonzalo; Sebastian
and Antonio in like manner attended by Adrian
and Francisco. They all enter the Circle which
Prospero had made, and there stand charm'd:
which Prospero observing, speaks.

A solemn Air, and the best Comforter
To an unsettled Fancy, cure thy Brain's
Now useless Boil within thy Skull. There stand,   60
For you are Spell-stopp'd.
– Holy Gonzalo, Honourable Man,
Mine Eyes, ev'n Sociable to the Shew of thine,

64   **Fall . . . Drops**   drop companionable tears. Compare line 16
      and I.ii.155. *Fall* recalls II.i.277–78.
      dissolves apace   quickly melts (IV.i.150, anticipating line 66) in
      the solution of our flowing 'Eyes'. Compare line 57.

66   **rising**   (a) dawning (sun-rising), (b) awakening, (c) uprising
      (aroused to defend themselves). Compare II.i.211–13,
      III.ii.10. *Melting* echoes IV.i.148–50. *Senses* recalls line 31.

67   **chase . . . mantle**   drive out the uninformed humours that
      enrobe. *Chase* echoes line 35; *Ignorant*, I.ii.18 and III.ii.29;
      mantle, IV.i.182.

69   **Sir**   signior, gentleman. *Clearer* (line 68) echoes III.iii.82.

70–71 **pay . . . Home**   repay your kindnesses completely. *Follow'st*
      echoes IV.i.269 and V.i.7.

73   **Furtherer**   second (III.iii.102–4), accomplice.

74   **pinch'd**   (a) trapped, (b) afflicted. See I.ii.328, II.ii.4, and
      compare III.iii.105–7, IV.i.233–35.

75   **entertain**   (a) give welcome to, and (b) continue to harbour.
      Compare II.i.14–18. In line 76 *whom* means 'who'.

80   **swell**   surge, like a rising 'Tide'. Compare lines 34–36, 56,
      64–68.

81   **fill . . . Shore**   fill the 'Sea-marge' (IV.i.69) of Reason.

82   **Foul and Muddy**   stinking with rotting debris and slimy with
      mud. *Muddy* recalls III.iii.102. *Foul* echoes II.i.124–25 and
      IV.i.181–84, 199–200.

83   **would know me**   either (a) is able to recognize me, or (b) wishes
      to acknowledge me [given the guilt they now feel about how
      they were willing to treat ('use', line 72) me in the past].

85   **discase me**   remove the 'Magic Garment' (I.ii.24) that disguises
      the Prospero they knew. Compare *The Winter's Tale*,
      IV.iv.650. *Discase* echoes *Case* in I.i.36, 57, II.i.272–73,
      III.ii.29–30.

86   **sometime Millaine**   at one time when I was the Duke of Milan.
      Free (line 87) echoes IV.i.268, and anticipates lines 96, 240,
      251, 317.

89   **Cowslip's Bell**   bell-shaped bloom of the cowslip flower.

90   **couch**   'lie', repose myself.

Fall fellowly Drops. – The Charm dissolves
   apace,
And as the Morning steals upon the Night,   65
Melting the Darkness, so their rising Senses
Begin to chase the Ignorant Fumes that mantle
Their Clearer Reason. – O good Gonzalo,
My true Preserver, and a loyal Sir
To him thou follow'st, I will pay thy Graces   70
Home both in Word and Deed. – Most cruelly
Didst thou, Alonso, use me and my Daughter;
Thy Brother was a Furtherer in the Act.
– Thou art pinch'd for't now, Sebastian. – Flesh
   and Blood,
You, Brother mine, that entertain Ambition,   75
Expell'd Remorse and Nature, whom, with
   Sebastian
(Whose inward Pinches therefore are most
   strong),
Would here have kill'd your King, I do forgive
   thee
Unnatural though thou art. – Their Understanding
Begins to swell, and the approaching Tide   80
Will shortly fill the Reasonable Shore
That now lie Foul and Muddy. Not one of them
That yet looks on me, or would know me. – Ariel,
Fetch me the Hat and Rapier in my Cell,
I will discase me, and my self present   85
As I was sometime Millaine: quickly, Spirit,
Thou shalt ere long be Free.
          Ariel sings, and helps to attire him.

[ARIEL]   *Where the Bee sucks, there suck I;*
        In a Cowslip's Bell I lie;
        There I couch when Owls do cry,   90
        On the Bat's Back I do fly

92 **After Summer** after the summer is over (when bats migrate south).

94 **Bow** bough; the Folio spelling, which rhymes with *now*, recalls the bowing boughs of IV.i.113. Compare I.ii.380–82, IV.i.80–81.

96 **so, so, so** Here *so* probably means 'thus', with Prospero expressing his satisfaction over Ariel's work in attiring him.

100 **enforce** spur, direct. Compare line 14 of the Epilogue.

103 **Or ere** before. Compare I.ii.11. *Beat* recalls IV.i.162–63.

104 **Amazement** maze-like bewilderment. Compare I.ii.14, 198, and III.iii.2–3.

106 **fearful** fear-full; frightening. See I.ii.466.

108 **For more Assurance** to give you more convincing evidence.

110 **thy Company** both (a) your 'Society' see (IV.i.90–92), and (b) those who accompany you. As he speaks lines 110–11 Prospero embraces Alonso and greets the four others who have been standing in the charmed circle with Gonzalo.

111 **Where** whe'er (whether).

112 **inchanted Trifle** charm-energized nothing. *Trifle* recalls II.ii.8.
abuse both (a) mislead, deceive, and (b) misuse.

113 **late** of late; very recently.

114 **Beats** throbs. Compare line 103.
saw thee (a) observed you, and (b) recognized you.

115 **amends** mends, heals. Compare lines 58–60. *Affliction* echoes line 22.

116 **held** (a) bound, and (b) 'stopp'd' (line 61).
crave require, call for.

118 **resign** relinquish. *Wrongs* echoes line 25.

   After Summer merrily.
   Merrily, merrily, shall I live now,
   Under the Blossom that hangs on the Bow.

PROSPERO Why that's my dainty Ariel; I shall miss
 thee,   95
 But yet thou shalt have Freedom; so, so, so.
 To the King's Ship, Invisible as thou art;
 There shalt thou find the Mariners asleep
 Under the Hatches. The Master and the Boatswain
 Being awake, enforce them to this Place,   100
 And presently, I prethee.
ARIEL I drink the Air before me, and return
 Or ere your Pulse twice beat.   *Exit.*
GONZALO All Torment, Trouble, Wonder, and
  Amazement
 Inhabits here. Some Heavenly Power guide us 105
 Out of this fearful Country.
PROSPERO   Behold, Sir King,
 The wronged Duke of Millaine, Prospero.
 For more Assurance that a living Prince
 Does now speak to thee, I embrace thy body
 And to thee, and thy Company, I bid   110
 A hearty Welcome.
ALONSO   Where thou beest he or no,
 Or some inchanted Trifle to abuse me
 (As late I have been), I not know. Thy Pulse
 Beats as of Flesh and Blood; and since I saw
  thee,
 Th' Affliction of my Mind amends, with which 115
 I fear a Madness held me; this must crave
 (And if this be at all) a most strange Story.
 Thy Dukedom I resign, and do entreat
 Thou pardon me my Wrongs. But how should
  Prospero
 Be living and be here?

122   **measur'd** calculated ('confin'd' to a finite sum). *Confin'd* echoes line 7. *Age* (line 121) echoes IV.i.191–92; compare I.ii.258–59, II.i.149–50, IV.i.261–64.

123–   **You . . . Isle** your senses still 'relish' (line 23) the deceptions
24   ('Subtleties') that have been your only taste of the island thus far. *Subtleties* recalls II.i.28–31.

124   **nor** neither, not.

126   **brace** yoked pair. Compare *Coriolanus*, II.i.43, II.iii.66.
      minded disposed. See I.i.41–42, II.i.248–49, II.ii.17.

127–   **I . . . Traitors** I could pull down King Alonso's displeasure
28   upon your heads and see you brought to justice for treason. *Frown* echoes lines 28–30; it thereby emphasizes that Sebastian and Antonio are not yet 'Penitent'. *Pluck* recalls I.ii.24.

129   **The . . . him** Sebastian's words echo II.ii.105–7. Lines 126–29 are often marked in today's editions for delivery as asides; that is by no means the only way they can be staged.

132   **rankest Fault** foulest crime. One meaning of *rankest* is 'most overgrown' (a sense that recalls I.ii.80–81, 85–87; II.i.253; IV.i.14–22).
      require request (suggesting 'demand', as in line 51).

133–   **which . . . restore** which of course I know you must return.
34   *Perforce* means 'of necessity'.

135   **Give . . . Preservation** explain just how you survived.

136   **whom . . . since** who only three hours ago. Compare *whom* in line 76.

137   **wrack'd** shipwrecked. Compare I.ii.26, 486; IV.i.156.

138   **Point** sword or knife point. But *Point* can also mean (a) 'import', meaning, and (b) punctuation (especially the point – the period or full stop – that concludes a sentence). It can also refer to the 'compunctious Visitings' of conscience, as in *Macbeth*, I.v.47. *Point* recalls I.ii.194 and III.i.4. *Remembrance* echoes II.i.213–20.

139   **woe** sorry; filled with woe (grief). Here *woe* suggests *woo*. Compare *The Winter's Tale*, III.ii.157, and *Love's Labour's Lost*, IV.iii.372, where *woe* means 'woo', and see *Romeo and Juliet*, III.iv.8, where Paris says that 'These Times of Woe afford no Times to Woo'.

PROSPERO   — First, Noble Friend,   120
  Let me embrace thine Age, whose Honour cannot
  Be measur'd or confin'd.
GONZALO   Whether this be
  Or be not, I'll not swear.
PROSPERO   You do yet taste
  Some Subtleties o'th' Isle, that will nor let you
  Believe things certain. — Welcome, my Friends
    all.   125
  — But you, my brace of Lords, were I so minded
  I here could pluck his Highness' Frown upon you
  And justify you Traitors. At this Time
  I will tell no Tales.
SEBASTIAN   The Divel speaks in him.
PROSPERO   No.
  — For you, most wicked Sir, whom to call
    Brother   130
  Would even infect my Mouth, I do forgive
  Thy rankest Fault, all of them, and require
  My Dukedom of thee, which perforce I know
  Thou must restore.
ALONSO   If thou beest Prospero,
  Give us particulars of thy Preservation,   135
  How thou hast met us here, whom three Hours
    since
  Were wrack'd upon this Shore? where I have lost
  (How sharp the Point of this Remembrance is)
  My dear Son Ferdinand.
PROSPERO   I am woe for't, Sir.

141   **Cure** This word echoes lines 58–60 and recalls I.ii.106; compare II.ii.73–85.

145–   **and . . . Loss** and to make the grievous loss bearable. The
46   phrase 'dear Loss' recalls I.ii.485–86, II.i.119, IV.i.204. *Supportable* recalls I.ii.152–58. *Comfort* (line 147) echoes line 58. *Weaker* alludes to the New Testament phrase 'weaker vessel' (1 Peter 3:7), referring to a woman.

149   **that** would that; if only. See the notes to II.i.307, 309.

151   **mudded . . . Bed** embedded in the seabed. Alonso's words fulfil the prophecy in I.ii.394–402. Compare lines 58–60, 79–82; I.ii.50, 252–53; III.iii.99–102.

154   **admire** wonder; gape in amazement. Compare III.i.37.

155   **devour their Reason** consume their reasoning powers [by overusing them in a vain attempt to puzzle out this mystery]. See the notes to III.iii.84, 105, IV.i.1. *Encounter* (line 154) recalls IV.i.137–38.

156   **do . . . Truth** function as servants of the truth. *Offices* recalls I.i.39–40, I.ii.84, 312–13.

157   **natural Breath** the 'Breath' of creatures whose natures are not uplifted by higher intellect (the 'Eyes' of Grace).

158   **justled . . . Senses** shaken from your normal ability to perceive and think. *Senses* echoes line 66; *justled* recalls III.ii.29–30.

160   **thrust forth of** cast out of (so also in line 204). Compare I.ii.62–63; II.i.233; II.ii.37–38, 99–100, 114–15, 130–33; III.iii.53–56.
    strangely inexplicably. This word recalls lines 116–17, and IV.i.234–35. *Wrack'd* echoes line 137. *Shore* recalls lines 79–82.

163   **a . . . Day** a story whose day-by-day circumstances are not to be related in a single setting.

ALONSO   Irreparable is the Loss, and Patience   140
  Says it is past her Cure.
PROSPERO   I rather think
  You have not sought her Help, of whose soft
    Grace
  For the like Loss I have her sovereign Aid
  And rest my self Content.
ALONSO   You the like Loss?
PROSPERO   As Great to me as Late, and Supportable   145
  To make the dear Loss have I Means much Weaker
  Than you may call to comfort you: for I
  Have lost my Daughter.
ALONSO   A Daughter?
  Oh Heavens, that they were living both in Naples
  The King and Queen there, that they were; I
    wish   150
  My self were mudded in that oozy Bed
  Where my Son lies. When did you lose your
    Daughter?
PROSPERO   In this last Tempest. – I perceive these
    Lords
  At this Encounter do so much admire
  That they devour their Reason and scarce think   155
  Their Eyes do offices of Truth. Their Words
  Are natural Breath. – But howsoev'r you have
  Been justled from your Senses, know for certain
  That I am Prospero, and that very Duke
  Which was thrust forth of Millaine, who most
    strangely   160
  Upon this Shore where you were wrack'd was
    landed
  To be the Lord on't. No more yet of this,
  For 'tis a Chronicle of Day by Day,
  Not a Relation for a Break-fast, nor
  Befitting this first Meeting. – Welcome, Sir: 165

167   **abroad**   outside my immediate 'Court'. Compare III.i.52–53.
       Subjects recalls I.ii.340–41.

169   **requite**   (a) repay, and (b) reward. Compare lines 70–71, and
       see III.iii.71. *Wonder* (line 170) recalls I.ii.424–25,
       II.ii.172–75, IV.i.122–24, V.i.104; *content* echoes line 144
       and recalls II.i.251–52.

S.D.   **discovers**   dis-covers; discloses [by pulling open a stage
       curtain]. Compare *discase*, line 85.

171– **play / Me False**   break the rules to beat me. Compare
72   I.ii.60–62, and see *The Winter's Tale*, IV.iv.146–53.

173– **Yes ... wrangle**   yes you would; for twenty kingdoms ('the
74   World') you would do everything you could to win.
       Miranda's words echo what Aemilia tells Desdemona in
       Othello, IV.iii.61–103.

175   **a ... Island**   a true sight (as opposed to a hallucination).
       Alonso alludes to what Prospero has said in lines 123–25.

176   **twice loose**   (a) lose, and (b) loose (release) a second time.
       Loose echoes IV.i.249; compare II.i.107–11.
       A ... Miracle   How this line is to be delivered is a matter of
       interpretation, but it is difficult (though not impossible) to
       imagine that Sebastian, any more than Antonio, has
       experienced a spiritual conversion; see line 129 for his only
       other speech in this part of the scene. In productions of the
       play Sebastian sometimes addresses this line to Antonio as a
       sardonic aside; at other times he speaks it openly, but in such
       a way as to encourage the theatre audience, if not the onstage
       audience, to hear in it a mixture of disappointment (that
       Alonso's crown now has a secure heir) and sarcasm (since
       what others will construe as a sign of providential
       intervention is, for Sebastian, merely another misfortune,
       another of fickle Fortune's blows to his frustrated ambitions).

177   **Merciful**   bestowing gracious favour when wrath was deserved.
       Compare I.ii.1–21, 62–63, 149–51, V.i.1–32. *Cause* (line
       178) recalls II.i.1–2, 110–11.

179   **compass thee about**   embrace you. Compare III.ii.63–64.

182   **brave**   (a) wondrous, (b) 'goodly', and (c) 'beauteous' (lines
       180–82). Compare III.ii.104. *Wonder* (line 180) echoes line
       170. *Goodly* (line 181) recalls I.ii.414, IV.i.113.

This Cell's my Court. Here have I few
  Attendants,
And Subjects none abroad. Pray you look in:
My Dukedom since you have given me again,
I will requite you with as good a thing,
At least bring forth a Wonder, to content ye   170
As much as me my Dukedom.

Here Prospero discovers Ferdinand and Miranda,
playing at Chess.

MIRANDA   Sweet Lord, you play
  Me False.
FERDINAND   No, my dearest Love, I would not for
  The World.
MIRANDA   Yes, for a score of Kingdoms you
  Should wrangle, and I would call it Fair Play.
ALONSO   If this
  Prove a Vision of the Island, one dear Son   175
  Shall I twice loose.
SEBASTIAN   A most high Miracle.
FERDINAND Though the Seas threaten, they are
  Merciful:
  I have curs'd them without Cause.
ALONSO   Now all the Blessings
  Of a glad Father compass thee about:
  Arise, and say how thou cam'st here.
MIRANDA   O Wonder!   180
  How many goodly Creatures are there here?
  How beauteous Mankind is? O brave new World
  That has such People in't.

183   **'Tis . . . thee**   Prospero speak with the wisdom of experience; he knows that even the 'new World' so amazing to Miranda has 'Creatures' who are neither 'goodly' nor 'beauteous', among them Prospero's own unrepentant brother. Compare III.iii.30–37.

186–   **Is . . . together?**   Alonso's words (which echo I.ii.419–20)
87   allude to a betrothal that has (a) established a new relationship between father and son (Genesis 2:24), (b) brought Alonso a new daughter, and (c) united Alonso and Prospero through their heirs. *Mortal* echoes I.ii.403–5.

189–   **when . . . Advise**   Compare *The Winter's Tale*, IV.iv.405–34,
90   where another son fails, for different reasons, to ask his father's advice and obtain his consent.

192   **Renown**   report, fame.

194   **a second Life**   Ferdinand refers to (a) the life of Miranda (which will now become 'one flesh' with his own, Genesis 2:24), and (b) his own psychological and spiritual renewal (see John 3:3–8) through his love for her.

195   **I am hers**   (a) I am her 'second Father', and (b) I too love her and belong to her [giving my consent to your marriage].

197   **ask . . . Forgiveness**   ask my new daughter to forgive me. Compare *King Lear*, IV.vii.69–73, 81–83.

198   **burthen our Remembrances**   (a) oppress our memories, and (b) load our expressions of affection (remembrances of others). *Remembrances* echoes line 138; *burthen* recalls IV.i.113.

199   **Heaviness that's gone**   woe that is now lifted. *Heaviness* recalls I.ii.306–7 and III.i.5; compare the stage direction following IV.i.138. Prospero hints at the 'rest' the Gospels promise to those 'who labour and are heavy laden'; see the note to III.iii.5.
  inly wept   experienced deep, silent sorrow. Compare line 77.

201   **drop . . . Crown**   deposit a heavenly crown. Compare II.i.189–91; IV.i.18, 76–86, 103–17, 233–35. *Drop* also recalls lines 16, 63–64, and I.ii.320–22; II.ii.20–22, 145; III.ii.144–47.

202   **chalk'd . . . Way**   marked the path. Compare *Henry VIII*, I.i.60.

204–5   **Was . . . Naples?**   Gonzalo's words recall the exchange in I.ii.59–63, a passage also echoed in lines 171–74.

PROSPERO   'Tis new to thee.

ALONSO   What is this Maid with whom thou wast at
    play?
    Your eld'st Acquaintance cannot be three Hours.   185
    Is she the Goddess that hath sever'd us,
    And brought us thus together?

FERDINAND   Sir, she is Mortal;
    But by Immortal Providence, she's mine.
    I chose her when I could not ask my Father
    For his Advise, nor thought I had one. She   190
    Is Daughter to this famous Duke of Millaine,
    Of whom so often I have heard Renown
    But never saw before; of whom I have
    Receiv'd a second Life; and second Father
    This Lady makes him to me.

ALONSO   I am hers.   195
    But O, how oddly will it sound that I
    Must ask my Child Forgiveness?

PROSPERO   There, Sir, stop:
    Let us not burthen our Remembrances
    With a Heaviness that's gone.

GONZALO   I have inly wept,
    Or should have spoke ere this. — Look down, you
        Gods,   200
    And on this Couple drop a blessed Crown;
    For it is you that have chalk'd forth the Way
    Which brought us hither.

ALONSO   I say Amen, Gonzalo.

GONZALO   Was Millaine thrust from Millaine, that
    his Issue
    Should become Kings of Naples? O rejoice   205
    Beyond a common Joy, and set it down
    With Gold on lasting Pillars: in one Voyage
    Did Claribel her Husband find at Tunis,
    And Ferdinand her Brother found a Wife
    Where he himself was lost, Prospero his Dukedom   210

211–   **and . . . own**   and all of us found our true selves when none of
12   us really recognized or owned himself before. See the notes to
         line 11 (and in its light lines 28–31, 53, 85) and lines 32, 149,
         and 194.

213   **still**   both (a) yet, and (b) forever.

215   **more of us**   more of our company.

217   **Blasphemy**   Gonzalo's name for the saucy, cursing Boatswain.
         Compare I.ii.365. *Gallows* recalls I.i.30–36, 49–51.

218   **That . . . o'er-boord**   who thrust 'Grace' overboard, both (a) by
         blaspheming the Gods, and (b) by showing so little reverence
         to their deputy on Earth (the King), and his Grace's
         counsellors. See I.i.17–19, 22–29.

219   **Hast . . . Land?**   Does your mouth utter no curses now that it is
         on shore? *Mouth* recalls I.i.55.

221   **next**   next (second) best news.

222   **Glasses**   hourglasses (that is, hours). Compare line 185 and
         I.ii.240–41.
         since . . . Split   ago we gave up for lost, thinking it was split in
         two. Compare I.i.63–64.

223   **Tight and Yare**   watertight and seaworthy. Compare I.i.3–4, 7.
         bravely Rigg'd   as handsomely equipped for sailing. *Bravely*
         echoes line 182. *Service* recalls I.ii.247, 286, II.i.133, III.i.65,
         IV.i.35, 269; compare I.ii.187, 271, III.i.85, IV.i.33.

227   **Strange**   'not Natural'; mysterious. Compare lines 116–17,
         160–62, 231.

229   **dead of Sleep**   so deeply asleep that we were aware of no more
         than corpses would have been. See II.i.262–69.

230   **clapp'd under Hatches**   tightly fastened under the closed
         hatches in the ship's deck. Compare I.ii.230.

231   **strange and several**   various inexplicable.

In a poor Isle, and all of us our Selves
When no Man was his own.

ALONSO   Give me your Hands:
Let Grief and Sorrow still embrace his Heart
That doth not wish you Joy.

GONZALO   Be it so, Amen.

Enter Ariel, with the Master and Boatswain
amazedly following.

O look, Sir, look, Sir, here is more of us: 215
I prophesied, if a Gallows were on Land,
This Fellow could not drown. – Now, Blasphemy,
That swear'st Grace o'er-boord, not an Oath
   on Shore,
Hast thou no Mouth by Land? What is the News?

BOATSWAIN   The best News is that we have safely
   found   220
Our King and Company; the next, our Ship,
Which but three Glasses since we gave out
   Split,
Is Tight and Yare, and bravely Rigg'd, as when
We first put out to Sea.

ARIEL   – Sir, all this Service
Have I done since I went.

PROSPERO   My tricksy Spirit.   225

ALONSO   These are not Natural Events, they
   strengthen
From Strange to Stranger. Say, how came you
   hither?

BOATSWAIN   If I did think, Sir, I were well awake,
I'd strive to tell you. We were dead of Sleep,
And (how we know not) all clapp'd under
   Hatches,   230
Where but even now, with strange and several
   Noises

232   **roaring, gingling** screaming, jingling. *Roaring* recalls line 44.

233   **moe** more. Compare *Mow* in IV.i.47

234   **straight . . . Liberty** immediately we were set free.

235   **in . . . Trim** all our uniforms in trim condition. Compare II.i.45–55. Many editors emend *our* to *her*.

237   **Cap'ring . . . her** dancing capers in his joy upon seeing her.

237   **On a Trice** in an instant.

238   **Even . . . them** as in a dream, we were separated from the others. See I.ii.484 and III.ii.139–47, and compare *A Midsummer Night's Dream*, IV.i.71–72, 190–202, 207–21.

239   **moping** in a still-dazed state. Compare IV.i.47.

240   **my Diligence** my industrious servant. Compare line 217.

241   **strange** insoluble. *Maze* recalls line 104 and III.iii.2–6.

242– **in . . . of** in this experience a pattern that points to the
43   guidance of an agency higher than 'Nature'. In line 244 *rectify our Knowledge* means 'correct and restore our understanding'. *Business* recalls III.i.94–96 and III.iii.69, and anticipates line 246. *Oracle* recalls IV.i.11–12.

245   **infest . . . on** overwhelm your mind with attempts to resolve. Compare I.ii.176, IV.i.162–63, V.i.103, 113–16.

246– **At . . . Accidents** when we have leisure to speak individually
49   (which opportunity to speak 'single' [alone] should occur soon), I'll give you a rational explanation of how all these events came to pass. In this passage *single* appears to mean 'selected' or 'singled out'; it recalls I.ii.430. Meanwhile *probable* carries the sense 'capable of being proven true'.

254   **Some few odd** a small number of peculiar. *Remember* echoes line 198.

Of roaring, shrieking, howling, gingling
   Chains,
And moe Diversity of Sounds, all horrible,
We were awak'd; straight way at Liberty,
Where we, in all our Trim, freshly beheld   235
Our royal, good, and gallant Ship, our Master
Cap'ring to eye her. On a Trice, so please you,
Even in a Dream, were we divided from them
And were brought moping hither.

ARIEL   – Was't well done?
PROSPERO   Bravely, my Diligence, thou shalt be
   Free.   240
ALONSO   This is as strange a Maze as ere Men trod,
And there is in this Business more than Nature
Was ever Conduct of. Some Oracle
Must rectify our Knowledge.
PROSPERO   Sir, my Liege,
Do not infest your Mind with beating on   245
The Strangeness of this Business. At pick'd
   Leisure
(Which shall be shortly single) I'll resolve
   you
(Which to you shall seem probable) of every
These happen'd Accidents; till when, be
   cheerful
And think of each thing well. – Come hither,
   Spirit.   250
Set Caliban and his Companions free;
Untie the Spell.   *[Exit Ariel.]*
       – How fares my gracious Sir?
There are yet missing of your Company
Some few odd Lads that you remember not.

   Enter Ariel, driving in Caliban, Stephano, and
      Trinculo, in their stol'n Apparel.

255   **shift for**   work on behalf of. Here *shift* is an unintended
       reminder that Stephano, Trinculo, and Caliban have shifted
       (changed) into stolen shifts (changes of apparel). What the
       drunken Stephano probably means to say is 'let every man
       shift for [take care of] himself'. Compare II.ii.65–67.

256–   **for . . . Fortune**   for Fortune (rather than anything we mere
57   humans can do to determine our fates) rules in all things.
       Compare *Twelfth Night*, II.v.27. See the second note to line
       176.

257   **Corasio**   a slurred, inebriated rendering of *Coragio* (Italian for
       'Courage').

258   **true Spies**   reliable observers (eyes). *Goodly* (line 259) recalls
       line 181.

260   **Setebos**   Caliban invokes the deity he had referred to in I.ii.371;
       he has now forsworn his faith in the divinity of Stephano.
       Here *brave* means 'Fine' (line 261); compare lines 223, 240.
       Lines 258–62 echo lines 180–83.

261   **Fine**   magnificent [referring to Prospero's ducal robes].

265   **a plain Fish**   a simple fish. Antonio could be referring to
       Stephano (see line 276), who is 'drowned' in sack; but he is
       almost certainly commenting on the appearance of Caliban;
       see II.ii.25–40, III.ii.14–17, 30–34, IV.i.249–50.

266   **Badges**   identifying devices (worn on their livery by servants to
       identify the household that employed them). Prospero's point
       is that the livery, the 'stol'n Apparel', these 'Men' (servants, as
       in II.i.256) are wearing proves them to be thieves, rather than
       'True' (honest) men. For other references to 'true men' see
       Much Ado About Nothing, III.iii.1, 54–55, and *Measure for
       Measure*, IV.ii.46–52.

269   **make . . . Ebbs**   make the tides rise and fall. Compare line 35.
       Ebbs recalls II.i.203–10. For a similar description of the
       Moon as 'the Governess of Floods' see *A Midsummer Night's
       Dream*, II.i.103.

270   **deal . . . Command**   act with the authority of the Moon
       Goddess (the 'Triple Hecate' of *A Midsummer Night's
       Dream*, V.ii.14, and *Macbeth*, II.i.51).

STEPHANO   Every Man shift for all the rest, and   255
　let no Man take care for himself: for all is
　but Fortune. – Coragio, Bully-Monster, Corasio.
TRINCULO   If these be true Spies which I wear in
　my Head, here's a goodly Sight.
CALIBAN   O Setebos, these be brave Spirits
　indeed: 260
　How Fine my Master is? I am afraid
　He will chastise me.
SEBASTIAN   Ha, ha, what things are these, my Lord
　Antonio?
　Will Money buy 'em?
ANTONIO   Very like: one of them
　Is a plain Fish, and no doubt marketable.   265
PROSPERO   Mark but the Badges of these Men, my
　Lords,
　Then say if they be True. This misshapen Knave,
　His Mother was a Witch, and one so strong
　That could control the Moon, make Flows and
　Ebbs,
　And deal in her Command, without her Power.   270

271 **rob'd** both (a) robbed, and (b) robed, by stealing the robes I
put out as 'Stale', and by doing your part to prepare for my
donning my old ducal robes (see lines 261–74, 291–92).
Compare *King Lear*, III.vi.38, for a similar *robbed/robed* pun.

274 **know, and own** recognize and claim responsibility for.
Compare lines 211–12. *Pinch'd* (line 275) echoes line 74.
this ... Darkness Caliban. Here *Darkness* probably refers to
Caliban's (a) complexion, (b) ignorance, (c) moroseness, and
(d) vengefulness. *Thing* recalls II.ii.125, and anticipates line
288.

276 **Butler** wine steward; servant in charge of the butts of wine and
beer and of other pantry items.

278 **reeling ripe** too drunk to stand without listing (III.ii.20).
Alonso implies that Trinculo is like an overripe fruit, ready to
fall of its own accord from the tree to which it is attached.

279 **gilded 'em** turned their faces blood-red (see *Macbeth*,
II.iii.118–21). Compare IV.i.171. Alonso may also be
referring to the golden tint that Stephano and his companions
have acquired from the 'mantled Pool' (IV.i.182) into which
Ariel has led them; see IV.i.199–200.

280 **Pickle** both (a) predicament, and (b) pickled (inebriated) state.

282–   **me ... Bones** I will never get the marinating 'Liquor' out of
83   my system.

283 **fear Fly-blowing** need to worry about having flies deposit their
eggs in my flesh and fill me with maggots. Compare
III.i.62–63.

286 **a Cramp** a walking convulsion. See IV.i.261–64.
Sirha sirrah, a mode of address for a social inferior.

287 **sore** (a) pain-racked, (b) cruel. Compare III.i.10–11.

291 **As you look** if you expect (hope).

292 **trim it handsomely** move quickly and decorously. *Trim* echoes
line 235.

293 **I** both (a) I, and (b) ay. Compare IV.i.167.

These three have rob'd me, and this demi-Divel
(For he's a bastard one) had plotted with them
To take my Life. Two of these Fellows you
Must know, and own; this Thing of Darkness I
Acknowledge mine.

CALIBAN   I shall be pinch'd to death.   275

ALONSO   Is not this Stephano, my drunken Butler?

SEBASTIAN   He is drunk now; where had he Wine?

ALONSO   And Trinculo is reeling ripe. Where
   should they
Find this grand Liquor that hath gilded 'em?
– How cam'st thou in this Pickle?   280

TRINCULO   I have been in such a Pickle since I
saw you last that I fear me will never out of
my Bones. I shall not fear Fly-blowing.

SEBASTIAN   Why how now, Stephano?

STEPHANO   O touch me not: I am not Stephano,   285
But a Cramp.

PROSPERO   You'd be King o'th' Isle, Sirha?

STEPHANO   I should have been a sore one then.

ALONSO   This is a Strange Thing as ere I look'd
   on.

PROSPERO   He is as Disproportion'd in his Manners
As in his Shape. – Go, Sirha, to my Cell: 290
Take with you your Companions. As you look
To have my Pardon, trim it handsomely.

CALIBAN   I, that I will; and I'll be Wise hereafter,

294   **Grace**   'Pardon' (line 292); forgiveness and favour. *Grace* can
       also mean 'salvation', of course, and that sense recalls
       Caliban's quest for a deity worthy of his worship; see the note
       to line 260, and compare lines 294–96 with I.ii.331–38,
       349–58, 370–72, II.ii.125–27, 134–35, 145–75, III.ii.60–62,
       107–10, III.iii.83–84, IV.i.216–20, 230–31, 240–41.

296   **Go to**   come now, begone.

297   **bestow your Luggage**   leave your regalia. Compare
       IV.i.231–32.

299   **Train**   entourage, 'company' (line 253). *Rest* recalls
       II.i.178–80, III.i.18–20, III.iii.1–6, V.i.144; compare line 255.

303   **quick**   both (a) quickly, and (b) in a quick (lively) fashion.

304   **particular Accidents**   individual occurrences. Compare lines
       134–35, 246–49.

307   **Nuptial**   wedding.

308   **solemnized**   ceremonially ratified; here to be pronounced
       'so-lém-ni-zéd'. To make the metre of this line seem less
       strained, some editions have emended *belov'd* to *beloved* and
       solemnized to *solemniz'd*.

309   **retire me**   retire myself. Prospero's phrasing echoes I.ii.89–97
       and IV.i.161. Once again he will subordinate 'Worldly Ends'
       to 'the bettering of [his] Mind', in accordance with Matthew
       16:24–27 and 1 John 2:15–17.

310   **Every . . . Grave**   a third of my thoughts will be directed
       towards my final retirement. Compare I.i.25–28, IV.i.1–4.

312   **Take . . . strangely**   seize hold on the listener in an
       extraordinary way. *Strangely* echoes lines 226–27, 231, 241.
       deliver all   discharge the burden that has been growing within
       me for twelve long years. Compare I.ii.156–58, II.ii.211–13,
       III.i.1–2, 13–15. See the notes to *Cymbeline*, V.v.370, and
       The Winter's Tale, V.ii.31, 35–36.

313   **auspicious**   favourable. Compare I.ii.182.

And seek for Grace. What a thrice double Ass
Was I to take this Drunkard for a God   295
And worship this dull Fool?
PROSPERO   Go to, away.
ALONSO Hence, and bestow your Luggage where
    you found it.
SEBASTIAN   Or stole it rather.
              [Exeunt Stephano, Trinculo, and Caliban.]
PROSPERO   Sir, I invite your Highness and your
    Train
  To my poor Cell, where you shall take your
    Rest   300
  For this one Night, which part of it I'll waste
  With such Discourse as, I not doubt, shall make
    it
  Go quick away: the Story of my Life,
  And the particular Accidents, gone by
  Since I came to this Isle. And in the Morn   305
  I'll bring you to your Ship, and so to Naples,
  Where I have hope to see the Nuptial
  Of these our Dear-belov'd solemnized,
  And thence retire me to my Millaine, where
  Every third Thought shall be my Grave.
ALONSO   I long   310
  To hear the Story of your Life, which must
  Take the Ear strangely.
PROSPERO   I'll deliver all,
  And promise you calm Seas, auspicious Gales,

314– **Sail . . . off**   a sail (voyage) so swift that it shall catch your sails
15   and carry your fleet far into the distance before you are aware
      of it.

316   **That . . . Charge**   you have completed your assignment, and I
      now release ('deliver', line 312) you from any further labour.
      Compare line 8. *Elements* recalls I.i.22–23 and III.iii.61–65.
      Free (line 317) echoes lines 86, 240, 251, and anticipates lines
      19–20 of the Epilogue.

317   **you**   it is not clear whether this pronoun refers to Alonso and
      his company (see lines 299–300) or to the audience. The Folio
      stage direction that concludes the scene suggests the former,
      with Prospero retiring briefly to his 'poor Cell' and then
      re-emerging to deliver his Epilogue to the audience.

And Sail so expeditious that shall catch
Your Royal Fleet far off. – My Ariel, Chick,   315
That is thy Charge: then to the Elements
Be free, and fare thou well. – Please you draw
  near.   *Exeunt omnes.*

EPILOGUE   Prospero now presents himself to the audience as a 'Single' mortal (I.ii.430, V.i.247) to deliver, and receive, a benediction.

2   **mine own**   both (a) the strength of any mortal [now that Prospero is reduced to an ordinary man without 'Charms'], and (b) the strength of a 'poor Player' (*Macbeth*, V.v.24) who has been a 'Deceiver' (line 7) impersonating the protagonist. *Charms* echoes V.i.2, 17, 31, 54.

4   **confin'd**   held prisoner in this 'Wooden O' (*Henry V*, Prologue, line 13), 'this bare Island' (line 8). Compare V.i.7, 122.

8   **your Spell**   your power to hold me in thrall unless (as I held Ariel) you 'release me' with your 'good Hands' (gracious applause) and 'gentle Breath' (generous bravos), lines 9–11. See the note to V.i.11. *Spell* recalls IV.i.127, V.i.252. *Hands* (line 10) echoes V.i.212.

11   **my Sails**   the sails that will allow me to depart from this now-barren setting for the life that awaits me in 'Naples' (line 5). Compare V.i.312–15. *Sails* for a theatre professional can be construed as a metaphor for sales, the receipts he receives from paying customers if his 'Project' succeeds and he and his companions 'please' their audiences. For another Shakespearean passage that relates 'Sale' to 'Pardon' (lines 19–20), see *King John*, III.i.162–68.

12–13 **else . . . please**   otherwise my 'Purpose of Playing' (*Hamlet*, III.ii.24) has been to no avail. *Project* recalls II.i.281, IV.i.175, and V.i.1. See the note on entertainment at II.i.17.

13   **want**   lack. Compare IV.i.116.

14   **Art to inchant**   power to 'enforce' my will with spells. *Art* recalls I.ii.1, 25, 28, 291, 370, II.i.279, IV.i.41, 120, V.i.50; *enforce* echoes V.i.100; *inchant* echoes V.i.112.

15   **my . . . Despair**   I die without any hope of redemption.

16   **reliev'd by Prayer**   assisted and mended by the kind of intercession. *Reliev'd* echoes II.i.105, II.ii.73–76.

17–18 **Which . . . Faults**   that is so penetrating that it pierces the heart of Mercy itself and thus secures my ransom from the 'Faults' (deficiencies, wrongdoings) that would otherwise consign me to an eternity of 'Perdition' (I.ii.30). *Pierces* recalls the play's many references to pinching and penetrating; see I.ii.327–29, II.ii.4–7, IV.i.233–35, and V.i.74, 77, 138, 275.

EPILOGUE

Spoken by Prospero

Now my Charms are all o'er-thrown,
And what Strength I have's mine own,
Which is most faint; now 'tis True
I must be here confin'd by you,
Or sent to Naples. Let me not,   5
Since I have my Dukedom got,
And pardon'd the Deceiver, dwell
In this bare Island by your Spell,
But release me from my Bands
With the Help of your good Hands: 10
Gentle Breath of yours my Sails
Must fill, or else my Project fails,
Which was to please. Now I want
Spirits to enforce, Art to inchant,
And my Ending is Despair,   15
Unless I be reliev'd by Prayer
Which pierces so that it assaults
Mercy it self and frees all Faults.

19–20 **As . . . free** Just as you pray daily for forgiveness of your sins (in keeping with Matthew 6:11–12, 14–15), I beseech you to grant me an 'Indulgence' (a pardon) and declare me 'free' (V.i.317) of the need for further incarceration. Prospero draws an analogy between his 'Project' as a man within the world defined by the play (to achieve at-one-ment with his fellow human beings, with the cosmos, and with God) and his objective as a performer (to receive the approbation of the theatre audience, which presides in judgement over the Globe playhouse in a way that imitates God's judgement over His creation). In the process he speaks for all the 'Actors' (IV.i.148), including a dramatist who was on the verge of retirement from 'this bare Island' (line 8) as he wrote these words. Like Prospero, the playwright has been functioning as a 'Deceiver' (line 7), charming impressionable patrons into accepting as somehow real what the magician himself knows to be an 'insubstantial Pageant' that will 'dissolve' as quickly as the 'Dreams' that epitomize 'our little Life' on this terrestrial globe (IV.i.148–58). In the person of Prospero, the author confesses that he is as frail as his 'all-unable Pen', and he begs us to bring 'fair Minds' to his actions and grant him our 'Acceptance' (*Henry V*, Epilogue, lines 1, 14). Here *Crimes* are equivalent to *Faults* (line 18), or sins; *pardon'd* echoes V.i.291–94.

As you from Crimes would pardon'd be,
Let your Indulgence set me free.   *Exit.*   20

FINIS

PERSPECTIVES ON
The Tempest

In the commentary accompanying his edition of Shakespeare's works (London, 1765) Samuel Johnson noted that *The Tempest* is unusual among the playwright's dramas in that 'its plan is regular' (in keeping with the classical 'unities' of time, place, and action). This, Johnson said, was probably 'an accidental effect of the story, not intended or regarded by our author'.

> But whatever might be Shakespeare's intention in forming or adopting the plot, he has made it instrumental to the production of many characters, diversified with boundless invention, and preserved with profound skill in nature, extensive knowledge of opinions, and accurate observation of life. In a single drama are here exhibited princes, courtiers, and sailors, all speaking in their real characters. There is the agency of airy spirits, and of an earthly goblin. The operations of magick, the tumults of a storm, the adventures of a desart island, the native effusion of untaught affection, the punishment of guilt, and the final happiness of the pair for whom our passions and reason are equally interested.

A few years later, a contemporary of Johnson's, John Potter, wrote in his *Theatrical Review* (London, 1772) that

> With respect to the Language put into the mouth of Prospero there are many Passages truly sublime, enriched with the finest images and dressed in the most nervous expression. . . . But there is one instance which sets a few objects before the eye without pomp of Language, yet is truly beautiful. It operates its effect by representing these objects in a climax, raising the mind higher and higher till it feels the emotion of grandeur in perfection.
>
> > The cloud-capt tow'rs, the gorgeous palaces,
> > The solemn temples, the great globe itself,
> > Yea all which it inherit, shall dissolve, &c.
>
> *The cloud-capt tow'rs* produce an elevating emotion, heightened by *the gorgeous palaces*, and the mind is carried still higher and

higher by the images that follow. Successive images, making thus stronger and stronger impressions, must elevate more than any single image can do.

... The elevation of the mind in the former part of [the quoted passage] makes the fall great in proportion when the most humbling of all images is introduced, that of an utter dissolution of the earth and its Inhabitants.

But there were some in the eighteenth century who deprecated the poetry of *The Tempest*. In *A Course of Lectures on Oratory and Criticism* (London, 1777), scientist Joseph Priestley observed that

The general rule for the use of metonymy is plainly this; that in all cases, provided the sense be in no danger of being mistaken, a writer is at liberty to substitute, instead of a proper term, any word which, by its associations, can bring along with it ideas that can serve to heighten and improve the sentiment. But it follows from this observation that when the sense doth not require to be heightened and improved, as in the ordinary forms of expression in conversation, on which no emphasis is ever laid, the figure is impertinent and useless: as when Prospero, in the *Tempest* of Shakespeare, speaking to ... Miranda, says

> The fringed curtains of thine eyes advance,
> And say what seest thou.

To mention the *eye-lids* at all, much more to denominate them by such a figurative periphrasis, was quite superfluous.

Early in the succeeding century an eminent Romantic poet and critic came to the defence of the image Priestley and several of his predecessors had found objectionable. In his 1811–12 lectures on Shakespeare and Milton, transcribed and in places adapted by John Payne Collier when he published them four decades later (London, 1856), Samuel Taylor Coleridge commended a passage that had 'fallen under the very severe, but inconsiderate, censure of Pope and Arbuthnot, who pronounce it a piece of the greatest bombast'. Coleridge allowed that

Taking these words as a periphrase of 'Look what is coming yonder', it certainly may appear to border on the ridiculous and to fall under the rule I formerly laid down – that whatever, without injury, can be translated into a foreign language in simple terms, ought to be in simple terms in the original language; but it is to be borne in mind that different modes of expression frequently arise from difference of situation and education: a blackguard would use very different words, to express the same thing, to those a gentleman would employ, yet both would be natural and proper; difference of feeling gives rise to difference of language: a gentleman speaks in polished terms, with due regard to his own rank and position, while a blackguard, a person little better than a brute, speaks like half a brute, showing no respect for himself nor for others.

But I am content to try the lines I have just quoted by the introduction to them; and then, I think, you will admit, that nothing could be more fit and appropriate than such language. How does Prospero introduce them? He has just told Miranda a wonderful story, which deeply affected her and filled her with surprise and astonishment, and for his own purposes he afterwards lulls her to sleep. When she awakes, Shakespeare has made her wholly inattentive to the present, but wrapped up in the past. An actress who understands the character of Miranda would have her eyes cast down and her eyelids almost covering them, while she was, as it were, living in her dream. At this moment Prospero sees Ferdinand and wishes to point him out to his daughter, not only with great, but with scenic solemnity, he standing before her and before the spectator in the dignified character of a great magician. Something was to appear to Miranda on the sudden, and as unexpectedly as if the hero of a drama were to be on the stage at the instant when the curtain is elevated. It is under such circumstances that Prospero says, in a tone calculated at once to arouse his daughter's attention,

> The fringed curtains of thine eyes advance,
> And say what thou seest yond.

Turning from the sight of Ferdinand to his thoughtful daughter, his attention was first struck by the downcast appearance of her eyes and eyelids; and, in my humble opinion, the solemnity of the phraseology assigned to Prospero is completely in character, recollecting his preternatural capacity, in which the most familiar objects in nature present themselves in a mysterious point of view. . . .

Of Miranda we may say that she possesses in herself all the ideal beauties that could be imagined by the greatest poet of any age or country; but it is not my purpose now so much to point out the high

poetic powers of Shakespeare as to illustrate his exquisite judgement, and it is solely with this design that I have noticed a passage
with which, it seems to me, some critics, and those among the best,
have been unreasonably dissatisfied. If Shakespeare be the wonder
of the ignorant, he is, and ought to be, much more the wonder of
the learned; not only from profundity of thought, but from his
astonishing and intuitive knowledge of what man must be at all
times and under all circumstances, he is rather to be looked upon as
a prophet than as a poet. Yet, with all these unbounded powers,
with all this might and majesty of genius, he makes us feel as if he
were unconscious of himself and of his high destiny, disguising the
half god in the simplicity of a child.

Coleridge categorized *The Tempest* as one of Shakespeare's
'ideal plays', and some of his most cogent remarks relate to Ariel,
the spirit who epitomizes the drama's emphasis on the transcendent.

Is there anything in nature from which Shakespeare caught the idea
of this delicate and delightful being, with such childlike simplicity,
yet with such preternatural powers? He is neither born of heaven,
nor of earth; but, as it were, between both, like a May blossom kept
suspended in air by the fanning breeze, which prevents it from
falling to the ground, and only finally, and by compulsion,
touching earth. This reluctance of the sylph to be under the
command even of Prospero is kept up through the whole play, and
in the exercise of his admirable judgement Shakespeare has availed
himself of it in order to give Ariel an interest in the event, looking
forward to that moment when he was to gain his last and only
reward – simple and eternal liberty.

Another instance of admirable judgement and excellent prepara-
tion is to be found in the creature contrasted with Ariel – Caliban,
who is described in such a manner by Prospero as to lead us to
expect the appearance of a foul, unnatural monster. . . .

The character of Caliban is wonderfully conceived: he is a sort of
creature of the earth, as Ariel is a sort of creature of the air. He
partakes of the qualities of the brute, but he is distinguished from
brutes in two ways: by having more understanding without moral
reason; and by not possessing the instincts which pertain to
absolute animals. Still, Caliban is in some respects a noble being:
the poet has raised him far above contempt: he is a man in the sense
of the imagination: all the images he uses are drawn from nature
and are highly poetical; images from the earth, Ariel images from

the air. Caliban talks of the difficulty of finding fresh water, of the situation of morasses, and of other circumstances which even brute instinct, without reason, could comprehend. No mean figure is employed, no mean passion displayed, beyond animal passion and repugnance to command.

In *Characters of Shakespear's Plays* (London, 1817), Coleridge's contemporary, William Hazlitt, said that

The Tempest is one of the most original and perfect of Shakespear's productions, and he has shown in it all the variety of his powers. It is full of grace and grandeur. The human and imaginary characters, the dramatic and the grotesque, are blended together with the greatest art. . . . Though he has here given 'to airy nothing a local habitation and a name,' yet that part which is only the fantastic creation of his mind has the same palpable texture and coheres 'semblably' with the rest. As the preternatural part has the air of reality, and almost haunts the imagination with a sense of truth, the real characters and events partake of the wildness of a dream. The stately magician Prospero, driven from his dukedom, but around whom (so potent is his art) airy spirits throng numberless to do his bidding; his daughter Miranda ('worthy of that name') to whom all the power of his art points, and who seems the goddess of the isle; the princely Ferdinand, cast by fate upon the haven of his happiness in this idol of his love; the delicate Ariel; the savage Caliban, half brute, half demon; the drunken ship's crew – are all connected parts of the story, and can hardly be spared from the place they fill. Even the local scenery is of a piece and character with the subject. Prospero's enchanted island seems to have risen from out of the sea; the airy music, the tempest-tossed vessel, the turbulent waves, all have the effect of the landscape background of some fine picture. Shakespear's pencil is (to use an allusion of his own) 'like the dyer's hand, subdued to what it works in.' Everything in him, though it partakes of 'the liberty of wit,' is also subjected to 'the law' of the understanding. For instance, even the drunken sailors, who are made reeling ripe, share, in the disorder of their minds and bodies, in the tumult of the elements, and seem on shore to be as much at the mercy of chance as they were before at the mercy of the wind and waves. These fellows with their sea-wit are the least to our taste of any part of the play; but they are as like drunken sailors as they can be, and are an indirect foil to Caliban, whose figure acquires a classical dignity in the comparison.

By mid-century the French poet and novelist Victor Hugo was championing the idea that *The Tempest* was 'the last creation of Shakespeare'. In his *Oeuvres complètes de Shakespeare* (Paris, 1859–66), Hugo asserted that

> There is in *The Tempest* the solemn tone of a testament. It might be said that, before his death, the poet, in this *épopée* of the ideal, had designed a codicil for the Future. In this enchanted isle, full of 'sounds and sweet airs that give delight,' we may expect to behold Utopia, the promised land of future generations, Paradise regained. Who in reality is Prospero, the king of this isle? Prospero is the shipwrecked sailor who reaches port, the exile who regains his native land, he who from the depths of despair becomes all-powerful, the worker who by his science has tamed matter, Caliban, and by his genius the spirit, Ariel. Prospero is man, the master of Nature and the despot of destiny; he is the man-Providence!
>
> *The Tempest* is the supreme donouement, dreamed by Shakespeare, for the bloody drama of Genesis. It is the expiation of the primordial crime. The region whither it transports us is the enchanted land where the sentence of damnation is absolved by clemency, and where reconciliation is ensured by amnesty to the fratricide. And, at the close of the piece, when the poet, touched by emotion, throws Antonio in the arms of Prospero, he has made Cain pardoned by Abel.

A few years later, in *Among My Books* (Boston, 1870), the American poet and essayist James Russell Lowell expanded upon Hugo's insights.

> If I read *The Tempest* rightly, it is an example of how a great poet should write allegory, – not embodying metaphysical abstractions, but giving us ideals abstracted from life itself, suggesting an under-meaning everywhere, forcing it upon us nowhere, tantalizing the mind with hints that imply so much and tell so little, and yet keep the attention all eye and ear with eager, if fruitless, expectation. Here the leading characters are not merely typical, but symbolical, – that is, they do not illustrate a class of persons, they belong to universal Nature. ... The whole play indeed is a succession of illusions, winding up with those solemn words of the great enchanter who had summoned to his service every shape of merriment or passion, every figure in the great tragi-comedy of life, and who was now bidding farewell to the scene of his triumphs.

Like Hugo and Lowell, Edward Dowden read the play in autobiographical terms. In *Shakspere – His Mind and Art* (London, 1875), Dowden wrote:

I should describe Prospero as the man of genius, the great artist, lacking at first in practical gifts which lead to material success, and set adrift on the perilous sea of life, in which he finds his enchanted island, where he may achieve his works of wonder. He bears with him Art in its infancy – the marvellous child, Miranda. The grosser passions and appetites – Caliban – he subdues to his service, . . . and he partially informs this servant-monster with intellect and imagination; for Caliban has dim affinities with the higher world of spirits. But these grosser passions and appetites attempt to violate the purity of art. Caliban would seize on Miranda, and people the island with Calibans; therefore his servitude must be strict. And who is Ferdinand? Is he not, with his gallantry and his beauty, the young [John] Fletcher in conjunction with whom Shakspere worked upon *The Two Noble Kinsmen* and *Henry VIII*? Fletcher is conceived as a follower of the Shaksperian style and method in dramatic art; he had 'eyed full many a lady with best regard,' for several virtues had liked several women, but never any with whole-hearted devotion, except Miranda. And to Ferdinand the old enchanter will entrust his daughter, 'a third of his own life.' But Shakspere had perceived the weak point in Fletcher's genius – its want of hardness of fibre, of patient endurance, and of a sense of the solemnity and sanctity of the service of art. And therefore he finally hints to his friend, that his winning of Miranda must not be too light and easy. It shall be Ferdinand's task to remove some thousands of logs and pile them, according to the strict injunction of Prospero. 'Don't despise drudgery and dryasdust work, young poets,' Shakspere would seem to say, who had himself so carefully laboured over his English and Roman histories; 'for Miranda's sake such drudgery may well seem light.' Therefore, also, Prospero surrounds the marriage of Ferdinand to his daughter with a religious awe. Ferdinand must honour her as sacred, and win her by hard toil. But the work of the higher imagination is not drudgery – it is swift and serviceable among all the elements, fire upon the topmast, the sea-nymph upon the sands, Ceres the goddess of earth, with harvest blessings, in the Masque. It is essentially Ariel, an airy spirit, – the imaginative genius of poetry, but recently delivered in England from long slavery to Sycorax. Prospero's departure from the island is the abandoning by Shakspere of the theatre, the scene of his marvellous works: 'Graves at my command Have waked their sleepers, oped, and let them forth By my so potent art.' Henceforth Prospero is but a man; no longer a great enchanter. He returns to the dukedom he had lost in Stratford-upon-Avon, and will pay no tribute henceforth to any Alonzo. . . .

For E. M. W. Tillyard, in *Shakespeare's Last Plays* (London, 1938), *The Tempest* was best approached as a drama that incorporated, and transcended, a 'tragic pattern'.

Prospero, when one first hears of him, was the ruler of an independent state and beloved of his subjects. But all is not well, because the King of Naples is his enemy. Like Basilius in Sidney's *Arcadia*, he commits the error of not attending carefully enough to affairs of state. The reason for this error, his Aristotelian *hamartia*, is his love of study. He hands over the government to his brother Antonio, who proceeds to call in the King of Naples to turn Prospero out of his kingdom. Fearing the people, Antonio refrains from murdering Prospero and his infant daughter, but sets them adrift in a boat. Now, except for this last item, the plot is entirely typical of Elizabethan revenge tragedy. Allow Prospero to be put to death, give him a son instead of a daughter to live and to avenge him, and your tragic plot is complete. . . .

In executing his work, Shakespeare chose a method new to himself but repeated by Milton in *Samson Agonistes*. He began his action at a point in the story so late that the story was virtually over; and he included the total story either by narrating the past or by re-enacting samples of it. . . .

For the re-enactment of tragedy it is possible to think with Dover Wilson that the storm scene does this. But it does nothing to re-enact the specific tragic plot in the play, the fall of Prospero; and one of its aims is to sketch (as it does with incomparable swiftness) the characters of the ship's company. The true re-enactment is in the long first scene of the second act where Antonio, in persuading Sebastian to murder Alonso, personates his own earlier action in plotting against Prospero, thus drawing it out of the past and placing it before us in the present. . . .

Dover Wilson greatly contributes to a right understanding of the play by stressing the first lines of the fifth act, when Prospero declares to Ariel that he will pardon his enemies, now quite at his mercy. . . . But when Dover Wilson would have this to represent Prospero's sudden conversion from a previously intended vengeance, I cannot follow him. It is true that Prospero shows a certain haste of temper up to that point of the play, and that he punishes Caliban and the two other conspirators against his life with some asperity. . . .

[But] Prospero does not change fundamentally during the play, [even] though, like Samson's, his own accomplished regeneration is put to the test. If he had seriously intended vengeance, why should he have stopped Sebastian and Antonio [from] murdering Alonso? That he did stop them is proof of his already achieved regeneration from vengeance to mercy. This act, and his talk to Ariel of taking part with his reason against his fury, are once again a re-enactment of a process now past, perhaps extending over a period of many years. I do not wish to imply that the re-enactment is weak or that the temptation to vengeance was not there all the time. Prospero's fury at the thought of Caliban's conspiracy, which interrupts the masque, must be allowed full weight . . . partly because Caliban's conspiracy typifies all the evil of the world which has so perplexed him, and partly because he is still tempted to be revenged on Alonso and Antonio. He means to pardon them, and he will pardon them. But beneath his reason's sway is this anger against them, which, like Satan's before the sun in *Paradise Lost*, disfigures his face. When Dover Wilson calls Prospero

> a terrible old man, almost a tyrannical and irascible as Lear
> at the opening of his play,

he makes a valuable comparison, but it should concern Prospero as he once was, not the character who meets us in the play, in whom these traits are mere survivals.

The advantage of this technique of re-enactment was economy, its drawback an inevitable blurring of the sharp outline. The theme of destruction, though exquisitely blended in the whole, is less vivid than it is in *The Winter's Tale*. Having made it so vivid in that play, Shakespeare was probably well content to put the stress on the theme of re-creation. And here he did not work solely by re-enactment. He strengthened Prospero's re-enacted regeneration by the figures of Ferdinand and Miranda. . . .

Not only do Ferdinand and Miranda sustain Prospero in representing a new order of things that has evolved out of destruction; they also vouch for its continuation. At the end of the play Alonso and Prospero are old and worn men. A younger and happier generation is needed to secure the new state to which Prospero has so painfully brought himself, his friends, and all his enemies save Caliban.

In his elegant study *Shakespeare* (New York, 1939) Mark Van Doren dissented from the assured tones of most of the critics who'd preceded him; he depicted *The Tempest* as a radically ambiguous play.

If Shakespeare thought of 'The Tempest' as the last play he would write he may have said to himself – silently, we must assume – that he could afford to let action come in it to a kind of rest; that its task was not so much to tell a story as to fix a vision; that the symbols he hitherto had defined his art by concealing might now confess themselves, even obtrude themselves, in measured dance and significant song; and that while he was at it he would recapitulate his poetic career. It is interesting to conjecture this, but it is perilous. 'The Tempest' does bind up in final form a host of themes with which its author has been concerned. It is a mirror in which, if we hold it very still, we can gaze backward at all of the recent plays; and behind them will be glimpses of a past as old as the tragedies, the middle comedies, and even 'A Midsummer Night's Dream.' Or it is a thicket of resonant trees, in an odd angle of the Shakespearean wood, which hums with echoes of every distant aisle. And certainly its symbols expose themselves as their ancestors in Shakespeare seldom or never did. The play seems to order itself in terms of its meanings; things in it stand for other things, so that we are tempted to search its dark backward for a single meaning, quite final for Shakespeare and quite abstract. The trouble is that the meanings are not self-evident. One interpretation of 'The Tempest' does not agree with another. And there is deeper trouble in the truth that any interpretation, even the wildest, is more or less plausible. This deep trouble, and this deep truth, should warn us that 'The Tempest' is a composition about which we had better not be too knowing. If it is one of Shakespeare's successes, and obviously it is, it will not yield its secret easily; or it has no secret to yield. Notwithstanding its visionary grace, its tendency toward lyric abstraction, it keeps that lifelike surface and that humor with which Shakespeare has always protected his meaning if he had one: that impenetrable shield off which the spears of interpretation invariably glance – or return, bent in the shaft and dulled at the point, to the hand of the thrower. It may well be that Shakespeare in 'The Tempest' is telling us for the last time, and consciously for the last time, about the world. But what he is telling us cannot be simple, or we could agree that it is this or that. Perhaps it is this: that the world is not simple. Or, mysteriously enough, that it is what we all take it to be, just as 'The Tempest' is whatever we would take it to be. Any set of symbols, moved close to this play, lights up as in an electric field. Its meaning, in other words, is precisely as rich as the human mind, and it says that the world is what it is. But what the world is cannot be said in a sentence. Or even in a poem as complete and beautiful as 'The Tempest.'

Separations and reconciliations are woven here within the circle of a remote and musical island where an enchanter, controlling the black magic of native witchcraft with the white magic of his liberal art, controls also a tempest until it brings to pass all things he has desired. The ship it founders on the shore, or seems to founder, carries his two chief enemies: his brother Antonio, whose treason has put the sea between them, and Alonso king of Naples, confederate to the treason. Prospero as duke of Milan had honored his brother with 'confidence sans bound.' But Antonio had abused his trust, and that is the first separation. The second has occurred likewise before the play begins, and nothing in the play can cure it. Alonso has lost his fair daughter Claribel by marriage to the King of Tunis, and indeed it is from that 'sweet marriage' that he is returning, bound sadly home for Naples, when he suffers shipwreck on Prospero's island. Alonso's loss of his remaining heir, his son Ferdinand, is temporary in so far as Prospero merely keeps them apart on the island until the separation has served its purpose, meanwhile entertaining the prince with the unearthly music of Ariel and with the charms of his own daughter Miranda; but it is permanent when Ferdinand and Miranda give themselves away to each other in love. And by the same blow, happy though it be, Prospero loses Miranda. The plot of 'The Tempest' is a complex of separations – and, swiftly and harmoniously, of reconciliations, so that Gonzalo can say:

> In one voyage
> Did Claribel her husband find at Tunis,
> And Ferdinand, her brother, found a wife
> Where he himself was lost, Prospero his dukedom
> In a poor isle, and all of us ourselves
> When no man was his own. . . .

Is Shakespeare Prospero, and is his magic the art with which he has fabricated thirty-seven plays? Is he now burying his book – abandoning the theater – and retiring where every third thought will be his grave? And does 'The Tempest' so signify? Answers are not too easy. Shakespeare has never dramatized himself before, and it may not have occurred to him to do so now. Also, 'The Tempest' is not a cantata; it is still a play, and it is ballasted with much life. It has snarling beasts and belching drunkards to match its innocent angels and white magicians. It contains two of Shakespeare's finest songs – 'Full fathom five thy father lies' and 'Come unto these yellow sands' – and two of his coarsest – ' 'Ban, 'Ban, Cacaliban' and 'The master, the swabber, the boatswain, and I.' And Ariel is more than an angelic musician; he is a mischief-maker, another Puck, unwilling at his work and restless under the burden of magic he bears. It can be doubted, in other words, that Shakespeare sat down solemnly to decorate his life's work with a secret signature. 'The Tempest,' pressed a little, yields this meaning as it yields most of the meanings ingenuity can insist upon, and yields it with grace. But a signature was the play itself, which, if its author had been given to such exercises, he might have recognized as one of the most beautiful literary objects ever made. He would scarcely, however, have been so conscious of what he had done. He is more likely to have let the moment go with four simple words: Now I will rest.

Somewhat more than a decade after Van Doren published his reflections on *The Tempest* Bonamy Dobrée expressed even more scepticism about the authorial self-references that many commentators had claimed to find in the play. In *Essays and Studies* (London, 1952) Dobrée asked whether 'in Prospero, Shakespeare himself [was] taking his farewell of the stage'.

I fear that some confusion has been caused by this ingenious conjecture, born some two hundred years after the play was acted. Perhaps as he wrote some of the passages a certain metaphorical resemblance between him and Prospero struck him whimsically, and he developed it a little, especially in the notorious farewell passage, which was a piece of common material about magicians he took almost verbatim from some lines in Golding's Ovid, and, as usual, transformed. Surely he would not have wished the likeness pushed too closely, in view of what Prospero is – a philosopher King, who like his prototype in *Measure for Measure*, was a disastrous ruler; a somewhat cruel, uncertain-tempered man, who far from renouncing anything, was going back to the enjoyment of worldly greatness; so we should not be pressed to regard the play as a kind of last will and testament, especially as Shakespeare did not break his wand or drown his book (*Henry VIII* followed, at least largely his, and portions of *Two Noble Kinsmen*). I admit it is possible that he had solved his problems on the plan of ordinary living, that he no longer wanted to write as he had done, and that he was moving into realms where he was finding, as Rimbaud was to find, that *paroles paiennes* would not express what now he had to say. However all that may be, I do not believe he was writing a kind of valedictory sermon; but that he was doing what every artist does in every work, exploring reality, here, in some ways, almost directly, and expressing the inapprehensible in symbols which he hoped might bring him illumination. . . .

. . . . I do not think that in dissecting a work of art we murder it, but it is possible that we may not be such skilful anatomists as we would like to think. . . . And if in the deliciously neat, humorous and perhaps deeply felt epilogue Prospero really is Shakespeare, what was it from that he was praying to be set free? May it not have been from what Lamb called the everlasting coxcombry of our moral pretensions? It is, certainly, always a difficult point to determine how far a great artist is conscious of what he is doing until he has done it. . . . What, as I believe, the poet does, is, by giving us a thing of delight, to release our spirits into a world of conjecture, freed of any immediate necessity for action. His materials are the thoughts, impulses, velleities which at the moment most occupy him; his symbols are the people he offers to our view, what happens to them, and the music of his utterance. The difference between works of art, in their importance, is the difference in the kind of realm into which we are released, to ponder and to muse, the degree of sensitive awareness induced in us. If we allow 'the meddling instinct,' as Wordsworth called it, to meddle too curiously, we prevent the work of art from giving us what it might. . . . So let us be a little delicate with this lovely thing which Shakespeare gave us, a thing composed of the impulses of love and forgiveness, of fear, of the sense of destiny, of the immateriality of our existence, of the brutality of matter; composed with grace of movement to the sound of entrancing music, a music sometimes terrible, sometimes miraculously sweet, but which brings the whole into a harmony which lies beyond contradiction.

For Reuben A. Brower the 'harmony' of *The Tempest* was best perceived in 'its metaphorical design, in the closeness and completeness with which its rich and varied elements are linked through almost inexhaustible analogies'. In *Fields of Light* (New York, 1951), Brower observed that

It is hard to pick a speech at random without coming on an

expression that brings us by analogy into direct contact with elements that seem remote because of their place in the action or because of the type of experience they symbolize. Opening the play at the second act we read,

> Four legs and two voices; a most delicate monster!

The last phrase is comic enough as used of Caliban and as issuing from the lips of Stephano, a 'most foul' speaker. But 'delicate' evokes a more subtle incongruity by recalling characters and a world we might suppose were forgotten. Stephano is parodying Prospero when he rebukes Ariel as 'a spirit too delicate / To act her [Sycorax's] earthy and most abhorr'd commands' and when he says,

> delicate Ariel,
> I'll set thee free for this!

We have in Stephano's words not only the familiar Shakespearean balancing of comic and serious, but a counterpointing of analogies that run throughout the play. 'Delicate' as the antithesis of 'earth' points to the opposition of Ariel and Caliban and to the often recurring earth–air symbolism of *The Tempest*. 'Delicate' used of this remarkable island creature echoes also the 'delicate temperance' of which the courtiers spoke and 'the air' that 'breathes . . . here most sweetly.' 'Monster' – almost another name for Caliban – balances these airy suggestions with an illusion to 'the people of the island . . . of monstrous shape' and thereby to the strain of fantastic sea lore in *The Tempest*, which is being parodied in this scene.

So viewed, Shakespeare's analogies may perhaps seem too much like exploding nebulae in an expanding though hardly ordered universe. But Shakespeare does not 'multiply variety in a wilderness of mirrors'; he makes use of a few fairly constant analogies that can be traced through expressions sometimes the same and sometimes extraordinarily varied. . . .

The surest proof of the pervasiveness of Shakespeare's design lies in the mere number of continuities that can be discovered in the play. . . . [Of these the six that are most important can be labelled] 'strange–wondrous,' 'sleep-and-dream,' 'sea–tempest,' 'music-and-noise,' 'earth–air,' 'slavery–freedom,' and 'sovereignty–conspiracy.'

All of these continuities appear during the second scene of Act I, which is an exposition of Shakespeare's metaphorical and dramatic designs for the entire play. . . .

By tracing two groups of 'tempest' expressions, metaphors of 'sea-swallowing' and images of 'clouds,' we may understand how these more complex analogies are built up. We may also see how Shakespeare moves from narrative fact to metaphor rich in moral and psychological implications. As in creating the analogies of 'strangeness' and 'sleep,' Shakespeare starts from a dramatic necessity: the audience must be told what the situation was in the storm scene with which the play opens, and they must learn through an actor (Miranda) how they are to take it. . . . Although there is a hint of magic in Miranda's vision of the tempest, she pictures it as a violent actuality:

> Had I been any god of power, I would
> Have sunk the sea within the earth, or e'er
> It should the good ship so have swallow'd and
> The fraughting souls within her.

As if there were an inner rhythm in these responses, this metaphor, like others we have been tracing, recurs in the plotting episode. Antonio is speaking of his sister Claribel, left behind in Tunis:

> she that from whom
> We all were sea-swallow'd, though some cast again,
> And by that destiny to perform an act
> Whereof what's past is prologue, what to come
> In yours and my discharge.

In this new context 'sea-swallowed' does several things at once. It brings back Miranda's horrified impression; but the magical nature of the storm now being known, the phrase reminds us that there was no 'sea-swallowing,' no actual sinking of 'fraughting souls.' Next, with a curiously Shakespearean 'glide and a jump' via the pun on 'cast,' 'sea-swallowed' merges into another metaphor (they are now 'cast' as actors in destiny's drama). 'Sea-swallowing' has become a metaphor that expresses destiny's extraordinary way of bringing Sebastian to the throne.

The irony of Antonio's words, which is clear to the audience, is made explicit later in the solemn speech in which Ariel explains the purpose of the tempest:

> You are three men of sin, whom Destiny –
> That hath to instrument this lower world
> And what is in't – the never-surfeited sea
> Hath caused to belch up you . . .

Few passages could show better how Shakespeare carries his analogies along and at the same time completely renews them. The 'belching up' recalls the wreck and the casting ashore and the earlier connection with destiny. But the sea's action is now described in much grosser terms and with grim sarcasm, while the oddly compact grammar makes 'the never-surfeited sea' very nearly a synonym for 'Destiny.' The violence though increased is now religious and moral; the imagery has become expressive of the strenuous punishment and purification of 'three men of sin.' So by the continuity of his varying metaphor Shakespeare has expressed an unbroken transition from actual storm to the storm of the soul. This sequence, which expresses both physical and metaphysical transformations, points very clearly to the key metaphor of *The Tempest*.

The recurrent cloud images present a similar sequence as they take on various symbolic meanings in the course of the play. 'Cloud' does not actually occur in the opening storm scene, but when Trinculo sees 'another storm brewing' and speaks of a 'black cloud,' we are reminded of the original tempest. The cloud undergoes an appropriate change in Trinculo's speech; it 'looks like a foul bombard that would shed his liquor.' This comic cloud is very different from 'the curl'd clouds' on which Ariel rides, though they too are associated with storms. The clouds of Caliban's exquisite speech are those of Ariel and the deities of the masque:

> and then, in dreaming,
> The clouds methought would open and show riches
> Ready to drop upon me . . .

Clouds – here linked with magical riches – become in Prospero's 'cloud-capp'd towers' speech a symbol for the unsubstantial splendor of the world. One of the subordinate metaphors there, the 'melting into air' and the 'dissolving' of the clouds, is picked up in Prospero's later words about the courtiers:

> The charm dissolves apace;
> And as the morning steals upon the night,
> Melting the darkness, so their rising senses
> Begin to chase the ignorant fumes that mantle
> Their clearer reason.

This dissolution of night clouds (suggested also by 'fumes') is a figure for the change from madness to sanity, from evil ignorance to the clear perceptions of reason. Although the cloud images of the play are so varied, they have a common symbolic value, for whether they are clouds of tempest or of visionary riches or of the soul, they are always magically unsubstantial. The reader is led to feel some touch of likeness among experiences as different as a storm at sea, a bit of drunken whimsy, a vision of heavenly and earthly beauty, and a spiritual regeneration. The cloud sequence, as an arc of metaphor, is in perfect relation to the gradual dramatic movement from tempest and punishment to fair weather and reconciliation, the images having meanings more and more remote from any actual storm. . . .

[But what] is the key metaphor through which the various continuities are linked, and how are they connected through it? Shakespeare's most direct expression of his key metaphor is 'sea change,' the key phrase of Ariel's song. But what does Shakespeare mean by 'sea change'? Ariel sings of 'bones' being made into 'coral' and of 'eyes' becoming 'pearls.' A change into something 'rich and strange,' we now understand, is a change 'out of nature.' 'Sea change' is a metaphor for 'magical transformation,' for metamorphosis. The key metaphor of the play is 'change' in this special sense, and 'change' is the analogy common to all of the continuities we have been tracing. . . .

. . . . The island is a world of fluid, merging states of being and forms of life. This lack of dependable boundaries between states is also expressed by the many instances of confusion between natural and divine. Miranda says that she might call Ferdinand

> A thing divine; for nothing natural
> I ever saw so noble.

Ferdinand cannot be sure whether she is a goddess or a maid, and Caliban takes Trinculo for a 'brave god.' There is a further comic variation on this theme in Trinculo's difficulty in deciding whether to classify Caliban as fish or man, monster or devil.

But 'change' is most clearly and richly expressed through the sequence of tempest images (especially 'cloud' and 'sea-swallowed') and through the noise-music antithesis. All kinds of sounds, harmonious and ugly, like the manifestations of sea and story, are expressive of magical transformation.

[As the protagonist addresses the other characters in the fifth act] Shakespeare makes us feel each shift in dramatic relationships as a magical transformation, whether it is the courtiers' return to sanity, or Prospero's restoration to his dukedom, or Ariel's flight into perpetual summer. While all of the 'slaves' and 'prisoners' are being freed, and while all of the 'sovereigns' are being restored, the sense of magical change is never wholly lost.

In '*The Tempest* and the Ancient Comic Tradition', an essay included in *English Stage Comedy*, edited by W. K. Wimsatt, Jr (New York, 1955), Bernard Knox elaborated on what Brower had written about 'slaves' and 'prisoners'. Knox began by noting that

> In *The Tempest* Shakespeare abandons the three familiar *milieux* in which most of his plays are set (classical antiquity, medieval England, and Renaissance Europe) for a nameless island which is remote even from that Tunis which is itself, according to Antonio, 'ten leagues beyond man's life.' This island is not only uncharted, it is one on which anything can happen; 'All torment, trouble, wonder, and amazement Inhabits heere.' The poet places his characters in a world which seems to be purely of his own creating; it seems in this respect significant that . . . no satisfactory source of *The Tempest* has yet been identified.
>
> In the so-called 'romances' of Shakespeare's last period there is an accelerated flight from probability; it is a movement beyond the 'probable impossibility' to the compete impossibility. In *The Tempest* the laws which govern objects existing in space and time as we know them are imperiously suspended. Until the solemn moment when Prospero abjures his rough magic, the action develops in a world which defies nature: 'These are not naturall events, they strengthen From strange, to stranger.' . . .
>
> But novel and fantastic effects (and in this play it is clear that Shakespeare was interested in producing them) have their dangerous side; they may, by trading too much on it, destroy that willing suspension of disbelief on which every dramatic performance depends – the audience may come to feel, with Gonzalo, 'Whether this be Or be not I'll not sweare.' The dramatist, by asking too much, may lose everything. Such a defiance of the normal laws of cause and effect in the operations of nature is especially dangerous in comedy, for comedy's appeal, no matter how contrived the plot may be, is to the audience's sense of solid values in a real world, to a critical faculty which can recognize the inappropriate. Tragedy, which questions normal human assumptions, may introduce the super- and the hyper-natural more safely than comedy, which depends on the solidity of those assumptions for a response. A comic poet who sets his characters in action, not in the world as we know it but in one which defies our expectation, must compensate for the strangeness of the events by making the essences and relationships of the characters immediately and strikingly familiar. To put it another way, the fantasy and originality of the setting

must be balanced and disciplined by a rigid adherence to tradition in character and plot.

This, I suggest, is a valid formula for *The Tempest*. It has certainly the most extraordinary and fantastic setting, for the sorcery of Prospero is a stranger thing than the familiar English fairy magic of *A Midsummer Night's Dream*. But in other ways it is the most rigidly traditional of all Shakespeare's comedies – with one exception. The exception is *The Comedy of Errors*, which is however apprentice work, a typical Renaissance *remaniement* of a Plautine original. *The Tempest* is as original as *The Comedy of Errors* is imitative; and yet they are the beginning and end of the same road. For the traditional foundation on which *The Tempest*'s cloud-capped towers are raised is the ancient comedy of Plautus, Terence, and (though the name would not have meant much to Shakespeare) Menander.

Like all proper foundations, this one is not conspicuous. But there are odd corners where its outline is visible in the superstructure. [Take, for example, Prospero's description of the torments Ariel suffered before his new master released him from the spell that Sycorax had imposed upon him.] The groans of a disobedient spirit imprisoned in a cloven pine by a 'blew ey'd hag' come 'as fast as Mill-wheeles strike': the simile illustrates the unfamiliar by appeal to an aspect of ordinary experience. Yet not, presumably, Ariel's ordinary experience: there are no mills in the strange economy of Prospero's island. ... The mill wheels of Shakespeare's simile come not from his own world but from the world of Plautine comedy, where with monotonous frequency the rebellious slave is threatened or actually punished with an assignment to the brutal labor of the mill. ...

Here the classical precedent is for a moment distinctly visible, but in general it does its work the more efficiently because it is not obtrusive. Below the strange and brilliant surface composed of medieval magic and Renaissance travel tales, the initial situation, the nature and relationships of most of the characters, the development of the action and its final solution are all conjugations of the basic paradigms of classical comedy.

One of the most influential of these paradigms relates to the existence in ancient society of a dividing line stricter and more difficult to cross than any social barrier has been since: the distinction between slave and free. The free man could not imagine a misfortune worse than slavery, nor the slave a greater blessing than freedom. Slave and free were not so much separate classes as separate worlds: Aristotle could go so far as to claim that they were separate natures. . . . Among other things [this division] provided a fixed contrast of condition and standards on which comedy could be based.

Ancient tragedy at the height of its development ignores the division and deals only with free men. . . . The place for slaves was comedy, which, says Aristotle, 'is an imitation of characters of a lower type'; and the lowest type imaginable was the slave.

When the dramatists of the Renaissance began to imitate the Roman comedies, slavery was a thing of the past in Europe (though not a few Elizabethan worthies made their fortunes by introducing it into the West Indies), but the ancient comic design was easily adapted to the conditions of a society which, like that of Elizabethan England, was based, however insecurely, on hierarchical social categories. Shakespearean comedy abounds in brilliant adaptations of the basic formula: the cruel reduction to his proper station suffered by Malvolio, who had 'greatness thrust' upon him; the exposure of Parolles 'the gallant militarist' as a 'past-saving slave'; above all the magnificent interpenetration of the two worlds of court and tavern in *Henry IV.* . . .

But in *The Tempest*, a Utopia which Shakespeare invented for himself (as Gonzalo invents his in the play), there is no need to translate the classic form: it can be used literally. Prospero is master (and incidentally an irritable old man with a marriageable daughter) and Ariel and Caliban are slaves. Prospero as sorcerer has the power to enslave and release the free men too: this contrast is relevant for all the characters of the play – one of its main components is what Brower has called 'the slavery–freedom continuity.' 'The "slaves" and "servants" of the play,' he points out, 'suffer various kinds of imprisonment, from Ariel in his "cloven pine" to Ferdinand's mild confinement, and before the end of Act IV everyone except Prospero and Miranda has been imprisoned in one way or another. During the course of Act V all the prisoners except Ferdinand (who has already been released) are set free. . . .'

[After his master threatens to return him to an even thicker tree than that from which he has earlier freed him,] Ariel acts as Prospero's eyes and ears, but, as befits the clever slave, with a certain initiative too. He rescues Alonso and Gonzalo from the conspirators, and his words suggest that, though he has a general commission to protect Gonzalo at any rate, the methods have been left to him. [Some of his speeches to Prospero sound] remarkably like the half-ironical servile exaggeration of the Plautine slave promising miracles of speed. . . . The comic aspects of Ariel's slavery are balanced by those of Prospero's mastery. . . . There is more than a touch in him of the Plautine old man, the irascible *senex* . . . , who may in the end turn out to have a heart of gold, but who for the first four acts has only a noticeably short temper and a rough tongue. . . .

Ariel, the slave whose nature is free, is balanced by Ferdinand, the free man and prince, who is enslaved. . . . The work he is doing is in fact Caliban's work. . . , and Ferdinand himself describes it as 'wodden slaverie.' But whereas Caliban has just declared his independence, and Ariel longs to be free, Ferdinand the free man is for the moment content to be a slave. . . . The service which he so willingly accepts is of course not that of his master, but that of his mistress. . . . And the multiple wit of these variations on the theme is dazzlingly displayed when he and Miranda plight their troth. . . . He accepts marriage (that is, bondage) with a heart 'as willing as bondage ere of freedome' (as willingly as Ariel, for example, would accept his liberty), but this acceptance, overheard by Prospero, is the signal for his release from the 'wodden slaverie' in which he is now bound.

Ferdinand, as we have seen, is contrasted to Ariel, but Ariel's real opposite is Caliban. . . . Caliban's employment is menial: while Ariel treads 'the Ooze of the salt deepe,' Caliban 'do's make our fire, Fetch in our wood, and serves in Offices That profit us.' . . .

Caliban's curses are highly original in expression – 'language as hobgoblin as his person,' says Dryden justly. Shakespeare has created a special vocabulary of invective appropriate to the savage apprehension of nature, but the expressions have the same dramatic characteristics as their venerable ancestors. . . . He 'needes must curse' because his cursing is vital to the comic essence of his nature; the scene in which he exchanges curses for Prospero's threats of punishment is a traditional feature of the comedy of master and slave.

Caliban is a sullen slave (a Sceparnio), a cursing slave (a Toxilus), and he is also a lecherous one. The only touch of low sexual humor in *The Tempest* is Caliban's unrepentant laughter when reminded of his attempt on Miranda's virtue: but that one laugh is enough to remind us that he has an ancestry reaching back through scurrilous Plautine slaves and Aristophanic comic actors wearing a leather *phallos* to the ithyphallic satyrs of the Greek vase paintings.

Caliban's meeting with Trinculo and Stephano is a servile parallel and parody of Miranda's meeting with Ferdinand; both mistress and slave are overcome with wonder at the vision of their counterparts in Neapolitan society. Miranda's worshiping remark, 'I might call him A thing divine,' is echoed in Caliban's 'that's a brave God, and beares Celestiall liquour'; while Ferdinand's 'My Language? Heavens' finds a base echo in Stephano's 'where the divell should he learn our language?' ... And Stephano the 'drunken butler' is a familiar figure; the slave in charge of his master's wine who drinks most of it himself is a standard character of the old comedy. In one of the better-known Plautine plays, the *Miles Gloriosus*, there is a scene with not one but two drunken butlers, one dead drunk on his back inside the house, the other drunk on his feet outside. . . .

The drunken butler dreams of a kingdom; he is not the first. It is instructive to compare his plans with those of Gripus, the Plautine slave who has fished a treasure out of the sea and intends to hang on to it:

> When I'm once free, I'll equip myself with property, an estate, a house. I'll go into trade with great ships; I'll be considered a King among Kings. . . .

This comic incongruity between the present and the imagined future, between station and ambition, is carried to hilarious lengths in the climactic appearance of Caliban and his associates. They 'do small all horse-pisse,' but Stephano's royal dignity is undisturbed. 'Wit shall not goe unrewarded while I am King of this Country,' he says, and Trinculo hails him in the titles of the old ballad, 'O King Stephano, O Peere: O worthy Stephano.' . . .

A few seconds later Stephano's kingdom melts into thin air. And on his last appearance he and Trinculo are ordered off with Caliban to perform menial tasks. . . . The stupid slaves, their wild ambitions foiled and their presumption suitably punished, are restored to their proper place and function.

Prospero has already been recognized as 'sometime Millaine' and restored to *his* proper station – 'thy dukedom I resigne' – the marriage of Ferdinand and Miranda is arranged; all that remains is to free the clever slave – 'to the elements Be free, and fare thou well' – and the play, except for a version of the conventional Plautine request for applause, is over, the traditional paradigm complete.

Since the late 1950s, when Frank Kermode published his influential edition of the play for the Arden Shakespeare (London, 1958), *The Tempest* has generally been discussed in terms of its genre (what Kermode labels 'pastoral tragicomedy'), its portrayal of Caliban ('the core of the play', in Kermode's opinion), its thematic relationships to the travel literature, both ancient and modern, that would have been familiar to Shakespeare and his contemporaries, its contrast between 'Art and Nature', its 'Masque Elements', and, increasingly in recent years, its allusions to, or echoes of, contemporary accounts of the New World. As Kermode observes,

> Prospero's assumption of his right to rule the island, 'to be the lord on't', is the natural assumption of a European prince. . . . The natives were worth some trouble; although they had no rational language, they did not lack certain mechanic arts, like the building of dams for fish, upon which the European settler long remained dependent. Many stratagems were devised to expedite the subjection of the natives. Stephano's claim to be descended from the moon was commonly made by unscrupulous voyagers who seized the chance of turning to account the polytheism of the Indians. There is ample testimony to the corrupting effect upon natives of contact with dissolute Europeans — Christian savages sent to convert heathen savages, as Fuller put it. . . . There are points in the play at which Shakespeare uses Caliban to indicate how much baser the corruption of the civilized can be than the bestiality of the natural, and in these places he is using his natural man as a criterion of civilized corruption, as Montaigne had done. . . .
>
> [Caliban is] the product of sexual union between a witch and an incubus, and this would account for his deformity, whether the devil-lover was Setebos (all pagan gods were classified as devils) or, as W. C. Curry infers, some aquatic demon. . . .
>
> . . . His origins and character are natural in the sense that they do not partake of grace, civility, and art; he is ugly in body, associated with an evil natural magic, and unqualified for rule or nature. He exists at the simplest level of sensual pain and pleasure, fit for lechery because love is beyond his nature, and a natural slave of demons. He hears music with pleasure, as music can appeal to the beast who lacks reason; and indeed he resembles Aristotle's bestial man. . . . [Even so] there is possibly a hint, for which there is no support in Aristotle, that the bestial Caliban gains a new spiritual dimension from his glimpse of the 'brave spirits'. Whether or no this is true, he is an extraordinarily powerful and comprehensive type of Nature; an inverted pastoral hero, against whom civility and the Art which improves Nature may be measured. . . .
>
> . . . [Prospero's] Art is supernatural; the spirits he commands are the daemons of Neo-Platonism, the criterion of whose goodness is

not the Christian one of adherence to, or defection from, God, but of immateriality or submersion in matter. He deals with spirits high in the scale of goodness, and if lesser spirits ('weak masters') are required, the superior daemon controls them on his behalf. He is '*divinorum cultor & interpres*, a studious observer and expounder of divine things', and his Art is 'the absolute perfection of Natural Philosophy'. Natural Philosophy includes the arts of astrology, alchemy, and ceremonial magic, to all of which Prospero alludes.

. . . [His magic], being the Art of supernatural virtue which belongs to the redeemed world of civility and learning, is the antithesis of the black magic of Sycorax. Caliban's deformity is the result of evil natural magic, and it stands as a natural criterion by which we measure the world of Art, represented by Prospero's divine magic and the supernaturally sanctioned beauty of Miranda and Ferdinand.

Writing a few years after the publication of the Arden edition of *The Tempest*, Northrop Frye reinforces many of Frank Kermode's conclusions. In his introduction to the Pelican text of the play (Baltimore, 1969), Frye argues that

we distort the play if we think of Prospero as supernatural, just as we do if we think of Caliban as a devil. Prospero is a tempest-raiser like the witches in *Macbeth*, though morally at the opposite pole; he is a 'white' magician. Anyone with Prospero's powers is an agent of fate, a cheating fate if evil, a benevolent fate or providence if motivated as he is. Great courage was required of all magicians, white or black, for the elemental spirits they controlled were both unwilling and malignant, and any sign of faltering meant terrible disaster. Ariel is loyal because of his debt of gratitude to Prospero, and because he is a very high-class spirit, too delicate to work for a black witch like Sycorax. But even he has a short memory, and has to be periodically reminded what his debt of gratitude is. . . .

. . . It has often been thought that Prospero is a self-portrait of Shakespeare, and there may well be something in him of a harassed overworked actor-manager, scolding the lazy actors, praising the good ones in connoisseur's language, thinking up jobs for the idle, constantly aware of his limited time before his show goes on, his nerves tense and alert for breakdowns while it is going on, looking forward longingly to peaceful retirement, yet in the meantime having to go out and beg the audience for applause.

Prospero's magic, in any case, is an 'art' which includes, in fact largely consists of, music and drama. Dramatists from Euripides to Pirandello have been fascinated by the paradox of reality and illusion in drama: the play is an illusion like the dream, and yet a focus of reality more intense than life affords. The action of *The Tempest* moves from sea to land, from chaos to new creation, from reality to realization. What seems at first illusory, the magic and music, becomes real, and the *Realpolitik* of Antonio and Sebastian becomes illusion. In this island the quality of one's dreaming is an index of character. . . .

Few plays are so haunted by the passing of time as *The Tempest*: it has derived even its name from a word (*tempestas*) which means time as well as tempest. Timing was important to a magician: everything depended on it when the alchemist's project gathered to a head; astrologers were exact observers of time ('The very minute bids thee ope thine ear,' Prospero says to Miranda), and the most famous of all stories about magicians, the story told in Greene's play *Friar Bacon and Friar Bungay*, had the warning of 'time is past' for its moral. The same preoccupation affects the other characters too, from the sailors in the storm to Ariel watching the clock for his freedom. . . .

. . . The scene of the play, an island somewhere between Tunis and Naples, suggests the journey of Aeneas from Carthage to Rome. Gonzalo's identification of Tunis and Carthage, and the otherwise tedious business about 'Widow Dido' in the second act, seems almost to be emphasizing the parallel. Like *The Tempest*, the *Aeneid* begins with a terrible storm and goes on to tell a story of wanderings in which a banquet with harpies figures prominently. Near the route of Aeneas' journey, according to Virgil, was the abode of Circe, of whom (at least in her Renaissance form) Sycorax is a close relative. Circe suggests Medea, whose speech in Ovid's *Metamorphoses* is the model for Prospero's renunciation speech. Echoes from the shipwreck of St Paul (Ariel's phrase 'Not a hair perished' recalls Acts xxvii, 34), from St Augustine, who also had associations with Carthage, and from Apuleius, with his interest in magic and imitation, are appropriate enough in such a play. Most of the traditional magical names of elemental spirits were of Hebrew origin, and 'Ariel,' a name occurring in the Bible (Isaiah xxix, 1), was among them.

[At the opposite extreme from Ariel is the character Prospero refers to as 'this thing of darkness'.] Nobody has a good word for Caliban: he is a born devil to Prospero, an abhorred slave to Miranda, and to others not obviously his superiors either in intelligence or virtue he is a puppy-headed monster, a mooncalf, and a plain fish. Yet he has his own dignity, and he is certainly no Yahoo, for all his ancient and fishlike smell. True, Shakespeare, like Swift, clearly does not assume that the natural man on Caliban's level is capable also of a reasonable life. But he has taken pains to make Caliban as memorable and vivid as any character in the play. . . .

. . . In the wedding masque of the fourth act and the recognition scene of the fifth . . . we find ourselves moving, not out of the world, but from an ordinary to a renewed and ennobled vision of nature. The masque shows the meeting of a fertile earth and a gracious sky introduced by the goddess of the rainbow, and leads up to a dance of nymphs representing the spring rains with reapers representing the autumn harvest. The masque has about it the freshness of Noah's new world, after the tempest had receded and the rainbow promised that seedtime and harvest should not cease. There is thus a glimpse, as Ferdinand recognizes, of an Earthly Paradise, where, as in Milton's Eden, there is no winter but spring and autumn 'Danced hand in hand.' In the last act, as in *The Winter's Tale*, there is a curious pretense that some of the characters have died and are brought back to life. The discovery of Ferdinand is greeted by Sebastian, of all people, as 'A most high miracle.' But the miracles are those of a natural, and therefore also a moral and intellectual, renewal of life.

Northrop Frye concludes his remarks with the exhortation that 'However we take it, *The Tempest* is a play not simply to be read or seen or even studied, but possessed.' Perhaps so, but most of the commentary that has appeared since Frye wrote has stressed how difficult it is merely to comprehend the play, let alone possess it. In 'Miraculous Harp: A Reading of Shakespeare's *Tempest*', *Shakespeare Studies*, 5 (1969), Harry Berger, Jr, focuses on what he regards as 'puzzling items' in the drama.

First, Prospero's language in describing the usurpation to Miranda encourages us to believe that he is partly responsible for what happened, yet *he* never seems to take this into account; throughout the course of the play, he acts the part of the good man wronged by villains, and he is not above an occasional reference to his injured merit. Second, Gonzalo, for all his goodness, was in effect Antonio's accomplice; as Alonso's counselor he mitigated the harshness of Prospero's exile, but the fact remains that he was master of the design, responsible for its execution. . . .

Third: a very important set of questions emerging from the exposition in I.ii have never, to my knowledge, been pursued. What are we really to do with Ariel, Sycorax, and Caliban? Why was Ariel punished by being stuck in a tree, why does he continually ask for his freedom, why the names *Sycorax* and *Caliban*, why the business about the witch's exile from Africa with its obvious echoes of Prospero's exile from Europe? What to make of a fact which many readers have noticed, the difference between Prospero's view of Caliban and ours? Why do we respond to certain qualities in Caliban which Prospero ignores, and why are we made to feel that the magician is more vindictive than he needs to be? . . . Finally, why the twenty-line epilogue, in which Prospero asks the audience for applause, sympathy, and release? . . .

. . . The name *Sycorax* means, among other things, *hooped together*: 'with age and envy grown into a hoop,' as Prospero says. [And as for Caliban,] to the familiar etymological interpretations of his name – *cannibal* and *blackness* (Romany, *cauliban*, E. K. Chambers) – I would add *Kali* (beauty) + *ban* or *bane*, and I would translate it in two ways: first, and most simply, 'the bane of beauty,' which is the way Prospero comes to see him. The second translation is a little more complicated, and it refers to what *we* – as opposed to Prospero – see in Caliban: 'banned from beauty, beauty is his bane.' . . .

The important point to be made about Caliban is that he can by no means be reduced to a figure of pure evil, the antithesis of Miranda or Ariel, the counterpart of Antonio. His baseness is shot through with gleams of aspiration, though the mixture is unstable and the diverse motives often undifferentiated. He displays the most transcendent, the most poignant, and the most natural urges of man as well as the most foolish and murderous and disloyal. . . . Situational parallels exist to Ferdinand (the logbearing), to Antonio (the plot), and to Prospero (who supplanted him on the island). His longings appear modulated into ideal civilized form in Miranda's capacity for wonder and Ferdinand's for worshipful service; his visions of riches are sublimed in Prospero's insubstantial pageant and cloudcapped towers. Prospero's original openness and subsequent antipathy to Antonio are reflected by both himself and Caliban in their island relationship. Finally, though it may seem odd, Caliban is not unlike Gonzalo in his attitude toward the island, and in the way his simpleminded good will is abused by Stephano and Trinculo (as Gonzalo's by Sebastian and Antonio). Childlike in his fears and passions, ingenuous in the immediacy of his responses to nature and man, open in the expression of feeling,

Caliban at his most evil and traitorous shows up as a mere puppy, a
comic Vice, a crude conspirator. . . .

. . . Prospero's ethnical and symbolic reduction of Caliban to a
figure of pure evil may suggest his share of guilt in encouraging
Antonio to his crime; for unwittingly he did everything he could to
cultivate whatever dram of evil his brother may have been heir to;
in that sense, he – no less than Antonio – new-created the creatures
that were his and gave them the occasion to say, with Caliban,
'have a new master; get a new man.'

In a way that complements Harry Berger's analysis of the
identities of Sycorax and Caliban, Karol Berger adduces some
illuminating background on Ariel's role in the execution of
'Prospero's Art'. Writing in *Shakespeare Studies*, 10 (1977),
Berger says that the Banquet Scene in III.iii

contains suggestive reminiscences of the Eucharistic ritual in which
God sends down his Holy Spirit (whom the Christian iconography
often represents as the dove) to bless the sacrificial offering, so that
the sacrifice may be efficacious. The rite commemorates the
sacrifice of Christ explained by him to the disciples during the Last
Supper [Matthew 26:26–28]. . . .

Prospero understands very well that the reconciliation, the new
covenant, and the purgation of sins (in particular the primordial
sin of violence) can be achieved only through a common sacrifice.
But Alonso is not ready yet. He is still the man of sin. . . . For this
reason the Communion of the sacrificial meal cannot be efficacious. D. P. Walker correctly observes that the Mass was the
fundamental influence behind medieval and Renaissance magic.
Prospero's spectacle is a mass *manqué*. The invisible magus (who
several times throughout the play is compared to God) sends down
his spirit on the banquet, only this spirit is not the dove but a harpy
and, instead of blessing the meal and transforming it into a true
sacrifice, he snatches it away, as the harpies did with Aeneas'
sacrificial banquet. Thus the Communion does not take place.
After the performance Prospero thanks Ariel: 'Bravely the figure of
this Harpy hast thou / Perform'd, my Ariel; a grace it had
devouring' (III.iii.83–84). This 'devouring grace' sums up Ariel's
role most amusingly. The spirit devours the meal instead of
blessing it with divine grace.

At least since the beginning of the nineteenth century, scholars
have recognized that Ariel's name figures conspicuously in the first
verse of Isaiah 29. . . . In the Geneva Bible (which is the translation

usually employed by Shakespeare), this verse reads: 'Ah altar, altar of the citie that David dwelt in . . .' The word 'altar' is explained in a marginal note: 'The Ebrewe worde Ariel signifieth the lyon of God, and signifieth the altar, because the altar seemed to devoure the sacrifice that was offred to God.' Ariel, explains this note, was the name of a voracious beast and, by association, also the name of the altar which 'seemed to devoure the sacrifice.'

The way Karol Berger reads the play, reinforcing a tradition that extends back at least to the eighteenth century, '*The Tempest* presents Prospero as the defender of legitimate power.' In the past two decades, however, that assumption has been subjected to a steady barrage of interrogation. As Charles Frey observes in an article entitled '*The Tempest* and the New World', *Shakespeare Quarterly*, 30 (1979), a new generation of scholars has called attention to

> how prophetic the play seems today, particularly in its depiction of sociopolitical problems within colonial and developing nations. As Leslie Fiedler, one of the more extreme proponents, would have it, by the time Prospero has put down the plot of Caliban, Stephano, and Trinculo,
>
> > the whole history of imperialist America has been prophetically revealed to us in brief parable: from the initial act of expropriation through the Indian wars to the setting up of reservations, and from the beginnings of black slavery to the first revolts and evasions. With even more astonishing prescience, *The Tempest* foreshadows as well the emergence of that democracy of fugitive white slaves, deprived and cultureless refugees from a Europe they never owned, which D. H. Lawrence was so bitterly to describe. And it prophesies, finally, like some inspired piece of science fiction before its time, the revolt against the printed page, the anti-Gutenberg rebellion for which Marshall McLuhan is currently a chief spokesman.

Writers in this mode tend to weave elaborate themes of colonialism, race relations, and cultural history out of *The Tempest*. But they sometimes work out themes of even broader design, as when Leo Marx, with convincing particularity, suggests ways in which 'the topography of *The Tempest* anticipates the moral geography of the American imagination.'

Frey insists that 'With many new worlds, including ours, *The Tempest* does, in truth, have much to do.' And he suggests that 'in order to explore the meanings implicit in the play's peculiar merger of history and romance, interpreters must travel and labor still onward.'

In that spirit Francis Barker and Peter Hulme advocate an orientation to the play in which 'the contextual background – which previously had served merely to highlight the profile of the individual text – gives way to the notion of *intextuality*, according to which, in keeping with the Saussurean model of language, no text is intelligible except in its differential relations with other texts'. In an essay entitled 'Nymphs and reapers heavily vanish: the discursive contexts of *The Tempest*' – published in *Alternative Shakespeares*, a collection compiled by John Drakakis (London, 1985) – Barker and Hulme express surprise that interpreters of the play have been so reluctant to scrutinize 'Prospero's version' of what happened on the island prior to the beginning of the action.

The play's second scene commences with Prospero's long narrative to his daughter. After she dozes off,

> Prospero is goaded by Ariel's demands for freedom into recounting at some length how his servitude began, when, at their first contact, Prospero freed him from the cloven pine in which he had earlier been confined by Sycorax. Caliban then offers his compelling and defiant counter to Prospero's single sentence when, in a powerful speech, he recalls the initial mutual trust which was broken by Prospero's assumption of the political control made possible by the power of his magic. Caliban, 'Which first was mine own King', now protests that 'here you sty me / In this hard rock, whiles you do keep from me / The rest o'th' island' (I.ii.344–6).
>
> It is remarkable that these contestations of 'true beginnings' have been so commonly occluded by an uncritical willingness to identify Prospero's voice as direct and reliable authorial statement, and therefore to ignore the lengths to which the play goes to dramatize its problems with the proper beginning of its own story. Such identification hears, as it were, only Prospero's play, follows only his stage directions, not noticing that Prospero's play and *The Tempest* are not necessarily the same thing. . . .
>
> . . . The purpose of Prospero's main plot is to secure recognition of his claim to the usurped duchy of Milan, a recognition sealed in

the blessing given by Alonso to the prospective marriage of his own son to Prospero's daughter. As part of this, Prospero reduces Caliban to a role in the supporting sub-plot, as instigator of a mutiny that is programmed to fail, thereby forging an equivalence between Antonio's initial *putsch* and Caliban's revolt. This allows Prospero to annul the memory of his failure to prevent his expulsion from the dukedom, by repeating it as a mutiny that he will, this time, forestall. But, in addition, the playing out of the colonialist narrative is thereby completed: Caliban's attempt – tarred with the brush of Antonio's supposedly self-evident viciousness – is produced as final and irrevocable confirmation of the natural treachery of savages. . . .

. . . The shakiness of Prospero's position is indeed staged, but in the end his version of history remains *authoritative*, the larger play acceding as it were to the containment of the conspirators in the safely comic mode, Caliban allowed only his poignant and ultimately vain protests against the venality of his co-conspirators.

That this comic closure is necessary to enable the European 'reconciliation' which follows hard on its heels – the patching up of a minor dynastic dispute within the Italian nobility – is, however, itself symptomatic of the text's own anxiety about the threat posed to its decorum by its New World materials. . . .

No adequate reading of the play could afford not to comprehend *both* the anxiety and the drive to closure it necessitates. Yet these aspects of the play's 'rich complexity' have been signally ignored by European and North American critics, who have tended to listen exclusively to Prospero's voice: after all, he speaks their language. It has been left to those who have suffered colonial usurpation to discover and map the traces of that complexity by reading in full measure Caliban's refractory place in both Prospero's play and *The Tempest*.

Like other exponents of the cultural materialist school of post-structural analysis, Barker and Hulme appear to be persuaded that, notwithstanding its sympathy to an anti-colonialist view of the political situation it depicts, *The Tempest* is finally complicit in the colonizing enterprise that was gathering momentum as Shakespeare's career drew to a close. But in a recent assessment, 'The Case of Colonialism in *The Tempest*' – see *Shakespeare Quarterly*, 40 (1989) – Meredith Anne Skura examines some of the assumptions behind such inferences. Skura grants 'the literal resemblance between' the plot of *The Tempest* 'and certain events and attitudes in English colonial history: Europeans arrive in the New World and assume they can appropriate what properly belongs to the New World Other, who is then "erased" '. Indeed,

> The similarities are clear and compelling – more so than in many cases of new historical readings; the problem, however, is that while there are also many literal differences between *The Tempest* and colonialist fictions and practice, the similarities are taken to be so compelling that the differences are ignored. Thus Caliban is taken to 'be' a Native American despite the fact that a multitude of details differentiate Caliban from the Indian as he appeared in the travelers' reports from the New World. Yet it does seem significant that, despite his closeness to nature, his naiveté, his devil worship, his susceptibility to European liquor, and, above all, his 'treachery' – characteristics associated in writings of the time with the Indians – he nonetheless lacks almost all of the defining external traits in the many reports from the New World – no superhuman physique, no nakedness or animal skin (indeed, an English 'gaberdine' instead), no decorative feathers, no arrows, no pipe, no tobacco, no body paint, and – as Shakespeare takes pains to emphasize – no love of trinkets and trash. . . . Caliban in fact is more like the devils Strachey expected to find on the Bermuda island (but didn't) than like the Indians whom adventurers did find in Virginia, though he is not wholly a monster from the explorers' wild tales either.
>
> [Nor does it seem to matter to those who read *The Tempest* as supportive of colonialist imperialism] that the play seems *anti*-colonialist to the degree that it qualifies Prospero's scorn by showing Caliban's virtues, or that Prospero seems to achieve some kind of transcendence over his own colonialism when at the end of the play he says, 'This thing of darkness I acknowledge mine.' . . .
>
> . . . In the effort to identify Caliban as one more colonialist representation of the Other, we fail to notice how remarkable it is that such a Caliban should exist. In 1611 there were in England no literary portrayals of New World inhabitants and certainly no fictional examples of colonialist discourse. Insofar as *The Tempest* does in some way allude to an encounter with a New World native (and I will for the remainder of this essay accept this premise), it is the very first work of nonliterary discourse. Outside of Shakespeare, however, there would be none in literature until two years after *The Tempest*, when they began to appear – feathers and all – in masques. And Shakespeare went out of his way to invent Caliban: [William] Strachey's [1610] account of the wreck on the

uninhabited Bermuda islands – Shakespeare's main New World source – contains, of course, no island natives. For these Shakespeare had to turn elsewhere in Strachey and in others who described the mainland colony in Virginia. Shakespeare was the first to show one of *us* mistreating a native, the first to represent a native from the inside, the first to allow a native to complain onstage, and the first to make that New World encounter problematic enough to generate the current attention to the play. . . .

Shakespeare's assimilation of elements from historical colonialist discourse was neither entirely isolated from other uses nor innocent of their effects. Nonetheless, the 'colonialism' in his play is linked not only to Shakespeare's indirect participation in an ideology of political exploitation and erasure but also to his direct participation in the psychological after-effects of having experienced the exploitation and erasure inevitable in being a child in an adult's world. He was not merely reproducing a pre-existent discourse; he was also crossing it with other discourses, changing, enlarging, skewing, and questioning it. Our sense of *The Tempest*'s participation in 'colonialist discourse' should be flexible enough to take account of such crossings; indeed our notion of that in which such discourse consisted should be flexible enough to include the whole of the text that constitutes the first English example of fictional colonialist discourse.

In a dazzling illustration of the kind of exegetical flexibility Skura pleads for, Stephen Greenblatt concludes *Shakespearean Negotiations* (Berkeley, 1988) with an essay, 'Martial Law in the Land of Cockaigne', that relates *The Tempest* not only to colonialist discourse but to contemporary events in which 'maimings and executions' were publicly displayed 'to arouse fear and to set the stage for the royal pardons that would demonstrate that the prince's justice was tempered with mercy'. According to Greenblatt,

> Renaissance England had a subtle conception of the relation between anxiety and the fashioning of the individual subject, and its governing institutions developed discursive and behavioral strategies to implement this conception by arousing anxiety and then transforming it through pardon into gratitude, obedience, and love. These strategies were implicated from their inception in the management of spectacles and the fashioning of texts; that is,

they are already implicated in cultural practices that are essential to the making and staging of plays. There was no need in this case for special modifications to adapt the techniques of salutary anxiety to the theater. Indeed the theater is a virtual machine for deploying these techniques in a variety of registers, from the comic anxiety that gives way to the clarification and release of marriage to the tragic anxiety that is at once heightened and ordered by the final solemnity of death. It was not surprising that the disguised duke of *Measure for Measure*, who fuses the strategies of statecraft and religion, has also seemed to many critics an emblem of the playwright. . . .

When near the close of his career Shakespeare reflected upon his own art with still greater intensity and self-consciousness than in *Measure for Measure*, he once again conceived of the playwright as a princely creator of anxiety. But where in *Measure for Measure* disguise is the principal emblem of this art, in *The Tempest* the emblem is the far more potent and disturbing power of magic. Prospero's chief magical activity throughout *The Tempest* is to harrow the other characters with fear and wonder and then to reveal that their anxiety is his to create and allay. . . .

. . . The rituals of humiliation and suffering through which Prospero makes Ferdinand and Miranda pass evidently have their desired effect: at the end of the play the couple displayed to the amazed bystanders are revealed to be not only in a state of love but in a state of symbolic war. The lovers, you will recall, are discovered playing chess, and Miranda accuses Ferdinand of cheating. The deepest happiness is represented in this play as a state of playful tension. . . .

[In a way that parallels the story William Strachey tells in his account of the providential rescue of the *Sea Venture* in Bermuda, and of the eventual arrival of Sir Thomas Gates as governor of the Virginia colony at Jamestown, *The Tempest* shows how a] crisis of authority – deposition from power, exile, impotence – gives way through the power of [the protagonist's] art to a full restoration. From this perspective Prospero's magic is the romance equivalent of martial law.

Yet *The Tempest* seems to raise troubling questions about this authority. . . . A Renaissance audience might have found the locus of these questions in the ambiguous status of magic, an ambiguity deliberately heightened by the careful parallels drawn between Prospero and the witch Sycorax and by the attribution to Prospero of claims made by Ovid's witch Medea. But for a modern audience, at least, the questions center on the figure of Caliban, whose claim to the legitimate possession of the island . . . is never really answered, or rather is answered by Prospero only with hatred, torture, and enslavement. Though he treats Caliban as less than human, Prospero finally expresses, in a famously enigmatic phrase, a sense of connection with his servant-monster, standing anxious and powerless before him: 'this thing of darkness I / Acknowle ' mine' (5.1.275–76). He may intend these words only as a declaration of ownership, but it is difficult not to hear in them some deeper recognition of affinity, some half-conscious acknowledgment of guilt. At the play's end the princely magician appears anxious and powerless before the audience to beg for indulgence and freedom.

As the epilogue is spoken, Prospero's magical power and princely authority – figured in the linked abilities to raise winds and to pardon offenders – pass, in a startling display of the circulation of social energy, from the performer onstage to the crowd of spectators. In the play's closing moments the marginal, vulnerable actor, more than half-visible beneath the borrowed robes of an assumed dignity, seems to acknowledge that the imaginary forces with which he has played reside ultimately not in himself or in the playwright but in the multitude. The audience is the source of his anxiety, and it holds his release quite literally in its hands: without the crowd's applause his 'ending is despair' (Epilogue, 15). This admission of dependence includes a glance at the multitude's own vulnerability:

> As you from crimes would pardon'd be,
> Let your indulgence set me free.
>
> (Epilogue, 19–20)

But it nonetheless implicates the prince as well as the player in the experience of anxiety and the need for pardon.

SUGGESTIONS FOR FURTHER READING

Many of the works quoted in the preceding survey (or excerpts from them) can be found in modern collections of criticism. Of particular interest are the following two anthologies:

Bloom, Harold (ed.), *William Shakespeare's 'The Tempest'* (Modern Critical Interpretations), New York: Chelsea House, 1988.
Palmer, D. J. (ed.), *Shakespeare, 'The Tempest': A Casebook*, Basingstoke: Macmillan, 1991.

The following publications also include valuable discussions of the play:

Adams, Robert M., *Shakespeare: The Four Romances*, New York: Norton, 1989.
Auden, W. H., 'The Sea and the Mirror: A Commentary on Shakespeare's *The Tempest*', *The Collected Poetry*, New York: Random House, 1945.
—— *The Dyer's Hand and Other Essays*, London: Faber & Faber, 1962.
Baker, Houston A.,' 'Caliban's Triple Play', *Critical Inquiry*, 13 (1986), 182–96.
Bender, John F., 'The Day of *The Tempest*', *ELH: English Literary History*, 47 (1980), 235–58.
Black, James, 'The Latter End of Prospero's Commonwealth', *Shakespeare Survey*, 43 (1991), 29–41.
Breight, Curt, ' "Treason doth never prosper": *The Tempest* and the Discourse of Treason', *Shakespeare Quarterly*, 41 (1990), 1–28.
Brockbank, Philip, '*The Tempest*: Conventions of Art and Empire', in *Later Shakespeare*, ed. John Russell Brown and Bernard Harris, London: Edward Arnold, 1959.
Brown, Paul, ' "This thing of darkness I acknowledge mine": *The Tempest* and the discourse of colonialism', in *Political Shakespeare: New Essays in Cultural Materialism*, ed. Jonathan Dollimore and Alan Sinfield, Ithaca, N.Y.: Cornell University Press, 1985.
Cartelli, Thomas, 'Prospero in Africa: *The Tempest* as Colonialist Text

and Pretext', in *Shakespeare Reproduced*, ed. Jean E. Howard and Marion F. O'Connor, London: Methuen, 1987.

Cheyfitz, Eric, *The Poetics of Imperialism: Translation and Colonization from 'The Tempest' to Tarzan*, New York: Oxford University Press, 1991.

Clark, Sandra, *William Shakespeare: 'The Tempest'* (Penguin Critical Studies), Harmondsworth: Penguin, 1988.

Comito, Terry, 'Caliban's Dream: The Topography of Some Shakespearean Gardens', *Shakespeare Studies*, 14 (1981), 23–54.

Curry, Walter Clyde, *Shakespeare's Philosophical Patterns*, Baton Rouge: Louisiana State University Press, 1937.

Daniell, David, *The Tempest* (Critics' Debate), Atlantic Highlands, N.J.: Humanities Press International, 1989.

Dawson, Anthony B., '*Tempest* in a Teapot: Critics, Evaluation, Ideology', in *'Bad' Shakespeare*, ed. Maurice Charney, Rutherford, N.J.: Fairleigh Dickinson University Press, 1988.

Dobson, Michael, ' "Remember / First to possess his books"; The Appropriation of *The Tempest*, 1700–1800', *Shakespeare Survey*, 43 (1991), 99–107.

Erlich, Bruce, 'Shakespeare's Colonial Metaphor: On the Social Function of Theatre in *The Tempest*', *Science and Society*, 41 (1977), 43–65.

Ewbank, Inga-Stina, '*The Tempest* and After', *Shakespeare Survey*, 43 (1991), 109–19.

Felperin, Howard, 'Making it "neo": The New Historicism and Renaissance Literature', *Textual Practice*, 1 (1987), 262–77.

—— *Shakespearean Romance*, Princeton: Princeton University Press, 1972.

Fiedler, Leslie A., *The Stranger in Shakespeare*, New York: Stein and Day, 1972.

Flagstad, Karen, ' "Making this Place Paradise": Prospero and the Problem of Caliban in *The Tempest*', *Shakespeare Studies*, 18 (1986), 205–33.

Frye, Northrop, *A Natural Perspective: The Development of Shakespearean Comedy and Romance*, New York: Columbia University Press, 1965.

—— *The Secular Scripture: A Study of the Structure of Romance*, Cambridge, Mass.: Harvard University Press, 1976.

Garber, Marjorie, 'The Eye of the Story: Structure and Myth in Shakespeare's *Tempest*', *Hebrew University Studies in Literature*, 8 (1980), 13–43.

Gillies, John, 'Shakespeare's Virginian Masque', *ELH: English Literary History*, 53 (1986), 673–707.

Greenblatt, Stephen, 'Learning to Curse: Aspects of Linguistic Colonialism in the Sixteenth Century', in *First Images of America*, vol. 2, ed. Fredi Chiapelli, Los Angeles: University of California Press, 1976.

Griffiths, Trevor R., ' "This Island's mine": Caliban and Colonialism', *Yearbook of English Studies*, 13 (1983), 159–80.

Gurr, Andrew, '*The Tempest*'s Tempest at Blackfriars', *Shakespeare Survey*, 41 (1989), 91–102.

Hamilton, Donna B., *Virgil and 'The Tempest': The Politics of Imitation*, Columbus: Ohio State University Press, 1990.

Harris, Anthony, *Night's Black Agents: Witchcraft and Magic in Seventeenth-Century English Drama*, Manchester: Manchester University Press, 1980.

Hartwig, Joan, *Shakespeare's Tragicomic Vision*, Baton Rouge: Louisiana State University Press, 1972.

Hawkes, Terence, 'Swisser-Swatter: Making a Man of English Letters', in *Alternative Shakespeares*, ed. John Drakakis, London: Methuen, 1985.

Hillman, Richard, '*The Tempest* as Romance and Anti-Romance', *University of Toronto Quarterly*, 55 (1985–86), 141–60.

Hirst, David L., *The Tempest* (Text and Performance Series), London: Macmillan, 1984.

Holland, Norman, 'Caliban's Dream', in *The Design Within: Psychoanalytic Approaches to Shakespeare*, ed. M. D. Faber, New York: Science House, 1970.

Hordern, Michael, 'The Tempest', in *Shakespeare in Perspective*, vol. 1, ed. Roger Sales, London: Ariel Books, 1982.

Howard, Jean E., 'The New Historicism in Renaissance Studies', *English Literary Renaissance*, 16 (1986), 13–43.

Hulme, Peter, *Colonial Encounters: Europe and the Native Caribbean, 1492–1797*, London: Methuen, 1986.

—— 'Hurricanes in the Caribees: The Constitution of the Discourse of English Colonialism', in *1642: Literature and Power in the Seventeenth Century*, ed. Francis Barker et al., Colchester: University of Essex Press, 1981.

Ide, Richard S., '*Macbeth* and *The Tempest*: The Dark Side of Prospero's Magic', in *Praise Disjoined: Changing Patterns of Salvation in Seventeenth-Century English Literature*, ed. William P. Shaw, New York: Lang, 1991.

James, D. G., *The Dream of Prospero*, Oxford: Clarendon Press, 1967.

James, Walter, 'From Tempest to Epilogue: Augustine's Allegory in Shakespeare's Drama', *PMLA*, 98 (1983), 60–76.

Kahn, Coppelia, 'The Providential Tempest and the Shakespearean Family', in *Representing Shakespeare: New Psychoanalytic Essays*, ed.

Murray M. Schwartz and Coppelia Kahn, Baltimore: Johns Hopkins University Press, 1980.

Kermode, Frank, *William Shakespeare: The Final Plays*, London: Longmans, Green, 1963.

Knight, G. Wilson, 'Caliban as a Red Man', in *Shakespeare's Styles: Essays in Honour of Kenneth Muir*, ed. Philip Edwards et al., Cambridge: Cambridge University Press, 1980.

—— *The Crown of Life: Essays in Interpretation of Shakespeare's Final Plays*, London: Oxford University Press, 1932.

Kott, Jan, 'The Tempest, or Repetition', *Mosaic*, 10 (1977), 9–36.

Latham, Jacqueline E. M., 'The Magic Banquet in *The Tempest*', *Shakespeare Studies*, 12 (1979), 215–27.

—— 'The Tempest and King James's *Daemonologie*', *Shakespeare Survey*, 28 (1975), 117–23.

Leininger, Lorie, 'Cracking the Code of The Tempest', *Bucknell Review*, 25 (1980), 121–31.

Levin, Harry, *The Myth of the Golden Age in the Renaissance*, Bloomington: Indiana University Press, 1969.

Loughrey, Bryan, and Neil Taylor, 'Ferdinand and Miranda at Chess', *Shakespeare Survey*, 35 (1982), 133–48.

McDonald, Russ, 'Reading The Tempest', *Shakespeare Survey*, 43 (1991), 15–28.

McNamara, Kevin R., 'Golden Worlds at Court: The Tempest and Its Masque', *Shakespeare Studies*, 19 (1987), 183–202.

Magnuson, A. Lynne, 'Interruption in The Tempest', *Shakespeare Quarterly*, 37 (1986), 52–65.

MANNONI, O., *Prospero and Caliban: The Psychology of Colonization*, New York: Praeger, 1964.

Marx, Leo, 'Shakespeare's American Fable', *Massachusetts Review*, 2 (1960), 40–71, later reprinted in *The Machine in the Garden: Technology and the Pastoral Ideal in America*, New York: Oxford University Press, 1964.

Mebane, John S., *Renaissance Magic and the Return of the Golden Age: The Occult Tradition in Marlowe, Jonson, and Shakespeare*, Lincoln: University of Nebraska Press, 1989.

Mowat, Barbara A., *The Dramaturgy of Shakespeare's Romances*, Athens: University of Georgia Press, 1976.

—— 'Prospero, Agrippa, and Hocus Pocus', *English Literary Renaissance*, 11 (1981), 281–303.

Nuttall, A. D., *Two Concepts of Allegory: A Study of Shakespeare's 'The Tempest' and the Logic of Allegorical Expression*, London: Routledge & Kegan Paul, 1967.

Orgel, Stephen (ed.), *The Tempest* (The Oxford Shakespeare), Oxford: Oxford University Press, 1987.

—— 'Prospero's Wife', in *Rewriting the Renaissance*, ed. Margaret Ferguson et al., Chicago: University of Chicago Press, 1986.

—— 'Shakespeare and the Cannibals', in *Cannibals, Witches, and Divorce: Estranging the Renaissance*, ed. Marjorie Garber, Baltimore: Johns Hopkins University Press, 1987.

Paster, Gail Kern, 'Montaigne, Dido, and *The Tempest*: How Came That Widow In?', *Shakespeare Quarterly*, 35 (1984), 91–94.

Pechter, Edward, 'The New Historicism and Its Discontents: Politicizing Renaissance Drama', *PMLA*, 102 (1987), 292–303.

Peterson, Douglas A., *Time, Tide and Tempest: A Study of Shakespeare's Romances*, San Marino, Cal.: Huntington Library, 1973.

Pettit, E. C., *Shakespeare and the Romance Tradition*, London: Staples, 1949.

Pitcher, John, 'A Theatre of the Future: *The Aeneid* and *The Tempest*', *Essays in Criticism*, 34 (1984), 193–215.

Roberts, Jeanne Addison, 'Ralph Crane and the Text of *The Tempest*', *Shakespeare Studies*, 13 (1980), 213–34.

Scofield, Marin, 'Poetry's Sea-Changes: T. S. Eliot and *The Tempest*', *Shakespeare Survey*, 43 (1991), 121–29.

Sharp, Sister Corona, 'Caliban: The Primitive Man's Evolution', *Shakespeare Studies*, 14 (1981), 267–83.

Siegel, Paul N., 'Historical Ironies in *The Tempest*', *Shakespeare Jahrbuch*, 119 (Weimar, 1983), 104–11.

Slover, George, 'Magic, Mystery, and Make-believe: An Analogical Reading of *The Tempest*', *Shakespeare Studies*, 11 (1978), 175–206.

Thompson, Ann, ' "Miranda, where's your sister?" Reading Shakespeare's *The Tempest*', in *Feminist Criticism: Theory and Practice*, ed. Susan Sellers, Toronto: University of Toronto Press, 1991.

Traister, Barbara Howard, *Heavenly Necromancers: The Magician in English Renaissance Drama*, Columbia: University of Missouri Press, 1984.

Traversi, Derek A., *Shakespeare: The Last Phase*, London: Hollis & Carter, 1954.

Vaughan, Alden T., and Virginia Mason Vaughan, *Shakespeare's Caliban: A Cultural History*, Cambridge: Cambridge University Press, 1991.

Vaughan, Alden T., 'Shakespeare's Indian: The Americanization of Caliban', *Shakespeare Quarterly*, 39 (1988), 137–53.

Vaughan, Virginia Mason, ' "Something Rich and Strange": Caliban's Theatrical Metamorphosis', *Shakespeare Quarterly*, 36 (1985), 390–405.

Willis, Deborah, 'Shakespeare's *Tempest* and the Discourse of Colonialism', *Studies in English Literature*, 29 (1989), 277–89.

Wilson, J. Dover, *The Meaning of 'The Tempest'*, Robert Spence Watson Memorial Lecture, published by the Literary and Philosophical Society of Newcastle upon Tyne, 1936.

Witt, Robert W., 'A Many-Faceted Jewel: Prospero's Masque', *Upstart Crow*, 9 (1989), 112–17.

Wittenburg, Robert, 'The *Aeneid* in *The Tempest*', *Shakespeare Survey*, 39 (1987), 159–68.

Wright, Neil H., 'Reality and Illusion as a Philosophical Pattern in *The Tempest*', *Shakespeare Studies*, 10 (1977), 241–70.

Wright, Rosemary, 'Prospero's Lime Tree and the Pursuit of "Vanitas" ', *Shakespeare Survey*, 37 (1984), 133–40.

Young, David, *The Heart's Forest: A Study of Shakespeare's Pastoral Plays*, New Haven: Yale University Press, 1972.

Background and general critical studies and useful reference works:

Abbott, E. A., *A Shakespearian Grammar*, New York: Haskell House, 1972 (information on how Shakespeare's grammar differs from ours).

Allen, Michael J. B., and Kenneth Muir (eds), *Shakespeare's Plays in Quarto: A Facsimile Edition*, Berkeley: University of California Press, 1981.

Andrews, John F. (ed.), *William Shakespeare: His World, His Work, His Influence*, 3 vols, New York: Scribners, 1985 (articles on 60 topics).

Barroll, Leeds, *Politics, Plague, and Shakespeare's Theater*, Ithaca: Cornell University Press, 1992.

Bentley, G. E., *The Profession of Player in Shakespeare's Time, 1590–1642*, Princeton: Princeton University Press, 1984.

Berry, Ralph, *Shakespeare and Social Class*, Atlantic Highlands, N.J.: Humanities Press, 1988.

Blake, Norman, *Shakespeare's Language: An Introduction*, New York: St Martin's Press, 1983.

Bullough, Geoffrey (ed.), *Narrative and Dramatic Sources of Shakespeare*, 8 vols, New York: Columbia University Press, 1957–75 (printed sources, with helpful summaries and comments by the editor).

Calderwood, James L., *Shakespearean Metadrama*, Minneapolis: University of Minnesota Press, 1971.

Campbell, O. J., and Edward G. Quinn (eds), *The Reader's Encyclopaedia of Shakespeare*, New York: Crowell, 1966.

Cook, Ann Jennalie, *The Privileged Playgoers of Shakespeare's London*: Princeton: Princeton University Press, 1981 (argument that theatre audiences at the Globe and other public playhouses were relatively well-to-do).

De Grazia, Margreta, *Shakespeare Verbatim: The Reproduction of Authenticity and the Apparatus of 1790*, Oxford: Clarendon Press, 1991 (interesting material on eighteenth-century editorial practices).

Eastman, Arthur M., *A Short History of Shakespearean Criticism*, New York: Random House, 1968.

Gurr, Andrew, *Playgoing in Shakespeare's London*, Cambridge: Cambridge University Press, 1987 (argument for changing tastes, and for a more diverse group of audiences than Cook suggests).

—— *The Shakespearean Stage, 1574–1642*, 2nd edn, Cambridge: Cambridge University Press, 1981 (theatres, companies, audiences, and repertories).

Hinman, Charlton (ed.), *The Norton Facsimile: The First Folio of Shakespeare's Plays*, New York: Norton, 1968.

Muir, Kenneth, *The Sources of Shakespeare's Plays*, New Haven: Yale University Press, 1978 (a concise account of how Shakespeare used his sources).

Onions, C. T., *A Shakespeare Glossary*, 2nd edn, London: Oxford University Press, 1953.

Partridge, Eric, *Shakespeare's Bawdy*, London: Routledge & Kegan Paul, 1955 (indispensable guide to Shakespeare's direct and indirect ways of referring to 'indecent' subjects).

Rabkin, Norman, *Shakespeare and the Common Understanding*, New York: Free Press, 1967.

Righter, Anne, *Shakespeare and the Idea of the Play*, London: Chatto & Windus, 1962.

Schoenbaum, S., *Shakespeare: The Globe and the World*, New York: Oxford University Press, 1979 (lively illustrated book on Shakespeare's world).

—— *Shakespeare's Lives*, 2nd edn, Oxford: Oxford University Press, 1992 (readable, informative survey of the many biographers of Shakespeare, including those believing that someone else wrote the works).

—— *William Shakespeare: A Compact Documentary Life*, New York: Oxford University Press, 1977 (presentation of all the biographical documents, with assessments of what they tell us about the playwright).

Spevack, Marvin, *The Harvard Concordance to Shakespeare*, Cambridge, Mass.: Harvard University Press, 1973.

Van Doren, Mark, *Shakespeare*, New York: Henry Holt, 1939.

Vickers, Brian (ed.), *Shakespeare: The Critical Heritage, 1623–1801*, 6 vols, London: Routledge & Kegan Paul, 1974–81.

Whitaker, Virgil K., *Shakespeare's Use of Learning*, San Marino, Cal.: Huntington Library, 1963.

Wright, George T., *Shakespeare's Metrical Art*, Berkeley: University of California Press, 1988.

PLOT SUMMARY

I.i   A ship is caught up in a tempestuous storm. As the sailors struggle to keep their vessel afloat, members of Alonso's, the King of Naples's, party try to find out what is happening. It seems that the ship will sink.

I.ii In a cell on an island Miranda is reassured by her father, Prospero, that – thanks to his magic art – no harm has come to the vessel she has just seen dashed to pieces.

He goes on to tell her who she is. He was once the Duke of Millaine (Milan). Wishing to pursue his scholarly studies, he gave the government of his dukedom to his brother, Antonio. Antonio, growing greedy for power, made a pact with Prospero's enemy, Alonso. Alonso sent an army to establish Antonio as the ruler of Millaine. Prospero, with the not yet three-year-old Miranda, was put on a ship, and later cast adrift at sea in the rotting carcase of a small boat. Through fortune, and the kindness of a Neapolitan called Gonzalo, who gave them food, fresh water and some of Prospero's books, father and daughter reached this island twelve years ago. Now fortune has brought Prospero's enemies to the island.

Miranda falls asleep, and Prospero calls Ariel, a spirit who serves him. Ariel tells how he frightened all who were not sailors into jumping off the ship. These he has brought to the island in several groups. The ship and the sailors he has left charmed in a harbour. The rest of the fleet, thinking the King's ship lost, are proceeding to Naples.

Prospero thanks Ariel and tells him there is more work to be done. Ariel asks when Prospero will set him free from his service. Prospero reminds Ariel how he found him in torment, imprisoned within a pine tree. He had been put there by the witch Sycorax before she died. She had been banished, for the various sorceries she practised, from Argiers (Algiers) to the island. She arrived pregnant, and later gave birth to Caliban.

Ariel thanks Prospero, and Prospero promises to free him within two days if he carries out the orders he is given. He sends Ariel away to make himself invisible.

Prospero wakes Miranda, and they call Caliban, their unwilling servant. Ariel returns, invisible, and Prospero sends him away with orders. Caliban enters, complaining at the way he is treated. Miranda tells how she looked after him and taught him language, and how he then tried to rape her. Prospero, threatening to inflict cramps upon him, sends him to collect fire-wood.

Ariel enters, leading Ferdinand, Alonso's son, by the sound of his singing. Miranda and Ferdinand fall in love. Prospero, saying that he mistrusts Ferdinand, leads him away to imprison him.

II.i   Somewhere near the shore of the island, the King's company discuss their escape from the storm and their present location. Gonzalo tries to cheer up Alonso, sad at the supposed loss of his son, by pointing out the good qualities of the island and with the hope that his son may still be alive. Sebastian tells his brother, Alonso, that he has brought the loss of his son on himself by marrying his daughter, Claribel, to an African in Tunis. It was from Tunis, and to Naples, that they were in the process of returning when the storm overwhelmed them.

Ariel enters, playing music, and soon all bar Antonio and Sebastian are asleep. Antonio suggests to Sebastian that he kill his brother and become King of Naples. As they are preparing to kill Alonso, Ariel returns and wakes Gonzalo who rouses the others. The party leaves to search for Ferdinand.

II.ii   In another place Caliban, carrying wood, mistakes Trinculo, a jester from the ship, for one of Prospero's tormenting spirits. He tries to hide from him by falling flat on his face. Trinculo finds him and assumes he has been hit by a thunderbolt. As a storm gathers he crawls under Caliban's gaberdine for protection. Stephano, a butler of the King's, appears drinking and sees the monstrous shape of Caliban and Trinculo. After examining the creature, and giving one of its heads (the frightened Caliban) some wine, he and Trinculo recognize each other. Caliban, delighted with the taste of wine, thinks Stephano a god, and offers to serve him and show him the island.

III.i   Near Prospero's cell Ferdinand has been set the task of piling thousands of logs. Miranda comes in, with her father unseen behind her. Miranda and Ferdinand declare their love for each other.

III.ii   Near the shore Caliban, Stephano and Trinculo are drinking. Caliban persuades Stephano to follow his plan to kill the tyrant Prospero and become King of the island. Ariel, who has been playing jokes on the group at Trinculo's expense, hears this. He leads the conspirators away by playing music.

III.iii   Elsewhere the King and his company, wearied, abandon their search for Ferdinand. Watched by Prospero, spirits bring in a banquet, which disappears when the King and his men try to eat it. Ariel, appearing as a harpy, explains that they are being punished for their treatment of Prospero and disappears. Prospero thanks Ariel and leaves. Alonso, driven to distraction by what he has seen and heard, runs away to seek his son in the depths of the sea. Antonio and Sebastian, equally distracted, run off to fight the spirits. Gonzalo orders the others to follow them and protect them from their guilt-ridden madness.

IV.i   In his cell Prospero gives his daughter in marriage to Ferdinand. He has Ariel put on a masque for the young couple. Iris, Juno and Ceres appear and offer blessings on the marriage, and afterwards nymphs and reapers dance. Towards the end of the dance Prospero, remembering the conspiracy of Caliban and the others, dismisses the spirits and calls Ariel.

Ariel recounts how he has led the enchanted conspirators through thorns and briars, and left them in a foul pond nearby. Prospero has him put out fancy pieces of clothing for them. The conspirators enter, complaining of their journey. Stephano and Trinculo, instead of going to kill Prospero as Caliban urges, try on the clothes. They are chased off-stage by spirits in the shape of dogs, set on by Prospero and Ariel.

V.i   Before his cell Prospero sends Ariel to release the King's company from his charms. Alone, he renounces his magic art. Ariel leads in the King's company, who begin to recover their senses. Meanwhile Prospero dresses himself as Duke of Millaine, and then sends Ariel to fetch the captain and bosun of the ship.

Prospero greets the waking King and his company, and explains who he is. Alonso gives him back his Dukedom, and asks his forgiveness. Prospero greets Gonzalo, and forgives Sebastian. He shows the company where Ferdinand and Miranda are playing chess. Ferdinand greets his father and explains that Miranda is to be his wife. Gonzalo celebrates their general good fortune.

Ariel leads in the captain and bosun. They greet the King and report that the ship is sound. Ariel fetches Caliban and his companions. Prospero explains their conspiracy and sends them into his cell.

Prospero then invites the King and his company to his cell for the night, promising to recount the story of his life. They will leave for Naples in the morning. Prospero sets Ariel free, and everyone leaves the stage.

Epilogue

Prospero, no longer possessing his magic arts, asks the audience to set him free from the island by giving their applause.

ACKNOWLEDGEMENTS

The editor and publishers wish to thank the following for permission to use copyright material:

Columbia University Press for material from Bernard Knox, 'The Tempest and the Ancient Comic Tradition' in English Stage Comedy, ed. W. K. Wimsatt, Jr. Copyright © 1955 by Columbia University Press; Charles Van Doren on behalf of his father's estate for material from Mark Van Doren, Shakespeare, Holt Rinehart, 1939; Random Century for material from E. M. W. Tillyard, Shakespeare's Last Plays, Chatto & Windus, 1938; Routledge for material from Frank Kermode, Introduction to The Tempest, Arden Shakespeare, Routledge and Kegan Paul, 1958; Shakespeare Quarterly for material from Meredith Anne Skura, 'The Case of Colonialism in The Tempest', Shakespeare Quarterly, Vol. 40, 1, 1989; University of California Press for material from Stephen Greenblatt, Shakespearean Negotiations: The Circulation of Social Energy in Renaissance England. Copyright © 1988 by The Regents of the University of California.

Every effort has been made to trace all the copyright holders, but if any have been inadvertently overlooked the publishers will be pleased to make the necessary arrangement at the first opportunity.

THE EVERYMAN SHAKESPEARE
EDITED BY JOHN F. ANDREWS

The Everyman Shakespeare is the most comprehensive, up-to-date paperback
edition of the plays and poems, featuring:

• face-to-face text and notes

• a chronology of Shakespeare's life and times

• a rich selection of critical and theatrical responses to the play over the centuries

• foreword by an actor or director describing the play in performance

• up-to-date commentary on the play

£2.99

AVAILABILITY

All books are available from your local bookshop or direct from
**Littlehampton Book Services Cash Sales, 14 Eldon Way, Lineside Estate,
Littlehampton, West Sussex BN17 7HE.** PRICES ARE SUBJECT TO CHANGE.

To order any of the books, please enclose a cheque (in £ sterling) made payable to
Littlehampton Book Services, or phone your order through with credit card details (Access,
Visa or Mastercard) on 0903 721596 (24 hour answering service) stating card number and
expiry date. Please add £1.25 for package and postage to the total value of your order.

In the USA, for further information and a complete catalogue call 1-800-526-2778.

DRAMA
IN EVERYMAN

A SELECTION

Everyman and Medieval Miracle Plays

EDITED BY A. C. CAWLEY
A selection of the most popular medieval plays **£3.99**

Complete Plays and Poems

CHRISTOPHER MARLOWE
The complete works of this fascinating Elizabethan in one volume **£5.99**

Complete Poems and Plays

ROCHESTER
The most sexually explicit – and strikingly modern – writing of the seventeenth century **£6.99**

Restoration Plays

Five comedies and two tragedies representing the best of the Restoration stage **£7.99**

Female Playwrights of the Restoration: Five Comedies

Rediscovered literary treasures in a unique selection **£5.99**

Poems and Plays

OLIVER GOLDSMITH
The most complete edition of Goldsmith available **£4.99**

Plays, Poems and Prose

J. M. SYNGE
The most complete edition of Synge available **£6.99**

Plays, Prose Writings and Poems

OSCAR WILDE
The full force of Wilde's wit in one volume **£4.99**

A Doll's House/The Lady from the Sea/The Wild Duck

HENRIK IBSEN
A popular selection of Ibsen's major plays **£4.99**

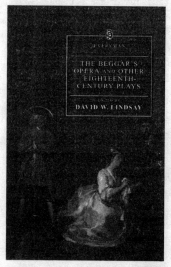

£6.99

POETRY
IN EVERYMAN

A SELECTION

Silver Poets of the Sixteenth Century

EDITED BY

DOUGLAS BROOKS-DAVIES
A new edition of this famous
Everyman collection **£6.99**

Complete Poems

JOHN DONNE
The father of metaphysical verse in
this highly-acclaimed edition **£6.99**

Complete English Poems, Of Education, Areopagitica

JOHN MILTON
An excellent introduction to
Milton's poetry and prose **£6.99**

Selected Poems

JOHN DRYDEN
A poet's portrait of Restoration
England **£4.99**

Selected Poems and Prose

PERCY BYSSHE SHELLEY
'The essential Shelley' in one
volume **£3.50**

Women Romantic Poets 1780-1830: An Anthology

Hidden talent from the Romantic era
rediscovered **£5.99**

Poems in Scots and English

ROBERT BURNS
The best of Scotland's greatest lyric
poet **£4.99**

Selected Poems

D. H. LAWRENCE
A new, authoritative selection
spanning the whole of Lawrence's
literary career **£4.99**

The Poems

W. B. YEATS
Ireland's greatest lyric poet
surveyed in this ground-breaking
edition **£7.99**

£5.99

AVAILABILITY

All books are available from your local bookshop or direct from
**Littlehampton Book Services Cash Sales, 14 Eldon Way, Lineside Estate,
Littlehampton, West Sussex BN17 7HE.** PRICES ARE SUBJECT TO CHANGE.

To order any of the books, please enclose a cheque (in £ sterling) made payable to
Littlehampton Book Services, or phone your order through with credit card details (Access,
Visa or Mastercard) on 0903 721596 (24 hour answering service) stating card number and
expiry date. Please add £1.25 for package and postage to the total value of your order.

In the USA, for further information and a complete catalogue call 1-800-526-2778.

WOMEN'S WRITING
IN EVERYMAN

A SELECTION

Female Playwrights of the Restoration
FIVE COMEDIES
Rediscovered literary treasures in a unique selection £5.99

The Secret Self
SHORT STORIES BY WOMEN
'A superb collection' *Guardian* £4.99

Short Stories
KATHERINE MANSFIELD
An excellent selection displaying the remarkable range of Mansfield's talent £3.99

Women Romantic Poets 1780-1830: An Anthology
Hidden talent from the Romantic era rediscovered £5.99

Selected Poems
ELIZABETH BARRETT BROWNING
A major contribution to our appreciation of this inspiring and innovative poet £5.99

Frankenstein
MARY SHELLEY
A masterpiece of Gothic terror in its original 1818 version £3.99

The Life of Charlotte Brontë
ELIZABETH GASKELL
A moving and perceptive tribute by one writer to another £4.99

Vindication of the Rights of Woman and The Subjection of Women
MARY WOLLSTONECRAFT
AND J. S. MILL
Two pioneering works of early feminist thought £4.99

The Pastor's Wife
ELIZABETH VON ARNIM
A funny and accomplished novel by the author of *Elizabeth and Her German Garden* £5.99

£6.99

AVAILABILITY

All books are available from your local bookshop or direct from
Littlehampton Book Services Cash Sales, 14 Eldon Way, Lineside Estate, Littlehampton, West Sussex BN17 7HE. PRICES ARE SUBJECT TO CHANGE.

To order any of the books, please enclose a cheque (in £ sterling) made payable to Littlehampton Book Services, or phone your order through with credit card details (Access, Visa or Mastercard) on 0903 721596 (24 hour answering service) stating card number and expiry date. Please add £1.25 for package and postage to the total value of your order.

In the USA, for further information and a complete catalogue call 1-800-526-2778.

SHORT STORY COLLECTIONS
IN EVERYMAN

A SELECTION

The Secret Self 1:
Short Stories by Women
'A superb collection' *Guardian* **£4.99**

Selected Short Stories
and Poems
THOMAS HARDY
The best of Hardy's Wessex in a
unique selection **£4.99**

The Best of
Sherlock Holmes
ARTHUR CONAN DOYLE
All the favourite adventures in one
volume **£4.99**

Great Tales of Detection
Nineteen Stories
Chosen by Dorothy L. Sayers **£3.99**

Short Stories
KATHERINE MANSFIELD
A selection displaying the remarkable range of Mansfield's writing
£3.99

Selected Stories
RUDYARD KIPLING
Includes stories chosen to reveal the
'other' Kipling **£4.50**

The Strange Case of
Dr Jekyll and Mr Hyde
and Other Stories
R. L. STEVENSON
An exciting selection of gripping
tales from a master of suspense **£3.99**

The Day of Silence and
Other Stories
GEORGE GISSING
Gissing's finest stories, available for
the first time in one volume **£4.99**

Selected Tales
HENRY JAMES
Stories portraying the tensions
between private life and the outside
world **£5.99**

EVERYMAN

THE SECRET SELF
Short Stories by Women

HERMIONE LEE

£4.99

AVAILABILITY

All books are available from your local bookshop or direct from
**Littlehampton Book Services Cash Sales, 14 Eldon Way, Lineside Estate,
Littlehampton, West Sussex BN17 7HE.** PRICES ARE SUBJECT TO CHANGE.

To order any of the books, please enclose a cheque (in £ sterling) made payable to
Littlehampton Book Services, or phone your order through with credit card details (Access,
Visa or Mastercard) on 0903 721596 (24 hour answering service) stating card number and
expiry date. Please add £1.25 for package and postage to the total value of your order.

In the USA, for further information and a complete catalogue call 1-800-526-2778.